MOVIE
& VIDEO
GUIDE

FOR CHRISTIAN FAMILIES

THE

MOVIE
& VIDEO
GUIDE

FOR CHRISTIAN FAMILIES

TED BAEHR
with Bruce W. Grimes and Lisa Ann Rice

THOMAS NELSON PUBLISHERS
Nashville

Published in Nashville, Tennessee, by Thomas Nelson, Inc., and distributed in Canada by Lawson Falle, Ltd., Cambridge, Ontario.

Printed in the United States of America.

Unless otherwise noted, Scripture quotations are from THE NEW KING JAMES VERSION. Copyright © 1979, 1980, 1982, Thomas Nelson, Inc., Publishers.

Scripture quotations noted NIV are from The Holy Bible: New International Version. Copyright © 1973, 1978, International Bible Society. Used by permission of Zondervan Bible Publishers.

Scripture quotations noted TEV are from the *Good News Bible*—Old Testament: Copyright © American Bible Society 1976: New Testament: Copyright © American Bible Society 1966, 1971, 1976. Used by permission.

Scripture quotations noted KJV are from the King James Version of the Bible.

ISBN 0-8407-3099-3

1 2 3 4 5 6 7 8 — 92 91 90 89 88 87

To Jesus—
and to Evelyn Peirce and Bob
Allen, great actors and my
beloved mother and father
Ted Baehr

To my mother and father, Alice
and Bill Grimes, and especially to
my wife Tish, without whose
continued support it would
not have been possible
Bruce Grimes

To my parents, Glen and Lee,
as well as to my beloved
husband Eric
Lisa Rice

CONTENTS

CONTENTS

ACKNOWLEDGMENTS

I want to thank the following for helping with this book: Tom Thompson, Michael Hyatt, George and Lucille Heimrich, Bill and Lenore Bronson, Andre and Helena Pieterse, Horton Foote, Ken Wales, Lisa and Eric Rice, Ken Kistner, Glennis O'Neal, Keith and Diane Grant, John and Pam Gradick, Bonnie and Don Voss, J. C. Jones, Diane Rich, Rebecca Wayt, Lauren Neal, Ralph Wofford, and Clyde Carrol.

I also want to thank Peter and Sandy Moore, Donna and David Jackson, Alan Karr, Ginny Litle, Fred Kelly, John Black, Jack and Linda Hanick, Ed Payne, Ken and Karen Boa, Dick and Carol Gourley, Grey Temple, Ryner and Evelyn Wittgens, Ralph and Susan Rathburn, Shorty Yeaworth, and all the directors and friends of Good News Communications, Inc.

Every opportunity has been made to ascertain the basic facts about each movie, but there will be gaps in some cases. Running times weren't always available, and it was hard to get all of the particulars on foreign films. It is our hope that as subsequent editions of this book come out we may be able to fill in missing information. What the reader has in this volume is as complete as we can make it.

Unsigned reviews were written by me, Ted Baehr. All other reviewers are noted by their initials in boldface at the ends of the reviews. My thanks to reviewers Bruce Grimes, Lisa Rice, Lili, Peirce and James Baehr, Rebecca Wayt, Diane Rich, J. C. Jones, Brandy Egan, Ken Kistner, Glennis O'Neal, Bonnie Voss, Kathy Day Gunter, Susan Klandt, Eric Rice, John Evans, Charlotte Ussery, Robert Allen, John Gradick, Erin Sherman, Keith and Diane Grant, Bret Senft, Vincenzo LaBella, and Richard Carlson.

The weapons we fight with are not the weapons of the world. On the contrary, they have divine power to demolish strongholds. We demolish arguments and every pretension that sets itself up against the knowledge of God, and we take captive every thought to make it obedient to Christ.

—2 Corinthians 10:4–5 NIV.

THE
MOVIE
& VIDEO
GUIDE
FOR CHRISTIAN FAMILIES

PART I

THE
FOUNDATIONS
OF
DISCERNMENT

MOVIES: A BIBLICAL PERSPECTIVE

The stewardess's voice came over the speakers in the crowded airliner: "Today, we are pleased to announce for your viewing pleasure that we will be showing the movie *Black Moon Rising*. This movie is rated PG–13, discretion is advised. For those who want to watch the movie, headsets will cost two dollars for adults and one dollar for children."

Suddenly, the screen at the front of the cabin lit up. Gory violence flashed across the screen. Blood and guts went everywhere. Then the scene cut to a man and a woman copulating. She was on top of him with her breasts visible.

How, I asked myself, *could children fail to watch this trash?* It was pure garbage, and it was being forced down every passenger's throat. As soon as I arrived at my destination, I dictated a letter to the president of the airlines. I had written him six months earlier on the same subject.

MOVIES ARE A FACT OF LIFE

This incident shows clearly that we cannot hide from motion pictures. Movies are an integral part of the fabric of contemporary society. They reflect and shape our culture and our vision. Either the larger-than-life images call us to take a stand for biblical principles, or they seduce us into perversion and senseless violence. Better than any other medium, movies capture the emotions and the imagination of the viewer.

As many Christian leaders have noted, movies and television have more influence on our society than all the preachers and ministries combined. Every time promiscuity or violence is portrayed on these media, it has an effect on the community. In fact, films affect some people by causing them to copy the immoral acts they see. There are many examples of this, such as *The Burning Bed,* where an abused wife sets her husband on fire. Programming such as this is a powerful role model working at the deepest levels of a person's perception of reality and acceptable behavior. Teenagers are especially susceptible to messages filled with drugs, sex, and violence that are communicated in movies and TV programs.

THE BAD FRUIT OF CURRENT TV/MOVIE FARE

Every teenager who gets swept up in drugs, sex, or violence because of the influence of mass media is a living testimony to their power. Because of this influence, the moral fabric of our society is eroding, as shown by the change in disciplinary problems at schools over the last forty years:

TOP OFFENSES IN PUBLIC SCHOOLS

1940	1982
1. Talking	1. Rape
2. Gum chewing	2. Robbery
3. Making noise	3. Assault
4. Running in halls	4. Burglary
5. Getting out of line	5. Arson
6. Improper clothing	6. Bombings
7. Not using wastebasket	7. Murder
	8. Suicide

—Indianapolis Tech Challenge, Jan. 1983

A *Time* magazine article (December 9, 1985) reported:

> Social workers are almost unanimous in citing the influence of the popular media—television, rock music, videos, movies—in propelling the trend toward precocious sexuality. One survey has shown that in the course of a year the average viewer sees more than 9,000 scenes of suggested sexual intercourse or innuendo in prime time TV.

In *The Atlanta Journal,* Charlotte Johnson reported that there is a direct link between violent, pornographic movies and antisocial behavior:

> In the early '70s, a group of Boston youths poured gasoline on a derelict and set him afire—a re-enactment of a scene they'd seen in the movie "Fuzz."
> In 1973, here in Atlanta, a young woman was killed by a 17-year-old boy who mimicked the actions of a suspect in the TV movie "The Marcus-Nelson Murders."
> In 1978, in California, four teenage girls assaulted a 9-year-old girl in imitation of a scene in a two-hour drama called "Born Innocent." In that drama, female reformatory inmates appeared to assault a teenage girl sexually with a wooden rod. The imitators used an empty beverage bottle.[1]

Whether we go to the movies or watch them on television, movies affect us and our society. A person who never watches television or goes to movies and who is a victim of rape, theft, or violence, committed by an impressionable person under the influence of a theatrical or television movie, is as affected by the medium as those who watch all the time and act accordingly. In fact, the whole country is affected, as was demonstrated by John Hinckley's attempted assassination of President Reagan, which was attributed to the influence of the movie *Taxi Driver*.

Study after study indicates that movies and television are the most powerful influences on our society. For instance, Dr. James L. McGough at the University of California has found that if a person is emotionally aroused at the time of seeing something, the chemical *epinephrin* is released into the brain and locks whatever the person was witnessing into the memory. As a result, that person has a vivid recall of the event, such as a sexually explicit act in a movie, that aroused him or her.[2] Since movies are made to arouse, our minds are filled with intense images that we may not want and that are often counter to our best interests. Movie scenes of sexual promiscuity and violence become time bombs in the minds of people who are particularly vulnerable to those images. The evening news broadcast frequently reports crimes, such as murder and rape, which the perpetrator blames on a particular movie, such as *Rambo,* or a television program, such as *The Burning Bed.* (Note: Sex, of course, is created by God and is beautiful in the context of love and marriage. However, movies rarely consider sex in these terms; thus, sex mentioned herein usually refers to perverted sex promoted by the media.)

The evil influence of pornography, which is all too frequently found in today's motion pictures and even on television when such movies are broadcast, is well documented. Many major studio feature films, such as *9 1/2 Weeks* and *Blue Velvet,* are, in fact, sexually violent, "soft-core" pornography, which Christians would oppose if they were shown in neighborhood theaters.

The final report of The Attorney General's Commission on Pornography, released in July 1986, cited a study indicating that in Cincinnati major sexual offenses (rape, robbery, and assault) had decreased 83 percent after the city had closed the soft-core movie theater along with all the other distributors of pornography.

The motion picture medium is not bad per se. Movies are tools of communication. Like any tool, they can be used for good or evil. A hammer can be used to build a church or to hurt someone. Movies can be used to uplift *(The Trip to Bountiful)* or degrade *(Emerald Forest* or *Cocoon).*

Like television (where movies play and play after they have made money in the theaters), movies are viewed with suspicion by the church; and it is true that too many movies are filled with nudity, profanity, and immorality, and they deserve our condemnation since we are called to "flee sexual immorality" (1 Cor. 6:18). On the other hand, there are many entertaining, uplifting movies (some with a biblical world view, such as *The Hiding Place)* that Christians should support, if only for the reason that our support will

17

cause producers, who are primarily interested in making money, to make more wholesome movies that will benefit society as a whole.

Trying to ignore movies and television has proved counterproductive. Rather than bury our heads in the sand, Christians should be careful about which movies we support at the box office. At the same time, we need to occupy the motion picture industry by producing entertaining movies from a biblical perspective so that every thought, including those communicated through this mass medium, is taken captive for Him.

The problem is that many Christians bemoan the vices of contemporary movies and then rush out to see the next immoral blockbuster of the year. Yet for years, the myth persisted that most Christians neither went to the movies nor watched television, except "Christian" television. Then the main-line denominations pooled their financial resources with the major television evangelists to commission the Annenberg-Gallup study of the media habits of Christians, in particular the impact of religious television programs on the local church. When George Gallup, Jr., summarized the study at a National Religious Broadcasters workshop that I chaired (February 6, 1985), I was surprised by the finding that most Christians watch *the same television programs* as non-Christians, sometimes adding to that media diet a dose of religious programs.

Taking a cue from Gallup, I have been conducting my own straw poll. While lecturing on how to communicate the gospel through the mass media, I used to ask my audience if they went to the movies or watched television. Most would say they did not. After Gallup's revelation about the television habits of Christians, I revised my question and asked if they had watched a particular program, such as the last episode of "Dallas," or if they had gone to see a particular movie, such as *The Trip to Bountiful*. Most of my audience would say yes to seeing a specific movie or television program, but they would claim that this was an aberration and that they seldom watched the medium in question. In point of fact, the overwhelming majority of the Christians in the United States have the same media habits as the non-Christian population! If Christians would redirect their entertainment dollars away from immoral entertainment toward moral movies, producers would take notice and produce movies and programs for us.

THE WAY WE WERE

Are you skeptical of that statement? The fact is that at one time the church did exert a powerful influence on the motion picture industry. Then, in the late sixties, the major denominations abandoned Hollywood, and the film industry deteriorated.

The church began to exert an influence on Hollywood when the Roman Catholic church formed the Legion of Decency in 1933; then, the whole industry suddenly sat up and took notice. It seems that one day Cardinal Dougherty of Philadelphia looked out his window and saw a particularly

18

lurid billboard that advertised an obnoxious Warner Brothers picture. The cardinal was so upset that he forbade Roman Catholics from entering a Warner Brothers theater (in those days, the theaters were owned by the distributor-producers). Then he left on a trip to Europe. Fearing a tremendous financial loss, Harry Warner conferred with a group of church leaders and the Legion of Decency was born.

Filmmakers quickly fell into line with the desires of the Legion, and the Legion and the Protestant Film Office, established fifteen years later, exercised influence over the industry for the next thirty-five years through the Motion Picture Code.[3] The motion picture studios and producers submitted scripts to the designated representatives of the major denominations who checked the scripts and other elements of the movies against the Code; approval meant that the picture could be distributed with the Motion Picture seal of approval, but approval was sometimes withheld until the script was cleaned up to meet the standards set forth in the Code. Monetary fines and the prospect of not being distributed to major theaters kept the Code enforced.

The Motion Picture Code was essentially the Ten Commandments adapted to the motion picture industry by several astute Roman Catholic priests under the auspices of the Legion of Decency. Section VIII of the Production Code of the Motion Picture Association of America, Inc., stated:

(1) No film or episode may throw ridicule on any religious faith.
(2) Ministers of religion in the character of ministers of religion should not be used as comic characters or as villains.
(3) Ceremonies of any definite religion should be carefully and respectfully handled.

This section of the Code was established so that movies would not undermine or lower respect for any religion. Since the abolition of the Code, it has become fashionable in Hollywood to attack and ridicule Christian ministers, as can be seen by the way ministers are portrayed in movies such as *Head Office* and *Poltergeist II*.

It should surprise no one that most of the best films ever made were produced during that thirty-five-year period; creativity and imagination had to replace the cheap lures of sex and violence to attract an audience into the theaters. Furthermore, it should not surprise Christians that movies with Christian themes have done very well at the box office. For instance, the 1959 movie *Ben-Hur* saved MGM from bankruptcy just as *The Ten Commandments* had saved Paramount from bankruptcy in 1956. What is surprising is that the heads of the motion picture studios continue to be amazed when movies with Christian themes and wide audience appeal, such as *Chariots of Fire* or *A Man Called Peter*, consistently make big money at the box office.

It would seem that someone in the studio would notice that Christian movies make money and are often blockbusters.

Of course, during the period of the Motion Picture Code and the Legion of Decency, Hollywood continued to try to use the lure of sex and violence to attract audiences through devious methods. As author James Wall noted:

> The end result was the cycle of Doris Day films that built on the classic dramatic technique that the audience knew something that the heroine did not—whether she had had intercourse with the leading man while she was intoxicated. This technique of enjoying immorality so long as the ending was moral was, in fact, created by the restrictions of the Legion and the Hays Office.[4]

However, the impact of the Legion and its Protestant counterparts convinced the moviemakers that they were at war with Bible-believing churches. Often this anti-Christian stance is not the result of conscious deliberation, but the result of a lack of faith in God, which blinds these men and women to the truth, combined with the knowledge that Christians oppose the promiscuity and violence of secular movies that so easily attract an unbelieving audience and therefore make money.

Here is how Hollywood and humanists portrayed the persons who sought cleaner movies:

> What was coming out of Hollywood irritated and dismayed them. Here was the realistic, the critical, the by-now merrily irreverent movie telling its audience that romantic love was hypocrisy, a biological joke; that the government ordained by the founding fathers was run by hypocrites in the interests of big business; that the "American way" in business itself was cut-throat competition but little removed from racketeering. . . . There slowly gathered during 1933 and 1934 a sentiment in the church, social and business organizations to use their power to muzzle and repress the screen.[5]

This vitriolic pen was then turned on the Legion and the churches who cooperated to clean up Hollywood:

> It hatched in the Roman Catholic Church, whose possession of the immemorial machinery of repression formed its nucleus and base. . . . At the same time, the [Roman] Church invited other denominations to join in this campaign, the object being to force Hollywood by mass boycott to give over its exposures and sensationalisms and make what were vaguely described as "good" films.[6]

This antichurch, anti-American, antieverything attitude prevails in Hollywood today because the churches have retreated. In the late sixties, the church and the movie industry shifted the burden to audiences and parents by moving from the Motion Picture Code to the ratings system. In 1968, the Motion Picture Association of America (MPAA) established a voluntary industry classification code to avoid any chance of state censorship and to replace the strict censorship of the Motion Picture Code. The ratings established were G, for general audiences without restriction; M (which has become PG), for parental guidance advised; R, for restricted with no one under seventeen allowed into the theater without parents or an adult guardian (this rating is seldom enforced and has become a come-on for teenagers); and X, for censored with no one under seventeen admitted (age of maturity varies from state to state).[7] Of course, the PG rating has recently been split into PG and PG–13, which denotes such excessive violence that a parent or guardian must accompany children under thirteen years old. Furthermore, the X rating has become XX and XXX as producers have tried to titillate their audiences.

Suddenly, everyone was taking the easy way out, with the pastor ignoring the fact that the parishioners were going to movies as part of their leisure-time entertainment. Not only did the church abandon movies to the philistines, but the mainline denominations acting together through the National Council of Churches (NCC) actually pushed movies into immorality. In the mid-1960s, the NCC started giving awards to outstanding movies. The first year of these awards was uneventful, but the next year the NCC gave an award to a movie that took the name of Jesus in vain, along with other profanities, and gave another award to a movie that featured a lingering look at bare breasts.

The major studios were completely perplexed because they had spent years trying to avoid nudity and profanity so as not to incur the wrath of the churches. The head of censorship at MGM called George Heimrich, the head of the NCC's West Coast Film Office who was opposed to the antibiblical actions of the NCC staff in New York, and complained that the NCC had "completely pulled the legs out from under" the studios that were trying to live by the Motion Picture Code.[8] In most instances, Hollywood studios enjoyed having the churches to blame for morality and wanted someone to say that they had gone far enough. Cecil B. DeMille had praised Protestant input when it first appeared in Hollywood in 1947. Unfortunately, those churches were blind to the impact of their actions and have only recently realized how evil the influence of sex and violence is on our culture.

Father Daniel Lord, who helped write the Motion Picture Code, was absolutely right when he said that "years of praising the good, had left the bad worse than ever."[9] Father Lord had emphasized that Christians must stay away from evil films, write indignant letters, and make it so hot that Hollywood would change its ways.

LET'S TAKE CHARGE!

We have largely forgotten these statements that Father Lord made in 1929 on the eve of the Legion of Decency. Too many Christian churches and organizations have avoided denouncing immoral movies and thereby have condoned the evil that has spewed forth from Hollywood. However now, by God's grace, Christians are again hearing His call to take every thought captive for Him. In our free society, we can again exercise our freedom to influence the motion picture industry to produce moral, uplifting movies. In spite of their ideological preferences for sex, violence, and anti-Christian messages, the producers in Hollywood are ultimately concerned about the bottom line. If Christians were to attend good films and avoid immoral ones, our impact would be felt quickly in Hollywood.

The devil often convinces us that we are powerless—that there is nothing we can do except complain, escape, or avoid. The truth of the matter is that we have great power. We *can* change the nature of television programs and films. Television programs and films are made to earn somebody money. They are not produced and distributed in a vacuum. The producers need our support, our dollars—directly at the box office or through our purchase of the products they are selling. Therefore, our actions of supporting the good movies and TV programs and boycotting the bad ones make a difference to producers and advertisers, even if they disagree with us philosophically. They need us; when we boycott bad programs and movies (and explain the reasons for the boycotts), they lose money. They may not understand Jesus Christ. They may bend the laws. But boycotting their products hits them where it hurts.

The power of the consumer to stop pornography and violence is illustrated by the recent success of two mothers, Kathy Eberhardt and Karen Knowles. They forced one of the giants in the motion picture industry, Tri-Star Pictures (owned by Columbia, which is owned by Coca-Cola), to pull from the theaters a grotesque movie called *Silent Night*, which had cost Tri-Star millions of dollars to produce.

Silent Night told the story of a crazed lunatic who dressed in a Santa Claus outfit and raped and chopped up unsuspecting women in front of their frightened children. These two outraged and courageous mothers picketed the Grand Theater in their home town, Milwaukee, Wisconsin. These protesters said they feared that the movie might cause the teenage viewers to emulate the violence in the film. They noted that after NBC-TV's movie *The Burning Bed* was shown in Milwaukee, a Milwaukee man murdered his wife by pouring gasoline on her and lighting a match, which was the way the wife in the TV movie had murdered her abusive husband.

The protest spread from Milwaukee to Chicago. After just a few days, the motion picture giant relented and pulled the multimillion dollar release from national distribution. Two women had defeated the modern Goliath simply by taking a stand.[10]

The protest against *Silent Night* shows that one or two people have the ability to stop the pollution of our minds. We can make a difference. National Federation for Decency has been able to get pornography removed from many drugstores and chain stores around the country. When the evil consequences of pornography were brought to the attention of Jack Eckerd of Eckerd Drugs, he fought his board to have all pornographic magazines removed from their stores.

Of course, some vendors refuse to pull the pornography from their stores, and some companies insist on advertising on television programs filled with sexual promiscuity and violence. However, most vendors and companies respond to marketplace pressure and do not want to alienate a significant portion of the American public.

More than once people have complained to me about obscene videotapes in the video stores where they rent movies for family viewing. One friend noted that the owner of one such store was a Christian. He discussed the pornographic tapes with the owner, who insisted that he had to survive and that those tapes attracted a substantial number of customers. At that point my friend should have made it clear that he would no longer do business there and that he would discuss the store's policy of carrying pornography with other Christians and advise them not to do business there either.

If we are going to make known our opinion that we will no longer support promiscuity and violence in movies and television programs, we should do so in love, hating the sin but loving the sinner. We should be able to tell the people who run the stores, manage the theaters, and produce and distribute the films that we have nothing against them, but that we cannot support programs and films that are polluting the minds of our peers and children.

IN THE KNOW RATHER THAN IN THE DARK

Furthermore, given the nature of our society, we need to be informed so that we can make godly choices, and each of us needs to be a film critic—a discerning viewer who can make wise judgments based on biblical principles. As God tells us, His people perish for lack of knowledge (Hos. 4:6). Although Christians have seen the same television programs and gone to the same movies as pagans, Christians now must support wholesome movies and programs. But we cannot depend on the ungodly to direct us and our families toward moral, uplifting movies and programs. Neither the ratings system nor most secular reviews will guide Christians in their choice of communication and entertainment.

The ratings assigned by the MPAA are based on a world view that is frequently opposed to Christianity. Their world view and their understanding that audiences are attracted by movies that explore new taboos prompt moviemakers to seek PG–13 and R ratings for films offering new titillations. Teenagers and young adults constitute the bulk of the movie-going public, and all those films with PG–13 and R ratings are attempting to attract those youths in spite of the warnings contained in the ratings. In fact, the ratings serve as a tempting enticement to curious young people.

The newspaper of the entertainment industry, *Variety*, shows that since the ratings system was inaugurated in 1969, the percentage of R-rated movies increased from 23 percent to 58 percent, while the percentage of G-rated movies decreased from 32 percent to 3 percent. If one were to include the new PG–13 category with the R-rated movies, the final percentage is 76 percent, with the movies becoming increasingly erotic, violent, and irreverent over the years.

On the other hand, quite a few movies are acceptable for Christian viewing and are powerful testimonies to the gospel. These include *Eleni* and *Tender Mercies*. Often, motion picture producers deliberately seek a negative rating for a movie that could have been fairly innocuous, as you discover by reading the reviews and examining the plot. The strong rating is sought, of course, to attract audiences to the box office.

Another example of the meaninglessness of ratings is *The Killing Fields*. This movie was given an R rating, even though there is practically no sex or obscene language in it. This film portrays the horrors that follow as a matter of course when communism takes over a country and systematically murders, destroys, and maims men, women, and children. *The Killing Fields* is a movie that Christians should see, but the R rating may have deterred many from considering it.

On the other hand, many teenage movies with a PG rating have language that nobody in his right mind would want children or young adults to hear. Two recent teen movies, *Goonies* and *D.A.R.Y.L.*, are examples of PG movies with excessively obscene language. Another example is *Beverly Hills Cop*, which is built on the premise that dishonesty triumphs over honesty when fighting the bad guys. Of course, when the good guys play fast and loose with the law, the question arises, Who are the bad guys?

G-rated movies hardly exist anymore. Moviemakers feel that people want to see more than G movies. Even executives at Walt Disney studios seek a PG rating for movies such as *The Return to Oz* to capture a broader audience (they think). To choose between PG, PG–13, and R is very difficult. To decide what movies to see, one must look carefully at the reviews and read between the lines to decide where the movie stands with respect to Christian values. There are many worthwhile movies that enlighten, uplift, and inspire, but it is difficult to find out which movies these are by reviewing secular ratings alone.

Reviewers have their own biases. Often, a critic's world view and the values he is advocating will be directly opposed to Christianity. Many critics have a very pronounced antibiblical, antireligious, and anti-Christian bias. They will criticize any movie that has a Christian world view. That is the reason *The Movie & Video Guide for Christian Families* has been written.

This book is intended to meet the need for a biblical guide to movies that will help Christians make the right choices when renting videotapes or watching television or going to the local theater. Coming from a biblical perspective, it will help you develop a sound standard for your viewing.

The Movie & Video Guide is a compilation of recent movie reviews that first appeared in "Movieguide: A Biblical Guide to Movies and Entertainment"—a daily two-minute radio feature and a monthly newspaper column. In addition to these reviews, Bruce Grimes has reviewed selected classic movies from the past, and we have added nearly one hundred fifty reviews written especially for this book.

As a special feature for the book, Lisa Rice has written a history of that American classic motion picture genre, the Western. In future volumes, other movie genres may be examined.

As Christians, by becoming informed we can turn the tide and influence the media for Jesus Christ, bringing them under biblical principles by refusing to support movies and television programs that go against God's Word.

Taking the media for Jesus is a must if we want to bring our nation under God. To change our culture and bring revival, we must commit our lives and our resources to His lordship and support those films and programs that honor Him while opposing those that deny Him and His truth. It is our hope and prayer that this book will help in this redemptive process.

---

1. Charlotte, Johnson, "Reel-Life Mayhem vs. Real-Life Madmen," *The Atlanta Journal* (April 2, 1981).

2. Victor Cline, "Psychologist Cites Porn's Effects on Children, Men," *NFD Journal* (November-December 1985): 15.

3. James A. Wall, *Church and Cinema* (Grand Rapids, Mich.: n.p., 1971), pp. 11–12.

4. Ibid., p. 73.

5. Paul Rotha, *The Film Till Now* (Great Britain: Spring Books, 1967), p. 445.

6. Ibid.

7. According to the Motion Picture Association of America, obscene language, violence, or drug use will earn a movie a PG-13. Heavy drug use, violence, or repeated four-letter words will earn a movie an R. However, the MPAA seems to think that taking the name of Jesus in vain is innocuous and acceptable dialogue in a movie; and the MPAA often labels sexual promiscuity and shadow nudity as PG. Please write to Jack Valenti, president of the Motion Picture Association of America in Sherman Oaks, California, and tell him that it is never acceptable to take the name of the Lord God in vain or to blaspheme Him in any way.

8. George Heimrich in an interview on June 21, 1986. For more revelations on the complicity of the church in destroying morality in the media, consult Heimrich's forthcoming book *The God Game*.

9. Ibid.

10. Recently *Silent Night* has been re-released by a small, independent film distributor. It, too, should be picketed.

ASKING THE RIGHT QUESTIONS

2

Scripture warns, "If anyone should cause one of these little ones to lose his faith in me, it would be better for that person to have a large millstone tied around his neck and be thrown into the sea" (Mark 9:42 TEV). Yet, how many little ones have been turned from faith in Jesus because of movies like *Elmer Gantry* and *Marjoe?* How often do we consider the negative impact of children's movies like *Labyrinth?* Of course, it is not just little ones, but also adults whose heads are turned from Christ by anti-Christian movies like *Poltergeist II,* which portrays preachers as evil, or *Head Office,* which ridicules Christians and prayer. As I watch movies, I am often saddened and shocked by the negative way Jesus and His church are presented.

All too often in this day of advanced spiritual decay, we are not aware of the false doctrines and gods that seduce us into the pits of damnation. What's worse, the church actively participated in the unleashing of perverted sex, violence, and false doctrine by retreating from actively overseeing the morality of the motion picture industry, as noted in the first chapter. In effect, the church caused millions of little ones to stumble by abandoning its responsibility to take a stand for biblical morality.

We can only thank God in fear and trembling that by His mighty grace "He chose us in Him before the foundation of the world" (Eph. 1:4), for our deeds as His church have fallen far short of His commands. Until the time comes when we once more drive immorality out of the mass communications media, we need to be discerning of the traps set for us, our children, and our friends in movies and television programs designed to keep so many of us alienated from Jesus Christ.

BE MORE DISCERNING

This chapter will help you ask the right questions about movies and television programs so that you can more readily discern the wheat from the chaff. Most of us tend to reduce the issues to promiscuity and violence, but the false gods and doctrines that beckon us with so much deadly appeal are often more dangerous.

Unlike the false, nominalistic religions such as Buddhism and Christian Science, which deny the existence of evil and treat reality as a figment of the imagination, biblical Christianity portrays reality as it is. Perverted sex and violence are real, and the Bible is quite outspoken about the evils of prostitution, homosexuality, murder, rape, plunder, greed, and other transgressions.

Chapter 16 of the book of Judges opens with the blunt, matter-of-fact report that "one day Samson went to Gaza, where he saw a prostitute. He went in to spend the night with her" (Judg. 16:1 NIV). Many Christians would be concerned by such language in a novel and would prefer to pretend that Samson's immoral act never happened. From a biblical perspective, however, we must present, and demand that others present, the truth about reality. Evil is real; sin is real; and our salvation from sin and death was bought and paid for by the death of Jesus on the cross. By ignoring Samson's immorality, we ignore his sinfulness and present him as a Christ figure without sin or as one who does not need the salvation only God attained for us.

Too many Christians demand saccharine movies and other communications that fail to capture an audience because they lie about the truth of man's corruption and fail God's Word because He is the truth. Any avoidance in any communication of the truth of sin, death, and evil ultimately discounts the reality of the gospel and cheapens the sacrifice that Jesus made for us.

Every communication should be clear about reality: Good is good and evil is evil; good must be chosen over evil; and evil is truly wrong and must be rejected in the name of Christ Jesus our Lord and Savior. Also, the real, undiluted message of redemption must be communicated, since all of creation is moaning and groaning for His salvation and for His sons and daughters to be revealed (Rom. 8).

At the same time, we must renounce the false dualism found in many movies that portrays the devil and evil as stronger than they are, as is the case with many horror movies such as *Psycho III* and *Big Trouble in Little China*. These movies and many other contemporary ones focus on evil to such a degree that evil becomes the norm and any victory over evil is merely a temporary respite in a war that evil has won. Of course, this is the other extreme from denying the reality of evil, but it achieves the same effect, which is to diminish the importance of the death and resurrection of Jesus Christ and the sovereignty of God.

Asking the right questions about the mass media requires a solid knowledge of Scripture and a working knowledge of how movies and television programs communicate. To go forward in the victory that Jesus has won for us and take every thought captive for Him, we must study His Word. Studying the Scriptures is a lifelong process; understanding movies and dramatic programs is much more simple.

Let us look briefly at the elements that make a motion picture work as a powerful, dramatic communication. This analysis will be framed as a series of questions to guide you in asking the right questions about the movies you, your children, or your friends consider viewing.

WHAT IS THE PREMISE OF THE MOVIE?

The premise of a movie is the dynamic, active, explosive nucleus that drives the story of the movie to its logical conclusion. Whether or not the audience is conscious of the premise as a statement per se, the premise implants the major message of the movie in the mind of each viewer.

The story line of an entertaining, successful movie logically proves the premise, which is stated or implied at the beginning of the movie. If the premise is "good triumphs over evil," the story line has to tell step by step in a logical manner how the good hero triumphed over the evil villain, or the movie will fail as a communication and as entertainment. Without a clear-cut premise, the characters will not live because it will be impossible for the moviemaker to know the characters and make them believable. A badly worded or false premise, multiple premises, or an ambiguous premise will almost certainly lead a movie to failure because the moviemaker will be unable to keep it on a clearly defined course.

In most cases, as far as the story line is concerned, a moviemaker will not be able to produce a successful movie based on a premise that he or she does not believe. For example, if the filmmaker has chosen the premise "poverty leads to crime," he or she must prove it. Obviously, this premise is not a universal truth; poverty does not *always* lead to crime. But for the purposes of this specific movie, all the elements must support the premise that it does.

The process of proving the premise dramatically and logically powers the story of the movie. In fact, a premise powers and drives every movie, every drama, and every powerful communication. The premise drives the plot, locks the characters in conflict, and forces the climax and the resolution of the story. Here are some sample premises:

- Grace triumphs over reason (example: *Death of an Angel*).
- Love conquers manners (example: *A Room with a View*).
- God triumphs over self-centeredness (example: *Mass Appeal*).
- Vision brings success (example: *The Glen Miller Story*).
- Intelligence defeats crookedness (example: *The Great Mouse Detective*).
- God's call triumphs over bondage (example: *The Trip to Bountiful*).
- Great faith conquers death (example: *Lady Jane*).
- Ruthless ambition destroys itself (example: *Macbeth*).
- Love conquers death (example: *Romeo and Juliet*).
- Love triumphs over selfishness (example: *Nothing in Common*).
- Strength defeats the forces of evil (example: *Cobra* and *Rambo*).
- Forgiveness brings reconciliation (example: *Desert Bloom*).

- A strong will defeats evil (example: *Labyrinth*).
- Innate talent triumphs over skill (example: *Top Gun*).

The *protagonist* initiates the action and carries that action through to the conclusion. The protagonist takes the lead in the movement of the story, creates the conflict, and makes the story move forward. The protagonist knows what he or she wants and is determined to get it. The protagonist can be the hero, the villain, or any other character—not necessarily the central figure—in the story.

The *antagonist* is the conflicting force who opposes the protagonist. The antagonist can be the hero, the villain, or any other character in the story. (However, the antagonist and the protagonist cannot be the same person.) The antagonist has to be as strong as the protagonist so that the conflict between the two will carry the story forward to its natural conclusion. If the antagonist gives up at any time, the story will die.

In every premise, *conflict* drives the communication forward. To prove the premise, the moviemaker must disprove the negation of the premise, and it is this process that propels the story line to the conclusion. If there is no negation and no conflict possible in the premise, the movie will be stillborn and will have no direction and no goal.

In every movie, the premise can be found by analyzing the story. In the *Star Wars* trilogy, the evil Empire is taking over the universe. A good young man, who courageously perseveres against all odds, is forced to fight the Empire, and he wins. "Good triumphs over evil" is clearly the premise. Every film or television program with that same clear-cut premise tells a different story by proving that premise in a different way. However, it is the process of proving the premise that satisfies the expectations of the audience.

Many well-produced movies fail not because of the quality of the production, but because of some defect in the premise. Though beautifully produced, the movie *2010* failed because three-quarters of the way through the story the premise changed, and the second premise was never proved to the audience's satisfaction. The first part told the story of how "cooperation triumphs over adversity"; then after proving that premise too soon in the story line, a second premise, "supernatural beings bring peace," was introduced, which took the movie in another direction.

Every one of Shakespeare's plays, every good movie, and even every commercial has a clear-cut premise, and that premise is the message the audience will receive from the communication. Try to find and state the premise of the next movie, television program, or commercial you see.

2 DOES THE PREMISE AGREE WITH, OR CONFLICT WITH, BIBLICAL TRUTH?

Once you have identified the premise, you need to evaluate whether the premise is consistent with a biblical world view. For example, the premise of

Labyrinth is "a strong will defeats evil," which does not square with the Christian world view that only Jesus has defeated evil, and we share in His victory only through faith, which is a gift from God. As a premise, our Christian perspective would be stated as "Jesus gives us victory over evil." Another example of a very popular contemporary premise is that of *Rambo*—"physical strength defeats the forces of evil"—whereas Christians know that "God's love defeats the forces of evil."

If the premise of the movie does not square with a biblical truth, you need to question the message the movie is leaving in the memory of the audience. In the case of *Labyrinth*, do we want people to practice magic, thinking, pretending that evil can be dismissed by a strong will? This type of thinking has allowed evil a free rein in our society and eroded the moral base of our culture. Evil must be recognized for what it is, no more and no less, so that salvation through faith in Christ Jesus will be sought by everyone who understands that through Him alone is the victory over evil.

The premise of *Impure Thoughts*, "good works take us to heaven," stands in contrast to the premise of the gospel, even though the movie appears to be overtly Christian in its trappings, setting, and moral statements. If good works did save us, as *Impure Thoughts* suggests, there would have been no need for Jesus to suffer and die on the cross. This movie openly espouses the old Pelegian heresy that incorrectly contends that something more than God's grace (what more could there be than the grace of the sovereign God?) is needed for our salvation, even if that "something more" is no more than our active acceptance of Christ. As biblical Christians, we know that we are saved by God's grace, even though we deserve damnation, and any faith in Him that we have is a gift from God.

It is interesting that secular critics have been enthusiastic about *Impure Thoughts,* even though it is set in purgatory and has many Christian references, but the same critics have been negative toward a powerful Christian film, *Death of an Angel*. This film clearly shows that we are saved and healed not by anything we do, but by the grace of God. *Death of an Angel* is one of the few movies with a solid Christian premise and story line that is entertaining and beautifully made. The reviews show that unconsciously or consciously the reviewers were reacting to a faithful presentation of a Christian story.

Another example of how a premise can undermine the truth is evident in *Rambo*. Too many impressionable viewers ended up believing that might makes right since Rambo demonstrates that strength, not goodness, triumphs over evil. We want movies to communicate the eternal truth that God's love alone secures the ultimate victory over the forces of evil.

HOW IS THE PREMISE SOLVED?

It is quite possible, given the modern mind-set, that the premise of a movie can agree with biblical truths, but the way that premise is solved may be anti-Christian, immoral, or evil. If that is the situation, the movie is not acceptable viewing for Christians.

In the children's film *The Dirt Bike Kid,* good triumphs over evil, but only by means of a magic bicycle. Therefore, although the premise ("good triumphs over evil") agrees with a biblical truth, the method by which the premise is solved (magic) is antibiblical (God condemns magic throughout the Bible), so the movie is suspect for anyone who does not understand that all magic is evil. If the magic were a literary device to point away from the manipulation of the supernatural for personal gain toward Jesus and God's grace, as in *The Chronicles of Narnia* (or the biblical story of the three Magi coming to lay down their ungodly authority at the feet of the baby Jesus), there would be a redemptive aspect to make the story acceptable. Many children's films adopt magic as a device to prove the premise that good triumphs over evil.

One Magic Christmas is a perfect example of a movie that has a biblical premise ("faith conquers death"), but the movie is anti-Christian because it calls for faith in Santa Claus, not in Jesus Christ. Santa is equated with God, which is both sacrilegious and idolatrous. That is why it is so important to think about the implications of how the premise is solved. A Christian viewer might initially think this is an acceptable movie just by identifying its premise.

4 WHAT ARE THE MORAL STATEMENTS?

Besides having the necessary premise that drives the story to its logical conclusion, many movies make moral statements. *Echo Park* has the premise "love triumphs over alienation" and the implicit moral statement that "the wages of sin is death." *3 Men and a Cradle* has the premise "love triumphs over selfishness" and the moral statements that "love is a decision," "hedonism is empty," and "caring for others is the true meaning of life."

Sometimes the premise of a movie is anti-Christian, while the moral agrees with a biblical world view. For instance, we noted that the premise of *Labyrinth,* "a strong will defeats evil," is contrary to the biblical world view; however, it makes the major moral statement that "possessions are worthless when compared to the value of the life of another human being," which agrees totally with God's written Word.

Therefore, you must think about the moral or the moral statements of a movie. Do they agree or conflict with biblical truths?

5 WHO IS THE HERO?

Malcom Muggeridge has expressed concern about today's heroes and heroines:

> Hollywood continued to furnish the heroes and heroines
> of our time. The ubiquitous cinema screen projected

> their images throughout the world. Sex is the ersatz, or
> substitute, religion of the 20th Century. These were the
> priests and priestesses. They were the American Dream,
> soon to be in technicolor—a Dream in terms of material
> satisfactions and sensual love, whose requisite happy
> ending was always a long drawn out embrace.[1]

As Christians, we would do well to share his concern and consider the kinds of heroes depicted in the movies we view.

Good guys may no longer wear white hats, but at least, the anti-hero of *Rebel Without a Cause* and *Easy Rider* has fallen out of favor with the Hollywood moviemakers. However, it is not safe to assume that the heroes of today's movies are the positive role models we want for our impressionable children, family, and society.

The number one macho hero at this writing is Sylvester Stallone, with Arnold Schwarzenegger and Chuck Norris nipping at the heels of his reputation. Even when a movie's premise is positive and the morals reflect a Christian world view, we must ask if the hero is compatible with a biblical role model. We need to look carefully at the character traits of the hero to see whether the individual is, in fact, a worthy role model or someone who will lead us into the abyss.

A comparison of Sylvester Stallone's three heroes—Rocky, Rambo, and Cobra—illustrates the different messages a hero can communicate through character traits in movies with basically similar premises. Rocky loves his family, prays, and tries to do the right things in life, although he is reduced to using brute force to prove his worth in our complex modern society. Rocky's use of force is mitigated by the fact that he prays before each fight, demonstrating his ultimate reliance on God and not on his own prowess. (Note that in *Rocky IV,* Rocky steps out of character and pursues vengeance for its own sake, when we know that vengeance belongs solely to the Lord.)

Rambo is a haunted man who strikes out at the country that abandoned him to die, and he tries to rescue his buddies who have suffered a similar fate. Rambo has lost his faith in everything except his pure animalistic strength and cunning, and he ends up asking why the rug of faith was pulled out from under him by the country he loved.

Cobra is a cruel, cynical killing machine who sets himself up as judge and jury, and he refuses to accept any authority other than himself. He is the ultimate humanist, who has neither the heart for God that Samson had nor the integrity of Gary Cooper in *High Noon.* Cobra is the worst type of hero.

Movies are not what they used to be, when the vestiges of a Judeo-Christian world view controlled the hero's "bone structure" (that is, the combination of the character's traits). Today the individual's bone structure is riddled with sins (which is biblically correct) and also with characteristics that tempt the viewer to repudiate the truth.

A good example of how far we've come from a Judeo-Christian base is the movie *The Kiss of the Spider Woman*, which has a male homosexual as the hero who seduces his cell mate. As an indication of how Hollywood glorifies homosexuality, William Hurt won an Academy Award for playing this hero.

Another Academy Award nominee, to which too many Christians gave their approval, is *The Color Purple*, whose heroine is a bisexual. All the men in this film are portrayed as wretched human beings; the women are the only ones who exhibit reason.

To understand who the hero is and whether we can approve of him and this movie he is in, we must analyze all of the characteristics that make him up. We need to look not only at physical characteristics, such as age, race, height, weight, and general appearance; background, such as occupation, marital status, political orientation, and social class; but also at psychological characteristics such as ambition, temperament, intelligence, and talents; and religious characteristics such as faith, hopes, cares, and world view. These characteristics can tell us a lot about the hero and what kind of role model the person is likely to be.

WHO IS THE VILLAIN?

As noted in the first chapter, the Motion Picture Code provided that ministers of any faith should not be portrayed as villains or in a comic role, because the framers of the Code understood that religion should not be ridiculed or demeaned in the minds of viewers. How far we have come since those reasonable days!

In *Poltergeist II*, the villain is a preacher. Called the Beast, this man leads evil spirits against a family he sets out to destroy. Not only does he fail in his attempt, but the family defeats him and his demons. The movie suggests that the family's love for one another is the reason for the victory. However, real love is impossible outside the redemption affected for us by Jesus; the family alone could not triumph over the Beast. Once again, a movie's premise conflicts with biblical truth.

Today, all too often the villain is a minister or even a layperson of faith. This is unacceptable because it undermines faith itself. As Christians, we need to analyze the characteristics of the villain and the other characters in a movie to determine whether they are being used to attack biblical truths. If they are being so used, we need to protest and even boycott the movie in question. We can use the same method to analyze these characters that we used to analyze the hero.

HOW ARE RELIGION, CHRISTIANS, AND THE CHURCH PORTRAYED?

It is important to be aware of how religion, believers, and the church are characterized for the same reasons that guided the writing of Section VIII of the Motion Picture Code mentioned earlier. Often in contemporary movies, religion, individual believers, and the church (whether the body of believers or the physical trappings, such as church buildings) are portrayed as evil, weak, insincere, obsequious, rotten, or foolish.

Although they had nothing to do with the movie's premise, some morning prayer meetings were inserted into the story line of *Head Office* and caricatured as gatherings of capitalist neo-Nazis who prayed with German accents about world conquest. Such was one screenwriter's attack on Christianity.

In *Hannah and Her Sisters,* Christianity, Roman Catholicism, and even Hinduism are mocked. Some people may think that mocking a false religion is okay, but that is a sign of pride and not of a godly desire to lift up the truth, who is Jesus the Christ. Furthermore, as history has constantly proved, mockery is certain to backfire.

Many movies, especially horror films such as *Vamp,* open with some satanic act taking place in a church building. Usually, it takes the audience some time to realize that the church service is not a real church service, but something sinister.

Direct attacks on the church and believers are inexcusable. Christians must not allow the work of the Holy Spirit, the church, and/or individual believers to be mocked. If a film portrays them in a negative manner, we have to rebuke that world view.

HOW IS THE WORLD PORTRAYED?

The environment in which the action of a movie takes place has an immense impact on the audience. Even omissions create powerful secondary messages in the minds of the viewers.

In an Annenberg School of Communications study, "Television and Viewer Attitudes About Work,"[2] it was found that blacks and other minorities portrayed on television were generally excluded from prestige professions. These omissions had a profound effect on specific demographic groups; some groups were demoralized by the exclusion, and others affirmed.

A State University of New York (SUNY) study found that the background environment of a television program had a tremendous impact on children. One little girl was asked what she wanted to be when she grew up. She said that she wanted to be a doctor. When asked why, she did not answer that she felt called to heal or help others; rather, she wanted a big house with a pool, a yacht, and plenty of money so she could travel. Her image of doctors was conditioned by the environment in which they are placed on television, not by the reality of medical practice.

Of course, the same is true for movies; the environment in which the story is set has a powerful effect. All around the world people see the United States in terms of the movies we export, which often portray the USA as a junkyard seething with crime. We must be aware of how a movie portrays the world so that we can counter any misconceptions created.

Movies, television, and the electronic audio media can distort the real world more easily than other media because the tampered product appears to be the truth. Editing, close-ups, shadow shots, reverse shots, and other conscious camera techniques can distort the meaning of a scene, and changing the meaning of a video, film, or audio recording is practically unnoticeable. Every film, video, or audio editor has condensed a real event on tape or film so that it fits into an allocated program time, and even the participants in the event seldom notice the editing.

Jerry Mander approaches what is the real world on television from a humorous perspective:

> There is a widespread belief that some things on television are "real" and some things are not real. We believe the news is real. Fictional programs are not real. . . . Talk shows are real, although it is true they happen only for television, and sometimes happen some days before we see them. . . . Are historical programs real? Well, no, not exactly.
>
> Our society assumes that human beings can make the distinctions between what is real and what is not real, even when the real and not real are served up in the same way, intercut with one another, sent to us from many different places and times and arriving one behind the other in our houses, shooting out of a box in our living rooms straight into our heads.[3]

The same holds true of movies. People will view an inaccurate historical movie such as *The Wind and the Lion* and consider that to be the truth. In fact the filmmaker took the liberty of placing the beautiful Candice Bergen in the role of the aged Greek-American male, Ion Perdicaris, who in real life was captured by the despicable Moroccan bandit Raisuli, who was portrayed by the dashing Sean Connery.

A common distortion of reality that contemporary moviemakers undertake is turning the savage, who is as sinful as the rest of fallen man, into the noble savage. *The Gods Must Be Crazy* presents the view that the world of the aborigine is idyllic while the world of civilization is a mess. With the same romantic intent, the New Zealand movie *Utu* canonizes the fierce Maori as the noble savages while criticizing the Christian colonists as pompous dimwits.

Aliens is a good example of the growing number of movies that establish a feminist world view, where the women are the strong, capable leaders and the men are mere obstacles or minor characters to get around. In *Alien*, the lone survivor of the battle with the aliens is a woman. In the sequel, *Aliens,* she goes back to the planet with a group of inept marines and a greedy businessman to save a human colony. The only survivors of this conflict are the heroine, a little girl, an android, and a marine who was good for nothing except his looks. The message is clear that women are superior to men.

Joshua Then and Now turns the world into a highly competitive, immoral, sleazy nightmare where the use of profanity is a sign of intelligence. The main character corrupts everything he touches. This sad, jaded view of the world passes for sophistication in some circles of society that have been cut adrift from the mooring of faith in the Creator.

So many films distort history and the nature of the world in which we live. Christians must discern how the world is portrayed in a movie and counter any lies and distortions discovered therein. Furthermore, Christians must demand historical accuracy in motion pictures.

9 HOW IS REALITY PORTRAYED?

Closely related to how the world is portrayed is how reality is portrayed. That is, how is the very nature of being presented?

We have already considered how important it is for communications to approach reality from a biblical perspective. We live in a real world, created by God, who saved us from evil, sin, and death through the death and resurrection of His Son, Jesus the Christ, who was both God and man. Any other view denies the gospel. For instance, classical Buddhism considers reality to be an illusion, which means that there is no evil and no need for redemption. In Christian Science the sinful, fallen world as we know it is only mortal mind, while reality is divine mind, which is the good universal consciousness. Therefore, Christian Science, like so many new-age religions and pagan religions such as Hinduism, sees reality as merely thought, projections of a divine mind that is a universal consciousness, and not the actual creation of the God of the Bible. Christian Science also denies the reality of sin and the need for salvation. Movies that reflect such views are to be avoided.

A universalist world view, such as that found in *A Passage to India* and *Enemy Mine,* has the same effect because it suggests that Jesus is not the only way to salvation. If that were the case, it was futile for Him to suffer a vicious death on the cross. This makes a mockery of the reality of His suffering, death, and resurrection.

We need to take stock of how reality is portrayed in movies and compare that with the biblical perspective. Nothing less than our faith is at stake.

10 HOW IS EVIL PORTRAYED?

We have already investigated how critical to an orthodox Christian world view is the correct presentation of the reality of evil and the fact that Jesus is victor over the forces of evil. False doctrine can often be traced to an incorrect view of evil, as is the case with humanism, which sees man as basically good and minimizes evil and sin, or new-age religions like TM and EST, which see evil as an illusion, or occultism and satanism, which view evil as strong as (if not stronger than) the ultimate good, God.

Sweet Liberty is a typical humanist movie. Neither God nor evil is a factor; everything is okay, in the right context; and man's actions don't have consequences. *Big Trouble in Little China* portrays evil as having power, but good can succeed only by participating in the magic whereby evil draws its strength. The *Star Wars* trilogy shows evil as being simply the other side of good, but the Force, the god of this environment, is ambiguous and ambivalent. *Agnes of God* distorts the gospel by making evil good and by portraying the nun Agnes as a spiritist who talks to departed spirits and worships the powers of the air. These movies demean the reality of our sinful situation and negate the truth of God and His sovereign goodness.

So many movies blur the line between good and evil that it becomes clear that the filmmakers themselves are adrift and trying to rationalize their own sinfulness and refusal to accept the reality of the righteous Lord of creation. Therefore, lest we be led astray by these false views, we must discern the manner in which evil is portrayed in a movie and counter any anti-Christian messages that may be aimed at our subconscious.

HOW IS GOVERNMENT PORTRAYED?

Because so many movies attack republican-democratic governments and promote socialism and/or communism, it behooves us to pay close attention to the way government is portrayed. Furthermore, to really analyze the world view being foisted upon us by a motion picture, we should also consider how private enterprise is portrayed.

As some studies have pointed out, the vast majority of those involved in the entertainment industry believe in socialism. Lichter and Rothman observe:

> Moreover, two out of three believe that TV entertainment [and movies] should be a major force for social reform. This is perhaps the single most striking finding in our study. According to television's creators, they are not in it just for money. They also seek to move their audience toward their own vision of a good society.[4]

But movies that lift up the state as savior and attack private property and industry are, in fact, promoting a very anti-Christian world view.

An actual attack on a legitimate government is found in some movies, such as *Salvador*. This film comes off as a dangerous piece of disinformation, which is infecting the minds of millions of viewers who don't know the truth. The rebels are the heroes, and all evil is laid at the feet of the government. The movie is constructed so that every questionable occurrence in Latin America is attributed to the government of El Salvador and conservative groups. The rebels, on the other hand, are a nice bunch of young people with no weapons except their good cause.

A good example of an attack on private enterprise is *Remo Williams: The Adventure Begins,* which is about a killer cop who is recruited by the president's supersecret, nice-guy SS to defend the state against unscrupulous free enterprise capitalists. The savior in this movie is an ancient Korean martial arts master who can walk on water; through mystical methods, he teaches Remo how to defeat his opponents. Unfortunately, this savior is dedicated to serving the state and death.

Secular critics have reacted strongly against movies that have been honest about the evils of communism. *White Nights* and *Eleni* were criticized for having a cold war mentality; in fact, they were written by people who had been directly affected by communism.

In *White Nights,* Mikhail Baryshnikov, who defected from the Soviet Union, tells the story of a dancer who has to escape for a second time from the USSR. Clearly, Baryshnikov is saying that if he had to escape again, he would; the Soviet system is that bad. Yet, some reviewers thought that this attitude was unrealistic.

Eleni is one of the most important movies of the century, yet critics have panned it because it tells the truth. It is the true story of a mother who was murdered by the Communists during the Greek civil war, and her son, Nicholas Gage, a *New York Times* reporter, searches for her murderer thirty years later. He discovers that his mother was murdered because she saved her children from the Communists who took twenty-eight thousand children from their families to re-educate them in Soviet satellite countries. Gage's story rings true because he was the producer and the author.

So that we can make our way through the minefield of antibiblical world views in movies, we need to ask how both government and private enterprise are portrayed. These questions will help us cut through the hidden political agenda of many films.

HOW IS LOVE PORTRAYED?

Love is at the heart of the gospel. God manifests perfect love; He loves us beyond the scope of our imagination. And He calls us to love Him with all our heart and all our soul and all our strength (Deut. 6:5).

The beauty of God's love is wonderful, yet most movies reduce love to one-night sexual relationships, tedious ordeals, eternal battles, or homosexual couplings. This desecration of love should be anathema to His people. Of course, we should not romanticize love; rather we should honor love because it is the greatest gift we have from God. Love marks us as His children, made in His image and likeness. In effect, we make the decision to love, which is a sacred commitment.

Numerous movies demean love and thereby strike at the heart of the gospel. *Nothing in Common* depicts the hero sleeping with one woman after another. *Ruthless People* shows the husband trying to murder his wife, while the wife is trying to blackmail the husband. In *Desert Hearts* a woman who is getting a divorce finds out that lesbian love is better than heterosexual love. *Heartburn* makes it clear that love is temporary and marriage can't last. *Twice in a Lifetime* proves the despicable premise that self-indulgence is more important than love.

Many horror movies capture an audience by luring them with the thought of forbidden love, such as necrophilia (fornication with the dead) and bestiality (fornication with animals). The comedy *Splash* lifts up the model of bestiality in a humorous way by having the hero fall in love with a mermaid. However, bestiality is not funny and is condemned by God.

Many movies suggest, or even promote, the idea of sex with a child. *Dreamchild* suggests that the Rev. Charles Dodgson (who wrote *Alice in Wonderland* under the pen name of Lewis Carroll) really had a sexual interest in Alice, which Alice realized many years later. Dr. Ann Burgess of the University of Pennsylvania School of Nursing says that child pornography was virtually unknown two decades ago, but now there are 280 magazines on the market that deal with child pornography. The motion picture industry has helped to promote this deplorable situation in our society.

Cocoon is the ultimate in promoting hedonism. A group of octogenarians sell their souls so that they can ride around the universe with some aliens and eat, drink, and be merry. In reality, this prospect seems tiresome and bleak in the extreme. To exchange the reality of eternal life with the Creator of the universe for such petty pleasures is inane.

The list could go on and on. However, the point is that we are being seduced, cajoled and brow-beaten into an anti-Christian view toward love that is destroying us. This has to stop, and the first step in stopping this attack on God's creation is recognizing the problem and rebuking it.

13 **HOW IS THE FAMILY PORTRAYED?**

Closely related to the way love is portrayed is the way the family is portrayed. Unfortunately, in our corrupt age, the situation is pretty much the same; both are under attack. Whether today's films are lifting up homosexuality, as is the case with *The Kiss of the Spider Woman* and *Desert Hearts,* or promoting free love, as in *Down and Out in Beverly Hills* and *Hannah and Her Sisters,* or tearing down marriage, as in *Heartburn* and *The Color Purple,* they are attacking the basic building block of our society—the family—and the will of God.

The Bible is quite clear about the importance of the family, so much so that when a man and a woman are married, they become one flesh (Gen. 2:24); a husband and a wife must not separate, except for the most extraordinary circumstances (Mark 10:1–12; 1 Cor. 7); children are a reward from the Lord (Ps. 127); children are commanded to honor their father and their mother (Exod. 20:12); and God gives blessing and inheritance not just to the individual who honors Him, but also to that person's family from generation

39

to generation (Num. 36). Also, the family is the focal point of God's economy and governance.

However, in the past few decades the family has been under attack by the mass media. In the Lichter and Rothman study previously mentioned, 87 percent of the motion picture elite feel that adultery, which is condemned in the seventh commandment, is okay. The recent revelations of sexual harassment in Hollywood indicate clearly that filmmakers are driven to a large degree by sexual desire,[5] and the movies they produce are a rationalization for their own conduct and an attempt to drag the rest of the world down to their level of immorality.

Twice in a Lifetime is a typical example of the overt attack on the family by many movies and television programs. By actively promoting divorce, it is a sad commentary on the state of our civilization.

In spite of the spate of antifamily movies, some refreshing films promote the family. *Eleni* is perhaps the best example. As a heroine, Eleni is a model of faith; she proclaims that "Christ is risen" on Easter, prays to God, and makes the touching statement before her execution that "it is such a joy to be a mother that I thank God for letting me know it." Christians should support movies like this one so that filmmakers will be guided by economic reality into producing better films. We must demand that families be portrayed in a biblical manner as an institution to be nurtured, defended, and loved because our society's future is so closely tied to the future of the family.

WHO ARE THE KEY PEOPLE IN THE FILM, AND WHAT ARE THEIR WORLD VIEWS?

The creative people behind the production influence the communication. Many excellent communicators make it a point to proclaim false gods, including sex, money, and even the forces of darkness, in their movies. Ever since a miraculous recovery from a childhood injury, George Lucas has had a mission to proclaim an occult-like force. Oliver Stone always inserts a sexual and a political bias into his movies. Jane Fonda interjects a political agenda into most of her movies. Ed Asner has a prohumanist perspective. The great director, John Huston, refuses to live in the United States because of his anti-American feelings. Paul Newman is very active in humanist-Socialist liberal causes. On the other hand, Charlton Heston has taken a very clear stand for traditional American republican democracy, which is reflected in the roles he plays.

If you follow the careers of any of the stars, directors, and other important motion picture production and distribution personnel, you will quickly discern in most cases a pattern in their communications. The biases of key people could be catalogued, but that would not be as effective as your developing the discernment to note the preferences of individual members of the media elite and understand how those preferences influence their communications.

Of course, many talented individuals have been able to separate their work from their personal preferences and prejudices. In preparation for writing this book, I had the pleasure of interviewing Horton Foote who wrote the screenplays for the great movies *To Kill a Mockingbird, Tender Mercies,* and *The Trip to Bountiful.* Foote is one of the greatest screenwriters of all time, and many of his movies have a solid, biblical Christian world view. In fact, his best-known movies have biblical Christians as heroes or heroines. In *The Trip to Bountiful,* the Christian mother is such a powerful figure that the audience roots for her right to sing hymns in her godless daughter-in-law's home where she lives. Yet Foote himself is not a Christian, which he readily admits; he is a Christian Scientist, whose theology is distinctly different from that of a biblical Christian.

Foote states with conviction that "I don't think that a real artist is a prose-lytizer. An artist tries to be honest and truthful. My characters are involved with the problems of faith and how to proceed in life. However, I don't think that many films are based on life—they are proselytizing."[6] He notes that his films have not been studio financed and that they are distributed modestly. His films seem to be breaking conventions, but that is not his purpose. His purpose is to capture a sense of truth and to be intellectually respectful. He says that to a large degree he is reporting on the people he knew as a child, many of whom were committed Christians.

Unlike Horton Foote, most of the media elite believe it is their responsibility to proselytize, as the Lichter and Rothman studies found. In fact, the lifestyles of the stars and the media elite communicate profound messages to the general public. Goldie Hawn, who has had a baby by Kurt Russell, says that marriage is ridiculous. The unwed Jessica Lange has given birth to two children fathered by two different famous men. These role models send a message that clearly goes against biblical mandates.

IS THERE ANY REDEEMING VALUE?

A movie can have many of the above-mentioned world views going against it and still be redemptive. *Nothing in Common* begins by focusing on an egocentric young advertising executive who pushes everyone around and plays fast and loose with every woman he meets; but he ends by giving up his job and his fast life to take care of his sick father. He makes a decision for love that costs him everything in the world's eyes, but gives him back his father and a new appreciation of life. Surprisingly, his boss lets him leave work to take care of his father with the insight that "there has been only one perfect son," or so he has been told. Therefore, *Nothing in Common* tells the story of a man who has been moved by the power of love from selfishness to selfless giving—a very redemptive message.

It is rare for a film to have a redemptive element that will transcend the negative elements. Some children's films, such as *The Dirt Bike Kid*, transcend their negative parts because those parts are treated lightly with deference and a lack of conviction as storytelling devices, while the redemptive elements of love, courage, and integrity are emphasized. If a motion picture succeeds in transcending its parts because of some redemptive element, we need to be aware of the good and the bad in the movie so that we can discuss both honestly and rebut the negative elements that may be detrimental to a Christian view.

WOULD YOU BE EMBARRASSED TO SIT THROUGH THE MOVIE WITH YOUR PARENTS, YOUR CHILDREN, OR JESUS?

Probably the most direct and important question we can ask ourselves is this: Would we be embarrassed to sit through the movie with our parents and/or our children and/or Jesus? When we are alone or with a friend, we often deceive ourselves regarding the true nature of a motion picture (or a television program for that matter). However, if we shift our perspective to that of our parents, our children, or the Lord who is always with us (which He is), the faults of the film will stand out clearly. If we ignore the faults, we will slowly be conditioned to condone, if not accept, a non-Christian point of view.

Of course, there are many other questions we could ask to evaluate a motion picture, but they all boil down to how we would like our loved ones to be affected by the messages being communicated. If we care about others and about the Lord Jesus, we will take a stand against anything being communicated that undermines biblical truths and mocks our Lord and Savior. Anything less than standing on His written Word denies our relationship with Him. "Fill your minds with those things that are good and that deserve praise: things that are true, noble, right, pure, lovely, and honorable" (Phil. 4:8 TEV).

---

1. *The International Dictionary of Thoughts* (Chicago: n.p., 1969), p. 503.
2. Stewart M. Hoover, "Television and Viewer Attitudes About Work," The Annenberg School of Communications (April 10, 1981).
3. Jerry Mander, *Four Arguments for Elimination of Television* (New York: William Morrow, 1970), pp. 250–54.
4. Donald Wildmon, *The Home Invaders* (Wheaton, Ill.: Victor Books, 1985), p. 22. This book provides an excellent analysis of the Lichter-Rothman studies of the entertainment industry.
5. Mary Murphy, "Sexual Harassment in Hollywood," *TV Guide* (March 29, 1986), pp. 2–11.
6. Telephone interview with Horton Foote, June 23, 1986, at 5:18 P.M.

"MY HEROES HAVE ALWAYS BEEN COWBOYS...."

by Lisa A. Rice

The old projector is resurrected from the shelf and gently threaded. The screen is carefully hoisted into position. The hot buttered popcorn and sodas are distributed. The lights are dimmed, and the show begins! Every Wednesday night for over twelve years, the Western heroes of yesteryear have ridden gallantly across the prairies in pursuit of insidious villains. Guns blaze, fistfights erupt, and bar stools are shattered across many a saloon counter.

These are the scenes one may find in the home of the owner of the world's largest Western movie collection. Clyde Carroll, of Atlanta, Georgia, owns over sixteen hundred Western movies, diligently collected and repaired over the last few decades. Together with his friend Ralph Wofferd (also an avid collector and Western trivia buff), the two families congregate to view two old Western films every Wednesday evening—at seven o'clock sharp!

As one enters the Carroll home, he is welcomed by a barrage of black-and-white photographs (many of them autographed), tastefully and lovingly positioned on the walls. The early stars are all there . . . Wild Bill Elliott with his backwards guns . . . Hopalong Cassidy with the famous crease down his hat . . . Buck Jones and his favorite horse. . . . The list goes on and on.

What makes these two men in their sixties care so much about these old black-and-white B Westerns? The answer is clear: The stars of the films were the great heroes of countless young boys, and they live on as heroes in many hearts today. Having met almost all of the first B Western film stars, Mr. Carroll attests to the fact that many were also heroes in real life. Some died fighting for their country; some died saving lives; and others are still living today—traveling the countryside and delighting their fans with film stories and tales of the Old West.

Ah, those grand B Westerns . . . low budgets, natural settings, simplistic hero-villain themes. The first Westerns filmed had none of the financial backing or Hollywood grandeur of the modern A Western. Yet, from the mid-1920s to the mid-1950s, their appeal and their success were undiminished.

What has happened to Westerns over the years? Where are these films headed now?

THE BIRTH OF THE WESTERN

To answer such questions, it is helpful to go back to the very beginning of the century. In 1903, the ingenious Edwin S. Porter directed *The Great Train Robbery*. This silent film, twelve minutes in length, gave birth to the enduring genre known as the horse opera . . . the oater . . . the Western!

A few facts about *Robbery* are worth noting. In the first place, most people were attracted to it because they anticipated a glimpse of the rugged countryside of the West. Little did many realize, however, that what they were seeing was a rugged New Jersey countryside.

As one would expect, the plot of the movie was abbreviated and quite simple. The film opened with four bandits entering a railroad depot and sandbagging the telegraph operator. After binding, gagging, and dragging him outside, they took over a train, robbed the mail car, shot a passenger, and forced a trainman to free the locomotive. The bandits dashed away with the loot, only to be followed by a posse formed by the telegraph operator and his daughter. The posse was triumphant, and the story ended. Dim and flickering as it was, *The Great Train Robbery* delighted young and old alike.

In addition to its unremitting action, this picture was to set many precedents in film production for years to come. It was here that the basic skeleton of the Western emerged—the good guys versus the bad guys; the grand conflict, or wrongdoing; the chase scene; and the final confrontation. All these elements were introduced by the skill and genius of Porter. Because *Robbery* was the first Western to tell a story, it has affectionately been dubbed "America's first real movie."

Another precedent set by Porter in this film was the use of parallel action, or "intercutting." This device enabled the film to portray simultaneous actions in different locations and even jump back and forth in time. A similar tool was the "ellipsis," allowing a surge forward in time by omitting non-essential material. Now two of the most basic film techniques, these elements were said to have been stumbled upon by accident.

The unique use of "histrionics," or the dramatic element, was also introduced. For example, the building of tension by using cutaways during action sequences or the "dance" of the cowboy being shot near the feet was a dramatic device that quickly caught on and became a standard feature of many Westerns. Along the same line, Porter initiated the cinematic mode of filming action. Previously, actors had been filmed as if on a stage, but Porter's lengthy pan shots were soon popularized with others in the industry.

These successful elements initiated by Porter in 1903 may be recognized in numerous films made throughout the next few decades. Besides *The Great Train Robbery,* the turn of the century brought American audiences such films as *Davy Crockett* (1910), *The Code of Honor* (1911), and *The Heart of an Indian* (1912)—to name only a few. These movies followed simple story lines, but they also showed a new attempt at dealing with social issues.

STARS OF THE WEST

In many of these films, "Bronco Billy" Anderson starred. After playing several supporting roles, including one in *The Great Train Robbery,* he distinguished himself as a dedicated and talented actor. Within seven years after this initial role, Anderson performed in almost four hundred films.

Bronco Billy (Gilbert M. Anderson, 1882–1971) is considered by most to be the genre's first major star. Formerly an unsuccessful vaudeville performer, Anderson tried his hand in the Western world . . . and won! Ironically, Bronco Billy was not the picture of a classic Western cowboy. A stout, sometimes uncoordinated actor, he learned to work at his roles twice as fervently as his companions.

After a few years of acting experience, Anderson joined up with a partner and formed his own film company. He starred himself in all the silent one- and two-reelers and averaged about one movie per week for seven years. His production crew was unique in that they filmed in the real West (not New Jersey), and they carried the film lab as they traveled. For bringing audiences an immense volume of short Westerns and for bringing the real West to the theater, Bronco Billy Anderson is most gratefully remembered.

Not long after Anderson's debut, the famous William S. Hart appeared on the scene; he was the first genuine Westerner to become a cowboy star. Having lived for years with the Sioux Indians, Hart worked his way out of the frontier and on to the New York stage. He toured with Shakespearean companies and soon established himself as a talented leading actor. The beginning of Hart's real fortune came in 1914, however, when producer Thomas Ince enlisted him as a villain in two short Westerns.

From there, it was a fairly easy road to stardom. Due to his vast experience with horses and harsh environments, Hart was immensely believable to his audiences. Unfortunately for Billy Anderson, though, this popularity began to manifest itself at the box office. Not only was Hart a more realistic cowboy, but the production values of his movies far outshone those of Anderson.

Just as Anderson made several significant contributions to the genre, Hart was to create some precedents of his own. As alluded to previously, his first contribution was the incorporation of realism into Western drama. Earlier films had often portrayed the lifestyle of the West as fairly easygoing and prosperous. From his own experience, however, Hart understood that this image lacked authenticity. For this reason, he insisted that his films truthfully depict the frontier as the bleak, austere domain that it was. Thus, barren, dim saloons often housed coarse cowhands whose language and demeanor were questionable. Shabby and soiled garments clothed tired, weather-worn bodies in many a William S. Hart film.

Along similar lines, Hart's second contribution involved the characterization of heroes and villains. Whereas once the villains had been viewed as crafty, rude, and completely devious in all respects, they began to be increasingly portrayed as middle-of-the-road characters. Often termed the "good-bad" man, the character would begin as a crooked troublemaker and eventually transform into a semi-moral, quasi-responsible citizen. The transformation would inevitably occur via a moral cause or the saving of the "virtue" of a woman. Films such as *The Bargain* (1914) and *The Texas Rangers* (1936) were excellent examples of this new characterization.

This progression from bad to good was not always a complete transformation, however. Often the good-bad man was still deviant after his reformation—in areas such as dishonesty in gambling and lust for disreputable women. This new kind of character being portrayed shocked many viewers, but ticket sales at the box office continued to soar. Other such films soon followed Hart's lead, and in the name of realism, the cowboy's basest nature was laid bare.

Not until 1935 did a Decency Code emerge, eliminating all nudity and limiting much of the suggestiveness the films had developed. Years before the Decency Code was enacted, however, public opinion had become weary of Hart's middle-of-the-road cowboy. "Give us heroes!" became the cry of the midtwenties audience. So, heroes they got!

Trailing on the heels of Mr. Hart came a likable sequence of stars, affectionately known as the Big Six. The major-action stars to follow Bronco Billy and William S. Hart were Tom Mix, Hoot Gibson, Ken Maynard, Buck Jones, Bob Steele, and Tim McCoy.

In the words of Clyde Carroll: "These men were true heroes—not only on the screen, but also in real life. On the screen, they played fair. They shot their enemy from the front, never the back. Their lifestyles were clean—on and off the screen. They didn't smoke, drink, or go back on their word. These men loved their families and were loyal friends." What a shining assessment of character!

REAL HEROES?

It is here, as Christian moviegoers, that we must stop and ask several probing questions. Should we always expect movies to give us a hero to admire? Must the villain be completely evil and amoral? Must the consequences of his deviant actions always be played out? After all, aren't real people simply mixtures of both good and bad elements? Why not lay the cards on the table and show humans as the weak creatures that we often are?

On the other hand, examine for a moment the movie star or hero who does have various character weaknesses. Don't films and television often condone or even glorify these weaknesses? Are our children developing hero images that are becoming less and less righteous? At what point, if any at all, do we draw the line? Must we apply biblical absolutes and moral standards to the theater? Or are movies simply good entertainment that Christians should leave in the hands of Hollywood? After all, what harm could come from displaying life at its rawest and heroes who are devoid of moral restraint? We will examine these questions in greater depth later, but for now we will move on through Western film history, but we should keep in mind that there were moral cycles in each decade.

THE BIG SIX

The mid-1920s ushered in the Big Six stars. The first was Tom Mix, possibly the most innovative of them all. Mix moved in the opposite direction from his predecessor, William S. Hart. Instead of showing a realistic West and detailed character development, Mix delighted his audiences with nonstop action, daring stunts, and unremitting heroics. Western film fans were more than ready for the change from the harsh frontier to the fast-paced Tom Mix adventure stories. *Texas Bad Man* (1933) and *Miracle Rider* (1935) were probably two of Mix's most widely remembered films. Unlike some of his contemporaries, this clean-cut cowboy was rumored to have had quite a colorful and rambunctious life off-screen.

Once a soldier and a Texas Ranger, Mix was known as a clever stunt man and daring risk taker. Throughout his career, he experienced several on-the-job accidents and eventually had to retire in the mid-1930s. Altogether, Mix made nine talkies and one serial.

Other genuine stunt riders included Hoot Gibson, Buck Jones, and Ken Maynard. Gibson began his career as a stunt man, but soon he developed his own comical character, which delighted countless audiences. Earlier he had made several silent movies, even as early as 1915. When it was discovered that he had a pleasant speaking voice, he was welcomed into the world of talkies.

Having actually been a cowboy for many years in Colorado, Gibson made good-humored films that involved a character who often used a sharp wit rather than a fast gun to resolve sticky situations. As a matter of fact, in most of his movies he carried his gun in his boot or carried no gun at all. His first major feature was *Action and Sure Fire* (1921), a silent directed by John Ford. Other favorites were *Clearing the Range* and *Wild Horse,* both filmed in 1931.

Buck Jones, also an expert rider, starred in many serials and B Westerns. His real name was Charles Gebhart, and he was probably most famous for his dry humor, his comical disguises, and his close relationship with his horse, Silver. Buck Jones was actually launched into fame by 20th Century films. In 1930, when Tom Mix was demanding more and more money for his films, 20th Century retaliated by bringing in the new face of Buck Jones. Not only was he an instant favorite, but he continued to rate in the Top Ten at the box office for over a decade.

Just as Buck Jones performed countless rescues on-screen, so was his life to end tragically in the same manner off-screen. In 1942, Charles "Buck Jones" Gebhardt died in a Boston fire while he was saving lives. Indeed, he was a true hero who is lovingly remembered. His last film, *Dawn on the Great Divide* (1942), was released prior to his death.

Another favorite was Ken Maynard. He spent much of his early off-screen years working the rodeo circuit and traveling with Wild West shows. His horse, Tarzan, was the most famous and loved trick horse of all. The animal could dance, free his front legs from a rope, and kneel down so that children could mount him. Maynard performed incredible riding stunts—with Tarzan's assistance, of course! A musician, stunt man, and talented entertainer, Maynard made films that revealed a remarkable knack for detail and top-quality production values. One of his best-known films was *Tombstone Canyon* (1932).

Also a stunt man and an extra, Tim McCoy was another of the Big Six. McCoy began his career by serving as a technical adviser for Indian extras in the 1932 hit, *The Covered Wagon*. Being an authority on Indian culture and customs, McCoy was able to add a fresh degree of authenticity to the screen. He fought in both world wars and retired as an army colonel. It is said that this actor could sit straighter in the saddle than any other man, undoubtedly due to his military training.

The last of the Big Six was Bob Steele. Born in 1907, Steele and his twin brother first acted in movies at the age of fourteen. Their father, Robert N. Bradbury, was a well-known producer at the time, and he encouraged his sons in their cinematic aspirations. Steele made his first talkie, *Near the Rainbow*, in 1930. Throughout his career, he worked with studios such as Worldwide, Tiffany, Supreme, Metropolitan, and PRC. He later acted in several John Wayne movies and played in television's "F Troop." Still living today, he made a total of sixty-five top-rated talkies.

RANGER BOB ALLEN

In addition to the Big Six heroes, other Western stars during the 1930s and 1940s had large followings. What true Western movie lover, for instance, could forget Bob "Tex" Allen and his *Bob Allen, Ranger* series? A talented Broadway actor, Bob Allen was not a Texan at all!

Born in Mount Vernon, New York, Allen received most of his horse-riding experience while in the cavalry at New York Military School. After graduation, he signed with Columbia Pictures and proceeded to make fifteen popular Western talkies. Some of his most well-remembered films were *Love Me Forever, Jealousy, Guard That Girl, Revenge Rider,* and *Lady of Secrets.* Columbia then featured him in the *Bob Allen, Ranger* series, which won immediate acclaim. Bob's shy smile and ruggedly handsome looks caused females across the country to swoon. The Hollywood critics loved him, too. As a matter of fact, the day after *The Unknown Ranger* was released in 1936, the

Hollywood Recorder headlines read, "Bob Allen Rides Ropes and Shoots with the Best of 'em!"

This cowboy from New York was rated right next to Tim McCoy on the Western film charts. Besides his acting abilities, Bob Allen could do all his own stunts. Films of today lack the knock-'em-down, drag-'em-out realism that characterized the fistfights he performed. His stuntwork also included jumping off buildings onto a horse's back and jumping through windows with his horse. Not until Buck Jones arrived on the scene was Allen's series put to rest.

Bob Allen's associates remember his aversion to working in the heat. After being clad in hot forty-pound buffalo chaps, he would often search for a cool place to rest between takes. The famous Spencer Gordon Bennet once remarked, "Don't move any trucks until we find Bob Allen!"

Today, Bob Allen resides on his spacious New York estate. He takes time off from participating in community activities to make trips to various Western film conventions, and he appears in numerous commercials and plays every year. At eighty, he is still going strong!

TAMING THE WEST IN THE 1930s

These first heroes set the stage for classic Western films to follow. Some of Hart's realism would reappear through the course of time, but the bent of Western film production since that time has mimicked the "standards" of the Big Six as well as the "epics."

What, exactly, was an epic? Simply put, Western epics told the tales of how the West was tamed. Features such as *The Covered Wagon* (1923) and *Tigerman* (1928) depicted the perils of wagon-train journeys across the rugged West. Pioneers were viewed crossing treacherous rivers and combating scores of ruthless Indians along the rugged Nevada mountains. Women were seen as strong, beautiful, brave trailblazers of the new frontier. Additionally, the mountains and expansive prairies allured many an early moviegoer. Audiences clamored for the epics, to be sure, but critics often remained skeptical.

William S. Hart, for instance, abhorred the lack of realism in many epics. Though the Indians were authentic, the countryside was untouched, and even the pioneers' beards were real, Hart argued that the plots of many epics were not too believable. His complaints included the fact that the epic woman's dress never quite got wrinkled . . . the hairdo stayed in place month after month . . . the love story was just a bit too perfect . . . and so on.

Fans ignored Hart's dissents, nevertheless, and the epic moved quickly along. A particularly notable one was *Cimarron*. Centered on the plains of Oklahoma, this 1931 Western epic was one of the first films to usher in the advent of sound.

Sadly and surprisingly, though, the Western world did not welcome the initiation of sound too readily. Many mistakenly believed that the audience's fascination with sound would distract from the Western's action shots and mitigate their effectiveness. The facts proved to be unfounded, however, in that most of the top-grossing films of the thirties and forties turned out to be epics. Examples of such successes were *Union Pacific* (1939), *Dodge City* (1939), and *Buffalo Bill* (1944). Later epics included such favorites as *The Wide Missouri* (1951) and *How the West Was Won* (1963). Not until about 1970 did the epic decline in popularity.

Thus, one of the things that marked the 1930 Western film era was the switch in taste by many audiences from the traditional action-packed Western with its Big Six stars to the dramatic journeys found in the epics, complete with numerous traumas and love stories. A large segment of the population, however, remained faithful and true to the declining traditional hero-villain action stories. As a matter of fact, these films continued to be shown across the nation in countless theaters and second-run movie houses. It is believed that the average traditional Western movie was shown over six thousand times in its lifetime—in one small town after another.

Another distinctive mark of the 1930s was the popularity of the low-budget picture. According to Ralph Wofferd and Clyde Carroll, average movies ranged in production cost from $4,000 to $35,000. One 1930s picture grossed $2 million at the box office, but the total salary for the star, Ken Maynard, was only $1,500.

Along the same lines, the thirties saw raw, authentic countryside. Studio sets were not used if they could be avoided. Actors performed their own stunts, and unions were almost nonexistent. For reasons such as these, costs of production could be streamlined more easily.

In addition, the Great Depression ushered in the quickie Western. Though often still maintaining their top-quality production values, the films were shot in six to ten days. "King of the Cowboys" Roy Rogers and Gene Autry, an eternal favorite, shot several singing cowboy films in six days!

Other hallmarks of the 1930s included the introduction of the double feature. As an enticement to get audiences to theaters and away from their homes and financial problems, the double feature was heralded as an immediate success. The second film shown was usually a B Western featuring a Big Six hero, but the first one was most likely a higher budget production such as Cesar Romero's *Cisco Kid* series at Fox.

New heroes also came on the scene at this time. The second group of B-film favorites included William "Wild Bill" Elliott, Donald "Red" Barry, Johnny Mack Brown, Ray "Crash" Corrigan, Tim Holt, William "Hopalong Cassidy" Boyd, Bob Livingston, and Lash LaRue.

It is reported that some of these actors (such as Mix and Boyd) quietly and consistently accumulated salaries that surpassed those of many major stars. Others, such as Tim Holt, went on to perform in studio successes of a much greater magnitude.

On the other hand, several major grade-A Western stars began careers in the realm of B filmmaking and slowly worked their way up to the A productions. For example, Lee J. Cobb and Robert Mitchum began with early B Westerns in roles such as a card player and a villain, respectively, before being recognized by major studios. John Wayne played minor roles in a long series of 1930s B Westerns before replacing Robert Livingston in *The Three Mesquiteers* and moving on to stardom.

According to film historians, however, the greatest successes of the 1930s were Gene Autry, Roy Rogers, William Boyd, and Randolph Scott. Gene Autry was a Texan who popularized the singing cowboy style of Western with *Tumbling Tumbleweeds* (1936). Considered to be a lighthearted, easygoing fellow, Autry made millions on his Westerns (1934 to 1954) and was even known as one of the Top Ten Hollywood money earners of his day. The singing cowboy retired from his acting career during World War II to join the armed forces.

Roy Rogers, on the other hand, began as a California migratory fruit picker in 1929. He played a small role in Autry's *Tumbling Tumbleweeds* and won immediate acclaim. Eventually, after Autry had departed for the war, Rogers was able to take over the title "King of the Cowboys."

Both Gene Autry and Roy Rogers adapted quickly to the changing American tastes. In the early 1950s, when the singing cowboy had run its cycle, the two men moved to television with their own production companies. Their pictures were fast paced and musically tight, and they combined elements of both the Old and the New West. For example, airplanes and cars were used just as much as horses in action sequences and chase scenes. Rogers's pictures were also responsible for developing the genre's most popular female star, Dale Evans. (As many who knew them expected, Rogers and Evans were married in 1947.)

The third giant Western success of the thirties was William Boyd. He began his career in 1920 with *Why Change Your Wife?* Other famous Boyd silents were *The Volga Boatman* (1926) and *King of Kings* (1927). His real launch into stardom, however, came with the 1935 picture, *Hop-A-Long Cassidy*. The Hop-a-long Cassidy character originally had been developed by writer Clarence E. Mulford for the *Saturday Evening Post*. After starring in sixty-six Cassidy episodes, Boyd purchased the rights to the character. The handsome Boyd came to realize the wisdom of his decision when he sold his features to television in the early 1950s. The episodes were such an instantaneous hit with youngsters that he was able to crank out fifty-two more half-hour television segments. Like Autry and Rogers, Boyd retired a rich man; he remained active until his death in 1972.

Randolph Scott was considered by many to be the greatest artistic success of this era. Spending the majority of the 1930s as the leading man in a variety of musicals, comedies, romances, and mysteries, Scott greatly loved the Western. Such films as *The Texans* (1938), *Frontier Marshal* (1939), *Western Union* (1941), and *Belle Starr* (1941) made the rugged, leathery Scott a smash at the box office.

One of his later contributions was the production of a series of high-quality B's between 1956 and 1960—featuring Scott as an aging, lonely, but still-tough hero. His last major success was the 1962 film *Ride the High Country* (MGM). It is said that one of the hallmarks of this film is the intricate way in which death was handled. To many viewers, it was a welcome switch from some of the glibness of the standard Western death scene.

Thus, the thirties saw low budgets, simplistic authentic Western settings, the entrance and exit of several B Western stars, and the emergence of some A Western hopefuls. The standard and the epic were the predominant choices of audiences of this era.

THE OLD WEST'S DECLINE IN THE FORTIES

In 1940, however, the personalized Western, or "character-mood" piece, was in greatest demand. The character-mood picture combined the drama of the epic with the action of the standard—in addition to placing a strong emphasis on character and mood. Though these elements had been integral in some films of earlier times, it wasn't until 1939 with John Ford's *Stagecoach* that their importance and popularity became widespread. This story of eight people traveling to Wyoming included elements of the epic, such as breathtaking shots of windswept wastelands, and elements of the standard Western, such as showdowns and chase scenes. However, above all else, this film was the first of its kind to boast of superior, even perfect, character portrayals.

The brilliant actors included Andy Devine, George Bancroft, John Carradine, Donald Meek, Louise Platt, Claire Trevor, and John Wayne. John Wayne, by the way, realized tremendous popularity in the wake of this great film.

An outstanding 1939 character-mood piece was *Destry Rides Again* with James Stewart. This period gave us *The Westerner* (1940)—a character study of Judge Roy Bean—and *The Ox-Bow Incident* (1943) starring Henry Fonda. Others were *Duel in the Sun* (1947), *Treasure of the Sierra Madre* (1948), *Red River* (1948), and *Rio Grande* (1948). In *Treasure of the Sierra Madre*, Humphrey Bogart costarred with the talented Walter Huston, father of famous actor-director John Huston.

One particular characteristic of these films was the widespread use of stunt men. Previously, the actors had to be excellent riders and daring risk takers. Now, they could concentrate fully on their acting performances, not their equestrian skills.

Another mark of the forties was the increased utilization of stock footage in films. Clips of the same landscapes could be spotted in numerous films. Identical shots of galloping herds of horses were shown in one Western after another. This technique saved money, but many fans caught on and protested.

Besides saving money, stock footage enabled the Old West to be portrayed in the day of its rapid decline. In the 1940s cities were being built at an unprecedented rate. Often the expansion overtook a prime Western shooting location. With few real Western towns left, producers found themselves succumbing to the expensive task of building sets and resorting to the use of stock footage.

Thus, the forties saw stunt men, stock footage, the disappearance of much of the barren West, and more expensively made movies. Whereas top movies of the thirties were made for about $35,000, the films of the forties averaged about $100,000 each. According to film experts Clyde Carroll and Ralph Wofferd, the 1940s movies were not as exciting or entertaining as some of those made earlier. Because it was getting harder to find the "real West," a certain atmosphere seemed to be lacking in the later Westerns.

CHANGING TASTES: SPICE AND SPAGHETTI

The fifties was a decade of great change for the Western. By 1953, the last B Western ever to be made had been completed. In total, 2,260 of the beloved movies had been filmed and released. By 1958, B Westerns quit running in theaters altogether. They were placed on television, however, numbering about ten per day. Though an immediate thrill to television audiences, the films quickly lost the atmosphere and luster that had characterized them on the big screen.

Other highlights of this period included the movie *Broken Arrow*—a 1950 James Stewart social treatise depicting the Indian–white man struggles. In 1957, Bronco Billy Anderson received a special Oscar for his contributions to motion pictures.

Two of the best 1950s productions were *High Noon* (1952) and *Shane* (1953). These films were considered to be the very best of the character-mood Westerns, and *Shane* grossed $9 million at the box office. Both films were nominated for Academy Awards, but *Shane* alone received the award for the Best Color Cinematography.

According to film historians, an apt description of the 1950s Western is "all things to all people." All three Western types—the standard, the epic, and the character-mood piece—were equally popular. Comedies and musicals had joined the Western ranks by this time as evidenced by films such as *Paleface* with Bob Hope (1950) and *Annie Get Your Gun* (1950). Small-screen series soon appeared with programs like *Gunsmoke*, *Rawhide*, and *Bonanza*.

By the 1960s, the Western was losing popularity. In the 1940s, westerns had accounted for one-quarter of Hollywood's output. By 1960, this figure had dropped to one-thirteenth!

To combat the waning popularity, producers decided to spice up Westerns by incorporating into story lines the elements of fear, violence, sex, and comedy. The violence could be seen in Randolph Scott's *The Tall T* (1957), Sam Peckinpah's *The Wild Bunch* (1969), and Clint Eastwood's "spaghetti Westerns," such as *The Good, The Bad, and The Ugly* (1966). (Spaghetti Westerns were so named because they were filmed in Italy.) The sexual element was seen in *McCabe and Mrs. Miller* (1971) and the humor element in *The Cheyenne Social Club* (1970).

What pulled the sagging Western back up, however, was the introduction of a handful of top-notch stars such as Paul Newman, Robert Redford, *(Butch Cassidy and the Sundance Kid),* and Jane Fonda *(Cat Ballou).* In addition, actors such as Dustin Hoffman *(Little Big Man),* Kirk Douglas *(The War Wagon),* and Burt Lancaster *(Hallelujah)* joined the Western scene.

The all-time favorite, though, was John Wayne. After ten years in B films and the success of *Stagecoach,* Wayne developed into an American hero and, eventually, a national institution. His films continued to appear on the industry's Top Ten money-making rosters from 1949 to 1974. By the early 1970s, however, Wayne's popularity was matched by Clint Eastwood and his spaghetti Westerns.

From the late seventies to the present, public taste has shifted away from the Western, except for a smattering of new releases, such as *Silverado.* It is the hope of many that moviemakers will start again to produce great stories of the rugged West.

HOW DO WESTERNS MEASURE UP?

Earlier in the chapter, we raised some questions to consider as Christian moviegoers. These questions can apply to Westerns and non-Westerns alike. It is important that we decide individually what stand we will take in regard to our viewing of films. The first question might be, "What elements should I look for (or avoid) as a Christian moviegoer? Let's take a look at what Scripture has to say.

The first Scripture that comes to mind in regard to movies is Philippians 4:8: "Finally, brethren, whatever things are true, whatever things are noble, whatever things are just, whatever things are pure, whatever things are lovely, whatever things are of good report, if there is any virtue and if there is anything praiseworthy—meditate on these things." Here we are encouraged, even commanded, to exert control over what we think about. And what do we think about? What we see and hear. Each of us must examine and evaluate the input allowed into the mind. Are the movies we watch pure, lovely, of good report, and praiseworthy? Or are they impure, dishonorable, unlovely, and not worthy of praise? The Bible tells us "as [a man] thinks in his heart, so is he" (Prov. 23:7). We become like what we worship. And what is our object of worship? Whatever occupies the majority of our time and energy.

If we spend our time worshiping the Lord, speaking to Him, reading the Word, and interceding for others, we soon develop the mind of Christ and become like Him. If, on the other hand, we spend our time molding ourselves to the humanistic patterns of this world, we gradually become like the world.

A pastor in Atlanta once gave his congregation a six-part test to evaluate questionable "gray" areas, or areas where Scripture is not specific. This test can be applied to anything from dancing to drinking to attending rock concerts and R-rated movies. Let's apply this test to the movies now on the market:

1. Does this object/activity bring glory to God?
2. Is this profitable to my Christian life? Will it aid me in my walk?
3. Will this edify me?
4. Does this object/activity have the potential of enslaving me?
5. Will this strengthen me against temptation or lead me deeper into it?
6. Is this activity characteristic of God or the world?

Narrowing our focus to Westerns in particular, let's examine how the films measure up to the test. How do Westerns stack up against other film types? The answer may be found by reviewing a history of the movies. Unlike other film types, the Western has usually sought to uphold basic Christian values such as honesty, integrity, boldness, the protection of the family, and the exposure and punishment of evil. Though not specifically Christian, most Westerns are considered to be family oriented and good, clean entertainment.

As we discussed earlier, B Westerns provided heroes who were gallant and good and villains who were clearly evil. These films showed children the difference between right and wrong, good and bad. How many films do that today?

The Westerns gave us heroes and role models, and so they should! Some critics may argue that it is unrealistic to have heroes who are completely good; they hold that real people are mixtures of good and bad. Many argue that we should see all films, regardless of their content and message, in order to be able to understand and counsel those in "the world."

The Bible teaches that we are to understand evil not through experience, but through the wisdom God gives us in His Word. We should avoid immoral movies, and we should look for the film heroes who are promoting clean lifestyles and moral values.

A final word. The "golden age" of Westerns is over, but it may someday return. When Christians rent or view in theaters movies such as the old Western classics, they are voting with their dollars for moral excellence in entertainment. Hollywood listens when we pay to see quality films. It listens even more carefully if enough of us avoid immoral films.

So, on the next rainy night, put away the complicated thoughts of this busy cement-and-skyscraper world, find a Western standard or two, and journey with your favorite hero back through those wonderful prairies and towns that make up the Old West of the movies.

PART II

REVIEWS
OF
SELECTED
MOVIES

REVIEWS

RATING SYSTEM

★★★★ EXCELLENT, RECOMMENDED

★★★ ACCEPTABLE, MUCH THAT IS GOOD, BUT NOTE RESERVATIONS

★★ POOR, SERIOUSLY FLAWED

NO RATING—**BAD, TOTALLY WITHOUT MERIT**

This book includes reviews of both good and bad movies so that you can have a better idea about their content and thus determine which ones are acceptable viewing, which ones should be avoided, and why. Ratings, no matter who determines them, have failed to guide individuals in their choice of motion pictures. Often, ratings have kept people from movies with a biblical world view, such as *The Prodigal,* or movies that are worthwhile viewing but have been given restrictive ratings for political, economic, or ideological motives, as was the case with *Eleni*. On the other hand, ratings have not kept people from movies they would have avoided if they had known more than what was touted in the advertisements and conveyed through word of mouth.

Parents often call me to ask if a movie is all right for teenagers to see with friends. The parents usually say that the teenagers have told them the movie isn't so bad and all their friends have seen it. However, when the parents hear the detailed review, they are armed with the right information to tell their teenagers exactly why they should not go to the movie in question.

Again, as I said in the Acknowledgments, not all of the particulars were readily available on every movie. Running times were not always available, but what you have before you is as complete as was available.

We have approached each movie from a biblical perspective, and the reviews reflect a biblical world view that should be reinforced within each Christian family. We pray that you will be blessed by this guide and that it will help you, your family, your friends.

ABOUT LAST NIGHT (1986), 116 min.

RATING: R
CONTENT: Profanity, sexual immorality, and nudity
INTENDED AUDIENCE: Teenagers
STARRING: Rob Lowe, Demi Moore, James Belushi, Elizabeth Perkins
DIRECTOR: Edward Zwik

This movie tells the story of two young people in Chicago who fall in love, move in together, break up, repent, and decide to get married. At its core, this story is about the need for marriage and honesty. However, it is ruined by some of the worst language I have ever heard in a film. Furthermore, the nudity and the premarital relationship make this movie unacceptable for anyone. Avoid this offensive romance.

THE ABSENT-MINDED PROFESSOR (1961) B&W, 104 min.

RATING: G   ★★★
CONTENT: Nothing objectionable
INTENDED AUDIENCE: All ages
STARRING: Fred MacMurray, Keenan Wynn, Tommy Kirk,
  Ed Wynn, Nancy Olson
DIRECTOR: Robert Stevenson

This Disney film is a sure winner with children and the young at heart. Fred Mac-Murray portrays Professor Brainard, a college instructor who accidentally invents a rubbery substance called "flubber." This material has the unusual property of giving things the ability to fly, and the professor becomes an instant sensation as his discovery becomes known to the United States military, corrupt school officials, and friends.

There are several well-crafted sequences in the film. In one of them Medfield college plays a rival school. Having one of the worst basketball teams in the conference, Medfield is getting beaten overwhelmingly until the professor decides to add a little "lift" to his school's players—by sticking flubber on the bottom of their shoes.

Even in black and white, *The Absent-Minded Professor* is entertaining because of the well executed special effects and polished script. **B.G.**

ABSOLUTE BEGINNERS (1986)

RATING: PG–13   ★★
CONTENT: Some obscenity and risqué settings
INTENDED AUDIENCE: Adults
STARRING: Eddie O'Connell, Patsy Kensit, James Fox, David Bowie
DIRECTOR: Julien Temple

This big, fresh, stylish, imaginative British musical based on the novel by Colin Mac-Innes captures the emergence of teenagers as postwar Britain's brassiest social group. The jaded love story of Colin, the boy photographer, and his pouty fashion model-designer, "Crepe" Suzette, is an exhilarating whirl through the decaying, decadent alleyways of London.

The opening two-thirds promises a unique, entertaining, new type of musical, but unfortunately, it collapses into a morality play that fails for immorality. The story revolves around Colin's search for love and happiness as a teenager who is disengaging himself from the problems of the real world. However, he is brought into the real world by Suzette who sells out for fame and fortune and marries a wealthy designer. Colin sells out to commercialism until he finds out that the powers who do the buying are mercilessly destroying the world where he lives and his friends. Colin comes to the aid of his friends, and Suzette realizes the error of her ways and returns to Colin. They end up in each other's arms, but they are no longer absolute beginners. They know the horrors of the real world.

Good triumphs over evil in this movie, but the good is mediocre and self-indulgent. The music and acting are excellent, especially by the supporting players, David Bowie and Sade. However, the setting is a portrait of hell—a den of thieves, prostitutes, and perverts that still exists in London. Although there are many things to recommend this film, background immorality and an amoral world view make it too risqué for Christians. Mark it down as a movie of unfulfilled potential.

THE ADVENTURES OF THE WILDERNESS FAMILY (1975), 101 min.

RATING: G   ★★★
CONTENT: Nothing offensive
INTENDED AUDIENCE: All ages
STARRING: Robert Logan, Susan Damante Shaw
DIRECTOR: Stewart Raffill

This convincing film tells the story of a beleaguered city family who escape from the harshness of urban Los Angeles to the realities of mountain living. Filmed in Utah, the movie offers beautiful vistas, and provides the audience with an insight into the "back-to-the-land" movement that occurred in the late sixties and early seventies.

The Adventures of the Wilderness Family tells the story of the Robinson family and their adventure on the land: how they build a log cabin, befriend orphaned bear cubs, and come face to face with grizzly bears and wolves. It also tells of their love, and how they bear their difficulties together. One of the better movies to come out of the "back-to-nature" films. **B.G.**

AFTER HOURS (1986), 96 min.

RATING: R
CONTENT: Nudity, profanity, sexual situations, and obscenity
INTENDED AUDIENCE: Adults
STARRING: Rosanna Arquette, Verna Bloom, Thomas Chong, Griffin Dunne
DIRECTOR: Martin Scorsese

This movie captures the essence of our fallen society. It shows a selfish young innocent who learns how to care for others by being thrown into the hell of the Soho district of New York City after hours. The young innocent pursues a young temptress only to be frustrated by his own scruples. Fleeing the temptress, he sets up a chain of events that threaten his life. By humbling himself, he is able to escape the forces of evil. In some respects it is an excellent picture because it challenges every film convention and succeeds, but in the process it employs sex, nudity, violence, and foul language to portray decadent, punk elements of city life. It's totally unsuitable viewing.

AFTER THE FOX (1966), 103 min.

RATING: G   ★★★
CONTENT: Nothing objectionable
INTENDED AUDIENCE: Adults
STARRING: Peter Sellers, Victor Mature, Britt Ekland, Akim Tamiroff, Martin Balsam
DIRECTOR: Vittorio De Sica

Peter Sellers portrays an ingenious criminal who masterminds a gold heist that in-volves smuggling gold into Italy. He poses as a famous movie director and engages an Italian village to help him make his next "epic." The film "crew" arrives in a van, and Sellers proceeds to "direct" his movie with everyone from the local policeman to the town mayor involved. A boat arrives with the gold, and the townspeople launch their various boats to off-load the cargo and carry it to the film van. Sellers then escapes with the gold, with the police in hot pursuit.

After the Fox is an interesting, but not great, movie that points out the sinfulness of fallen man in a humorous manner. **B.G.**

AGNES OF GOD (1985), 99 min.

RATING: PG–13
CONTENT: Spiritism, profanity, and obscenity
INTENDED AUDIENCE: Adults
STARRING: Jane Fonda, Anne Bancroft, Meg Tilly
DIRECTOR: Norman Jewison

This cinematic distortion of the gospel makes evil good. Jane Fonda portrays a chain-smoking psychiatrist trying to rescue an innocent from God and from the protec-tion of the convent; she wants the innocent to know the world. The title character, Agnes, is a spiritist, not a Christian, who talks to departed spirits and worships the powers of the air. The movie is full of superstition, and the language is obscene. The plot focuses on Agnes's killing of her newborn baby and on everyone's attempt to cover up her heinous crime. Not recommended.

ALICE IN WONDERLAND (1951), 80 min.

CONTENT: Nothing objectionable   ★★★★
INTENDED AUDIENCE: Families
STARRING: Ed Wynn, Richard Hayden, Sterling Holloway, Jerry Colonna,
    Kathryn Beaumont
DIRECTOR: Clyde Geronimi, Hamilton Luske, Wilfred Jackson

Alice in Wonderland is Walt Disney's wonderful, fanciful, screen adaptation of Lewis Carroll's famous book. It begins when Alice sees a white rabbit with a cashmere coat and watch, who says, "I'm late. I'm late for a very important date." She follows him through the hole in a tree into Wonderland. There she meets all the interesting characters of Lewis Carroll's fertile imagination: the Cheshire cat, Tweedle Dee and Tweedle Dum, the Queen of Hearts, the Mad Hatter, and all the rest. In the end, Alice comes back to the present realizing that fantasy is no substitute for reality and the closeness of one's loved ones. A masterpiece, well worth watching. **P.B.** and **J.B.**

ALIENS (1986), 135 min.

RATING: R
CONTENT: Profanity and violence
INTENDED AUDIENCE: Teenagers and adults
STARRING: Sigourney Weaver, Lance Henrikson
DIRECTOR: James Cameron

Like most sequels, *Aliens* is not the thriller that *Alien* was, even though it is in many ways better crafted, because the element of surprise is missing. Ripley (Sigourney Weaver) is rescued by a spaceship after being in hypersleep for fifty-seven years. Almost no one believes her story about vicious aliens. Eventually, however, a man named Burke, Ripley, and a detachment of marines investigate the planet where she found the aliens. Sure enough, the aliens are still implanting eggs inside humans where they incubate. Burke turns against everyone so that he can make money by bringing back an alien alive. Everyone gets killed except Ripley, one of the marines, an android, and a little girl. Ripley is the one who saves the little girl for whom she has motherly feelings (note that the little girl allows Ripley to enjoy motherhood without having a man in her life). In fact, Ripley seems to be the only commendable character of the bunch. The message is clear that women are superior to men, and feminism is the only valid world view.

Aliens would be a good movie, even with its lopsided gender emphasis, if it were not for the excessive profanity. Because of that, avoid it so that the entertainment industry will realize that it cannot profit from cursing God.

ALL THE KING'S MEN (1949) B&W, 109 min.

CONTENT: Nothing objectionable, but adult themes   ★★★
INTENDED AUDIENCE: Adults
STARRING: Broderick Crawford, Joanne Dru, Mercedes McCambridge,
John Ireland, John Derek
DIRECTOR: Robert Rossen

This film is a thinly veiled account of the life of a former governor of Louisiana, Huey Long, a power hungry dictator who reigned above the law during the Depression.

The story opens with Willy Stark's (Long's) beginnings in a small, rural town and follows his meteoric rise to power as a corrupt politician. The film shows how Stark becomes corrupted by the power of his position, and how he slides into a world of shady back room maneuvering, corrupt deals, betrayed confidences, and ruthless undermining. In the end, Stark loses everything, but not without pulling many people down with him. An important, powerful film you will want to see. **B.G.**

ALLAN QUATERMAIN AND THE LOST CITY OF GOLD (1987)

RATING: PG   ★★
CONTENT: Mild violence
INTENDED AUDIENCE: Youth
STARRING: Richard Chamberlain, James Earl Jones, Sharon Stone
DIRECTOR: Gary Nelson

This film is the sequel to the adventure yarn *King Solomon's Mines*. Allan, his girl friend, and his sidekick, played by James Earl Jones, set off to find Quatermain's younger brother and the legendary "Lost City of Gold." Allan and his friends manage to find the lost city in a remote region of Africa, but only after one harrowing episode after another.

The saving element in these movies is Richard Chamberlain whose professionalism makes the films worth watching in spite of the cheap production value of these films.

AMADEUS (1984), 158 min.

RATING: PG ★★★★
CONTENT: Some lewdness
INTENDED AUDIENCE: Adults
STARRING: F. Murray Abraham, Tom Hulce
DIRECTOR: Milos Forman

Christians should welcome this profound study of the sin of envy, even though the historical accuracy of the events is debatable. Antonio Salieri, the protagonist who is the villain in the movie, recognizes that God has given Wolfgang Amadeus a great musical gift. He had prayed for such a musical gift for himself, ostensibly so that he could honor God, but it is clear that he is more concerned with lifting up himself. Salieri rejects God because he is affronted that God could give such talent to someone so frivolous and ungodly as Mozart. The evil of envy drives him to destroy Mozart, to try to kill himself, and finally to condemn himself to eternal damnation by consciously rejecting God.

Viewers learn all these things as Salieri, a decrepit, bitter old man, tells an abbreviated story of his life to a listening priest. Music is used throughout the production, as if to support the validity of Salieri's recognition of Mozart's musical talent and his own mediocrity. Amadeus, whose name means "love of God," is shown as a mixture of genius and eccentric instability. Even as he works to destroy Mozart, Salieri grows more and more appreciative of Mozart's flawless music. After Mozart dies and is buried in a pauper's grave, Salieri lives on in agony, haunted by the evil he has done.

AMERICAN ANTHEM (1986)

RATING: PG–13
CONTENT: Profuse profanity and sexual promiscuity
INTENDED AUDIENCE: Teenagers and young adults
STARRING: Mitch Gaylord, Janet Jones
DIRECTOR: Albert Magnoli

This gymnastic flashdance features rock music with very little real dialogue. The characters talk *at* each other rather than *to* each other. Laura is a gymnast who is accepted on a potential Olympic gymnastics team, the Tops. A great gymnast and a football star who gave it all up to go to work, Steve also joins the Tops. In the end perseverance and commitment win out. At a gymnastics meet he comes in third for the men, and Laura comes in first for the women. The members of the team do so well that they are chosen for the Olympics. Even Steve's father attends the meet, and they are reconciled after a long period of alienation from each other. There are some positive aspects, but they are overshadowed by the thin characterizations, the profuse profanity, and the promiscuity. All in all, this film cannot be recommended. **R.W.**

AMERICAN FLYERS (1985), 113 min.

RATING: PG–13
CONTENT: Profanity, promiscuity, and pro-Eastern religious references
INTENDED AUDIENCE: Young adults
STARRING: David Grant, Kevin Costner, Rae Dawn Chong
DIRECTOR: John Badham

Good acting and beautiful filming cannot overcome the profanity, promiscuity, and pro-Eastern religious references that make this touching tale of bike racing unacceptable for Christians. Two brothers come back together through the valor of one who is on the verge of dying of an incurable brain disease. The story of reconciliation is very moving, but the setting and realization are strictly 1960s hippie. *American Flyers* is not the powerful movie that *Breaking Away* was, even though both share the same scriptwriter, Steve Tesich. You can miss this one.

AN AMERICAN IN PARIS (1951), 113 min.

CONTENT: Nothing offensive   ★★★★
INTENDED AUDIENCE: All ages
STARRING: Gene Kelly, Oscar Levant, Nina Foch, Leslie Caron
DIRECTOR: Vincente Minnelli

This glittering musical, based on the music of Ira and George Gershwin, is one of the best films of this genre. The film takes place in Paris with Gene Kelly as an ex-GI who wants to become a painter. There is a simple love-story angle to the film, with Kelly falling for Leslie Caron, then losing her and getting involved with local painters.

Kelly's fluid and energetic dance routines culminate in a unique ballet ending, lasting over twenty minutes. During this finale, Kelly dances to different styles to reflect the styles of different great painters. Also, his dance conveys his anguish over his love for Caron. Highly recommended. **B.G.**

AN AMERICAN TAIL (1986)

RATING: G   ★★★
CONTENT: Nothing objectionable
INTENDED AUDIENCE: All ages
DIRECTOR: Don Bluth

This beautifully animated movie is a delightful story about the Mousekowitz family—father, mother, sister, baby, and brother, Feivel, the little boy mouse who is the main character in the story. The family is routed out of their homes in Shasta, Russia, by mean Russian cats during a war in 1885. They escape with some other mice to Hamburg, Germany, and make plans to board a ship sailing for America. Dreams are high as they all compare stories and sing together that "there are no cats in America and the streets are paved with cheese."

The boat runs into rough seas and little Feivel is swept overboard and separated from his family. The Mousekowitz's grieve their loss, but Feivel ends up in a bottle alive and floats to Ellis Island where he is rescued and given shelter by a friendly pigeon named Henri who is helping to build the Statue of Liberty.

An American Tail is a great movie for all the kids in the family. There are some very good songs in it that creatively give a mouse point of view. Strong family ties are emphasized. **D.R.**

THE ANDROMEDA STRAIN (1971), 131 min.

RATING: PG   ★★★
CONTENT: Mild off-color language
INTENDED AUDIENCE: Adults
STARRING: James Olson, Arthur Hill
DIRECTOR: Robert Wise

An alien virus comes to earth as a small satellite crashes into a small, remote desert town. Scientists arrive in their protective suits, finding everyone in the town dead, except for an infant baby and an old man. The search for clues also uncovers the fact that in some of the victims the blood has crystallized. The pursuit for a vaccine almost ends in total disaster, however, as the virus mutates into an organism that affects the rubber seals of laboratory specimens, permitting the organism to escape. Highly entertaining, and one of the best science fiction thrillers ever produced. **B.G.**

ANIMAL CRACKERS (1930) B&W, 98 min.

CONTENT: Nothing objectionable   ★★★★
INTENDED AUDIENCE: Adolescents and adults
STARRING: The Marx Brothers, Lillian Roth, Margaret Dumont
DIRECTOR: Victor Heerman

Animal Crackers is the second of the thirteen Marx Brothers comedies and has many of the most memorable lines and gags ever uttered by the Marxes. Groucho portrays Captain Jeffrey T. Spaulding, the famous African explorer. As a guest at the Long Island estate of Margaret Dumont, Spaulding, with Zeppo, as his secretary, and Chico and Harpo as entertainers, becomes embroiled in the events surrounding the theft of a valuable Beauregard painting.

This film, now more than 50 years old, continues to sell in video stores, attesting to its drawing power and the inherently fine script. As Captain Spaulding observes: "One morning I shot an elephant in my pajamas. How he got in my pajamas, I'll never know." Great comedy. **B.G.**

ANNIE (1982), 128 min.

RATING: PG   ★★★
CONTENT: Nothing objectionable
INTENDED AUDIENCE: Families
STARRING: Albert Finney, Aileen Quinn, Carol Burnett, Anne Reinking
DIRECTOR: John Huston

Annie is a big family film based on the successful Broadway musical, which, in turn, was based on the famous comic strip. Annie is an orphan who is always in trouble with the mistress of the orphanage, Miss Hannigan. Annie runs away and during her escape, rescues a dog being chased by a gang of boys. She names the dog "Sandy" but is caught and returned to the orphanage.

Daddy Warbucks's secretary comes to the orphanage to find a boy for Daddy to adopt. After screening the children, she decides that Annie is the best child to take, mainly because she has red hair.

Daddy Warbucks begins to like Annie, and he says he will help her find her parents. He puts up a $50,000 reward to find her parents. However, Miss Hannigan concocts a scheme to get two of her friends to pretend they are Annie's parents so they can collect the reward. Of course, this scheme fails in the end, and everybody lives happily ever after. Children will love it. **P.B.** and **J.B.**

APRIL FOOL'S DAY (1986)

RATING: R
CONTENT: Sex, profanity, and violence
INTENDED AUDIENCE: Teenagers
STARRING: Griffin O'Neal, Deborah Foreman
DIRECTOR: Fred Walton

When some young people inherit a house on a New England island, they decide to turn it into a morbid fantasy island to attract tourists. They try out the idea on two straight young people and scare them almost to death with a series of mock murders. At the end, the tables are turned, however. Too much sex, profanity, and violence fill this film to make it acceptable. **J.C.J.**

THE ARISTOCATS (1970), 78 mins.

RATING: G   ★★★
CONTENT: Nothing objectionable
INTENDED AUDIENCE: Children and all ages
STARRING (Voices): Scatman Crothers, Paul Winchell, Lord Tim Hudson, Vito Scotti, Thurl Ravenscroft, Dean Clark, Liz English, Gary Dubin, Nancy Kulp, Pat Buttram, George Lindsey, Monica Evans, Carole Shelley, Charles Lane, Hermione Baddeley, Roddy Maude-Roxby, Bill Thompson
DIRECTOR: Wolfgang Reitherman

A kind eccentric millionairess, Madame Bonfamille, wills her entire fortune to her cats: Duchess, and her three kittens, Marie, Toulouse, and Berlioz. The butler, Edgar, hears Madame telling her elderly lawyer friend, Monsieur Hautecourt, that when her cats die, the remainder of her fortune passes to him, the butler. Normally a gentle soul, Edgar's greed drives him to try to kill the cats.

Eva Gabor plays Duchess, the aristocratic cat heir to a wealthy estate. Veteran singer/actor Phil Harris lent his voice to a Casanova cat-about-town named, O'Malley. *The Aristocats* is a positive, fun Disney movie that does not suffer from the magical thinking that pervades most Disney films. Good triumphs over evil in an enjoyable way. Highly recommended for the whole family. **B.E.**

AROUND THE WORLD IN EIGHTY DAYS (1956), 170 min.

CONTENT: Nothing objectionable   ★★★★
INTENDED AUDIENCE: All ages
STARRING: David Niven, Shirley MacLaine, Cantinflas, Robert Newton
DIRECTOR: Michael Anderson

This lavish, charming film version of the Jules Verne novel is a wonder with its many foreign locations and scores of cameos by famous actors and actresses. Phileas Fogg

(David Niven) makes a bet with fellow colleagues at his club that he can circle the globe in less than eighty days, which would be a first in 1872. Fogg travels with his companion valet, Passepartout, and the two of them surmount every obstacle man and nature can place in their path. The movie won Oscars for Best Picture and Best Screenplay. **B.G.**

AT CLOSE RANGE (1986), 115 min.

RATING: R   ★★
CONTENT: Profanity, violence, sexual situations, and obscenity
INTENDED AUDIENCE: Adults
STARRING: Sean Penn, Christopher Walken
DIRECTOR: James Foley

Thanks to *Rambo, Commando,* and other big moneymakers, violence is "in" in Hollywood movies. *At Close Range* could have been good if it hadn't been torpedoed by excessive violence and foul language. The acting is excellent, the photography is beautiful, and the premise of this true story is uplifting—"a son can make the decision to renounce the sins of his father."

The erstwhile father-husband of a down-and-out Pennsylvania family is the leader of a vicious gang of thieves. One son tries to follow in his father's footsteps as a low-life robber, but he is redeemed by falling in love. Aware that his father is also a rapist and a murderer, the son turns state's evidence to the police. The father goes on a killing spree that the son manages to survive, but he cannot kill his father. The son transcends the sins of the father because he has found love for others in his heart. The movie provides good insights into selfishness and love, but overall there are too many negatives to place it in the "acceptable" category.

BACK TO SCHOOL (1986), 94 min.

RATING: PG–13
CONTENT: Profanity, nudity, and vulgarity
INTENDED AUDIENCE: Teenagers and adults
STARRING: Rodney Dangerfield, Sally Kellerman, Keith Gordon,
   Adrienne Barbeau, Ned Beatty
DIRECTOR: Alan Metter

Some aspects of film criticism are a matter of taste, some depend upon the reviewer's world view, and some are totally unexplainable, as in the case of this mediocre film that has received good reviews from secular critics. Dangerfield doesn't deserve any respect for this movie, which is almost like a nightclub act on film.

Dangerfield's character has made millions with a string of "Tall and Fat" clothing stores, but he decides to go to college. When he doesn't qualify, he buys a building for the business school, and they admit him. He turns into a party animal. He redesigns his dormitory into a bachelor pad. He hires a stenographer to take notes at his classes. When he has to write a paper on astronomy, he hires someone from NASA. Kellerman plays a college literature professor who tries to upgrade Dangerfield in spite of his nonstop, downgrading one-liners. There is really nothing to commend this movie: lowbrow humor, thin plot, undeveloped characterizations. It's not even fun, must less interesting. **K.K.**

BACK TO THE FUTURE (1985), 116 min.

RATING: PG   ★★
CONTENT: Profanity
INTENDED AUDIENCE: Teenagers and adults
STARRING: Michael J. Fox, Christopher Lloyd, Lea Thompson
DIRECTOR: Robert Zemeckis

This charming, exciting little picture has a myopic world view, but it is not misanthropic or anti-Christian. A teenager, Marty (Michael J. Fox), goes back in time to the week when his parents met. The lovable eccentric inventor of a timemobile makes Marty's excursion possible. The events that occur when he goes into the past change the present, but it is all for the better. There are one or two cruel moments in the beginning when Marty's parents are caricatured, but they, too, turn out all right in the end. All in all, it would be good entertainment if it were not for the profanity and lack of respect for parents.

BAND OF THE HAND (1986)

RATING: R
CONTENT: Profanity and violence
INTENDED AUDIENCE: Teenagers
STARRING: Stephen Lang, James Remar
DIRECTOR: Paul Michael Glaser

Band of the Hand is a *Billy Jack* type of movie. After five guys are released from a Miami jail, they meet an Indian who turns them into heroes. The Indian gets killed fighting for good, and the five bury him before setting out to crush a big drug pusher and his operation.

Too savage and violent, the film portrays people in a constant state of war. It is an attempt to cash in on tough teens. Also, it is full of profanity. The only redeeming feature is that it shows how bad drugs are. Avoid it. **G.O. and J.C.J.**

THE BEAUTY AND THE BEAST (1987), 90 minutes

RATING: G   ★★★
CONTENT: Some magical thinking
INTENDED AUDIENCE: Children and families
STARRING: Rebecca de Mornay, John Savage
DIRECTOR: Eugene Marner

This film is an accurate rendition of the story "The Beauty and the Beast." Beauty takes care of her family and her father indulges all of his children, except Beauty on whom he leans for support. The father is a very wealthy man, but he loses his money through a series of misfortunes. Attempting to retrieve his fortune, he goes off to find one of his lost ships. But the ship has been sold out from under him, and he returns home down-trodden.

On the way home, he gets lost. Just before he faints, he stumbles across an elegant, empty castle where he eats and sleeps like a king. The next day, he picks a rose for Beauty, only to be confronted by Beast, who asks why the father is stealing a rose when he had been fed and lodged so magnificently. Beast says that the father either

69

has to give his life for his crime, or his daughter has to come and live with the Beast. Naturally, Beauty is horrified but obeys to save her father. She ultimately learns that the Beast is an enchanted handsome prince she has dreamed about. They get married and live happily ever after.

The Beauty and the Beast is recommended with the caution that it should be carefully explained to children that magical thinking is not true.

BEING THERE (1979), 107 mins.
RATING: PG   ★★★
CONTENT: Some implied sexual perversion
INTENDED AUDIENCE: Adults
STARRING: Peter Sellers, Shirley MacLaine, Melvyn Douglas, Jack Warden
DIRECTOR: Hal Ashby

Being There is a poignant, comic fable about the self-deception and foolish madness that flows from a lack of a moral world view. Peter Sellers gives a great performance as the slow-witted innocent, appropriately named Chance, who is mistaken for an aristocratic millionaire because he is wearing his benefactor's clothes. Before his guardian died, leaving him with no one to care for him, Chance spent his life watching television and gardening. All of his statements, which are couched in gardening terms, are interpreted as being the height of wisdom by the wealthy family who finds him wandering the streets and by the television interviewers who pick up on his "genius." Eventually, Chance is elected president of the United States by the gullible public that falls for the media hype around this poor, mentally retarded man.

This film shows what happens when we are set adrift in a turbulent sea of people's prejudices and imperfect perceptions. This is the situation we find ourselves in today. Unfortunately, *Being There* has one risqué, off-screen, sexual moment. Therefore, Christians should exercise caution in deciding to view this interesting insight into the folly of our time. **B.G.**

BELIZAIRE, THE CAJUN (1986)
RATING: PG   ★★★
CONTENT: Vigilante brutality
INTENDED AUDIENCE: Adults
STARRING: Armand Assante, Gail Young, Michael Schoeffling
DIRECTOR: Glen Pitre

When the French lost Nova Scotia to the British in 1779, her colonists wandered in exile. By 1859, a settlement of those colonists, called cajuns, struggled for permanent roots in southwest Louisiana. Conflicts arose between southern landowners and the cajuns, who were victims of torch-bearing night raids by vigilante lynch mobs ordering them out of Louisiana—"or else." This movie focuses on the conflict over the Perry family plantation, which is slipping from the fingers of an ailing founder to his two sons. Matthew regularly fathers the illegitimate children of a cajun woman, Belizaire's cousin. As insurance against losing the plantation to these "heirs," second son James, recklessly ambitious, kills his favored brother and blames it on the cajun woman. Hero Belizaire risks his life to save his cousin, and he exposes and captures the real murderer.

Other than minimal overtones of cajun black magic, moments of lust, and vigilante brutality, this movie could be rated inoffensive. There is no bad language or nudity. An entertaining movie, full of good scenery, it is for mature Christians who can see beyond the flaws. **G.O.**

BEN-HUR (1959), 217 min.

CONTENT: No swearing and no nudity, but some violence,   ★★★★
  with two graphic scenes
INTENDED AUDIENCE: All ages
STARRING: Charlton Heston, Stephen Boyd, Hugh Griffith,
  Jack Hawkins, Sam Jaffe
DIRECTOR: William Wyler

Nominated for twelve Academy Awards and winner of eleven, *Ben-Hur* stands as one of the most honored films in motion picture history. The story involves Rome, Christ, and the complicated friendship and falling out between Judah Ben-Hur and the Roman tribune, Messala. Judah Ben-Hur, a noble Jew of learning and wealth, is a close friend of Messala, who becomes the Roman commander of Jerusalem. After a confrontation between the two men, their friendship dissolves, and soon afterward, so does the House of Hur. An accident occurs as the Roman governor and his entourage pass the house; some roof tiles fall and startle the governor's horse, causing the animal to rear and crush the governor's head against a brick wall. Messala's soldiers burst into the house and arrest everyone.

This sets the stage for the remainder of the action. Ben-Hur, imprisoned falsely by the Romans, spends years in misery and torture, and his mother and sister linger in a miserable dungeon. Ben-Hur's final confrontation with Messala occurs in the chariot race. All the years of hatred reach a climax as the two men take out their vengeance on the dirt track of the arena. During the famed race (which took three months to film), Messala is thrown from his chariot and trampled by horses.

This film provides an interesting approach to Jesus of Nazareth. His face is never shown, and He is a minor character in the life of Ben-Hur, until the concluding scenes of the film. Only at that time, as Jesus is crucified, does Ben-Hur realize who He is—not for his divine origins, however, but for his human kindness. Earlier in the film, Jesus had given Ben-Hur a drink of water when he was a Roman slave. Ben-Hur tries to reciprocate as Jesus, who has been severely beaten and is carrying His cross to Golgotha, passes by Ben-Hur and his leprous mother and sister. When the time of death occurs for Jesus and Ben-Hur's mother and sister are instantly and miraculously healed, Judah Ben-Hur becomes a believer. This poignant climax, where Christ dies to save others and Ben-Hur becomes one of the first benefactors of Christ's death and salvation, is one of the most moving scenes ever recorded about the passion of Jesus. Judah Ben-Hur becomes a Jew who knows Christ as his Lord and Savior. You must see this film with your family. **B.G.**

BEST OF TIMES (1986)

RATING: PG–13
CONTENT: Obscenity, profanity, and sexual situations
INTENDED AUDIENCE: Adults
STARRING: Robin Williams, Kurt Russell
DIRECTOR: Roger Spottiswoode

Why Robin Williams would play in this dimwitted movie is beyond me. Except for an angel and a Bible quote at the end, this movie has no redeeming qualities. A broken-down banker has never recovered from his fumble that lost his town a critical football game. The town has never recovered either. He dreams up a plan to replay the game. When he does, the town wins, and life starts anew.

In spite of the corny attractiveness of the plot, the movie is slow and dull. Promiscuity is taken for granted, immorality is the norm, and bad language is prevalent.

THE BEST YEARS OF OUR LIVES (1946), 172 min.

CONTENT: Nothing objectionable   ★★★★
INTENDED AUDIENCE: All ages
STARRING: Myrna Loy, Fredric March, Dana Andrews, Virginia Mayo
DIRECTOR: William Wyler

"Last year, it was kill Japs; this year, it's make money." This one sentence, the words of one returning World War II veteran, capsulizes the theme of this picture that received seven Academy Awards. The story focuses on three veterans who return home from overseas duty: an air force captain who finds his wife a tramp; a middle-aged sergeant who discovers that his children have grown up in his absence; and a sailor who comes home without any hands, only hooks, to his fiancée and family. (Harold Russell, a real-life vet who actually lost his hands in combat, played the sailor.)

From the family reunions to the dashed, crushed hopes to the renewal of commitments, this film generates incredible emotion, a tear-jerker if ever there was one. We follow the three men's adjustments to civilian life and see how they are considered almost as outsiders, even within their families. Memories of the war return in their dreams to haunt them, each man suffering a different nightmare, yet the same in its cost to psyche, spirit, and ability to adjust. When they seek civilian employment, they meet unexpected reactions and unwanted rejection.

Eventually, the separate lives of the men become intermingled. The film ends on a note of hope as the three men meet at the sailor's wedding. Each man is learning to come to terms with his past and cope with his life. This profoundly moving picture is recommended. **B.G.**

BETTER OFF DEAD (1985), 97 min.

RATING: PG   ★★★
CONTENT: Mild obscenity
INTENDED AUDIENCE: Teenagers
STARRING: John Cusack, David Ogden Stiers, Diane Franklin
DIRECTOR: Savage Steve Holland

Although the title of this comedy leaves much to be desired, the story line is very encouraging. The teenage hero is devastated by the loss of his curvaceous, opportunistic girlfriend to the new star athlete in the school, but the hero finds true love by learning to be himself. In other words, humility triumphs over conceit.

As in any comedy, there are some flat moments, and some routines are too broad. There is very little off-color language. However, there is the hint of an illicit love scene between our hero and his former flame, but this affair is portrayed as being wrong. All in all, it rates above other teenage comedies and is an extraordinary effort for a low-budget film.

BIG TROUBLE IN LITTLE CHINA (1986)

RATING: PG–13
CONTENT: Foul language, magic, and violence
INTENDED AUDIENCE: Teenagers and adults
STARRING: Kurt Russell, Kim Cattrall, Dennis Dun, James Hong
DIRECTOR: John Carpenter

Though billed as "an adventure-comedy-kung fu-monster-ghost story about an imaginary world underneath [San Francisco's] Chinatown," the movie is a drag. The action may move at a brisk clip, but there is very little real tension because Jack Burton (Kurt Russell), a truck driver caught up in a war between Chinese white magic (Christians know there is no such thing as white magic) and Chinese black magic, is never really in jeopardy. Instead, this is more of a choreographed kung fu epic, straight out of Taiwan—slightly intriguing and slightly foolish. Reality is an afterthought.

Although the spiritism, occultism, and magic depicted are bad, they are muted by the absurdity of the plot. The story does not hold together because there are great gaps in it. This is not *Indiana Jones and the Temple of Doom,* but it is a feeble attempt to capture the same audience. The language is dreadful. Avoid *Big Trouble in Little China.*

THE BLACK CAULDRON (1985), 80 min.

RATING: PG
CONTENT: Spiritism, sorcery, mysticism, and occultism
INTENDED AUDIENCE: Children
STARRING: Animated characters
DIRECTOR: Ted Berman

Although many critics have complained that *The Black Cauldron* is uncharacteristic of Disney films, many movies from this studio have been preoccupied with sorcery. Spiritism, mysticism, and occultism are the basic elements of this second-rate movie. Don't allow your children to see it.

BLACK MOON RISING (1986)

RATING: R
CONTENT: Profanity, obscenity, sexual situations, and violence
INTENDED AUDIENCE: Adults
STARRING: Tommy Lee Jones, Robert Vaughn, Linda Hamilton
DIRECTOR: Harley Cokliss

This powerful, suspenseful movie is destroyed by sex, violence, and obscenity, and its setting and realization of the story line are evil in spades. The story involves a hired gun the FBI pushes to destroy an evil megalomaniac, who makes his fortune selling stolen cars. This is straight action adventure, well done and well acted, but spoiled by a fixation with things more suitable for the gutter than the movie screen.

BLISS (1986)

RATING: R
CONTENT: Nudity, sex, lewdness, and profanity

INTENDED AUDIENCE: Adults
STARRING: Barry Otto, Lynette Curran, Helen Jones
DIRECTOR: Ray Lawrence

Christians should avoid this strange, surrealistic movie from Australia in spite of the rave reviews it has received in this country. Harry Joy, a successful advertising man, has a heart attack, dies, and comes face to face with heaven and hell. But Harry returns to his body and decides he wants to find out if he is still alive or in hell. As time passes, he forgets his confrontation with death and looks for the answers to the ultimate questions. Though his conversation with a liberal clergyman never introduces him to the gospel of Jesus Christ, he decides to be good so he can go to heaven. His goodness is not consistent, but when he dies a second time, he goes off to heaven.

There are hints of Christianity throughout this movie, but the gospel is never clearly presented; what is presented is a new-age religious perspective. This may have been done to show how sinful people are; however, it is more likely that the moviemaker is confused about the fact that Jesus is the only way to heaven. In effect, *Bliss* never fulfills its potential as an adequate treatment of death, heaven, and hell. Nudity, lewdness, and profanity make this picture unacceptable for Christians, despite its amusing moments. Immorality is shown to be evil, but the good is not much better because it is removed from the redemptive power of Jesus Christ and His principles.

BLUE ANGEL (1930) B&W, 98 min.

CONTENT: The portrait of a man who is led by his desires ★★★
INTENDED AUDIENCE: Adults
STARRING: Emil Jannings, Marlene Dietrich, Kurt Gerron
DIRECTOR: Josef Von Sternberg

A self-righteous, middle-aged professor, Immanuel Rath, pursues a group of schoolboys to their nightclub haunt, the place they go after school for fun and recreation. He plans to chastise them for smoking and for going to the nightclub, but, instead, he sees the leading singer, Lola-Lola, and immediately falls for her. He turns from being an intelligent person to being an utter fool under her influence. She wraps him around her little finger, marries him and quickly tires of him. Soon, she puts him into her act as a clown and robs him of all character and grace.

A powerful movie, *The Blue Angel* is a movie that Christians might want to see for its message: the wages of sin is death.

BORN FREE (1966), 96 min.

RATING: PG ★★★★
CONTENT: Minor swearing
INTENDED AUDIENCE: Families
STARRING: Bill Travers, Virginia McKenna
DIRECTOR: James Hill

Game warden George Adamson and his wife Joy raise a lioness named Elsa as a pet and eventually return her to the wild. Their task is a complicated one because they have to turn their tame lioness into an animal capable of killing her own food. After a disastrous first attempt, the Adamsons return her to the wild again, this time successfully. Later, as the Adamsons prepare to leave the district, Elsa wanders into their camp, the proud mother of three cubs.

Born Free is a wholesome family movie with no nudity, no violence, and no profanity. The off-color language is minimal, and although Hollywood must learn to rely on better dialogue devices, the objectionable language is overshadowed by the love and caring that form the heart of the message. Filmed in Kenya, the movie contains some great footage of animals in the wild. **B.G.**

THE BOY IN BLUE (1986)

CONTENT: Foul language and sexual situations
INTENDED AUDIENCE: Adults
STARRING: Christopher Plummer, Nicholas Cage
DIRECTOR: Charles Jarrott

The Boy in Blue opens with the announcement that before baseball and soccer, there was sculling (rowing competitions). However, only baseball terms do justice to this poor imitation of *Chariots of Fire:* strike one for a set-up story; strike two for poor acting; and strike three for surface theme. There are no hits and no runs, but plenty of errors (mattress aerobics and foul language). When will producers get it through their thick heads that sweaty biceps and fierce facial straining for a split-second finish do not make a champion? The heart of a true champion focuses on the inner spiritual man in answer to his highest calling, but the highest calling depicted here was self. Sex and skulduggery make this movie unacceptable for Christians. **G.O.**

THE BOY WHO COULD FLY (1986)

RATING: PG ★★★★
CONTENT: Very mild bad language
INTENDED AUDIENCE: All ages
STARRING: Lucy Deakins, Bonnie Bedelia, Jay Underwood, Fred Savage
DIRECTOR: Nick Castle

The good news is that this big-budget movie has no profanity, no nudity, and very mild bad language. It's all heart—a good tear-jerker. When a teenage girl moves next door to an autistic boy who just wants to sit on his roof, she learns he has been autistic since his mother and father were killed in an airplane crash. There are rumors that he can fly, and as the girl tries to help the boy who now lives with his alcoholic uncle, she suspects that he really can fly. Events prove her to be correct.

This positive story of love and faith is a fable, not to be taken seriously—almost like a 1980s *Dumbo*. Christians who take their children to see it should point out that mind over matter does not work and that the children cannot fly no matter how hard they think about it. I recommend that you see it as pure fantasy, rather than some subtle philosophical message. It's a good, entertaining film for the whole family. **B.G.**

THE BOYS NEXT DOOR (1986)

RATING: R
CONTENT: Obscenity, profanity, violence, and sexual situations
INTENDED AUDIENCE: Adults
STARRING: Maxwell Caulfield, Charlie Sheen
DIRECTOR: Penelope Spheeris

This is a foul movie full of sex and violence. Two young men go on a killing spree for no good reason except the demons inside them. From crowbarring a gas station attendant to death to mutilating a homosexual, their actions seem all too real. There is no conscience or moral perspective evident in this film. Don't even consider viewing it. **R.W.**

BRAZIL (1986)

RATING: R ★★
CONTENT: Violence
INTENDED AUDIENCE: Adults
STARRING: Robert De Niro, Jonathan Pryce, Katherine Helmond
DIRECTOR: Terry Gilliam

A unique, breakthrough movie that has been grabbing awards from critics, *Brazil* is a nightmare, a dark vision of a Socialist bureaucracy where individuality and love are crushed by the state. It's the movie that *1984* should have been—a retrofuturistic film that sees the present through a future predetermined by the worst of the past. This satire is marred by a misguided view of Christianity, which sees the institutional church as an instrument of the state's oppression (unless this is the false church of the Antichrist). Furthermore, there is too much profanity. However, the acting is excellent, and the nightmare quality of the film takes it beyond traditional points of view.

What begins as a very funny movie quickly becomes a disquieting story of the helplessness of a man in love who is trying to overcome the oppression of the state. The ending is very painful. Yet for someone with a stout heart, it might be an interesting insight into statism run wild. For most people, it is too strong.

BREAKER MORANT (1980), 107 min.

CONTENT: Minor swearing, no nudity, no sexual situations, ★★★★
one off-color joke, and some violence that is not gory or graphic
INTENDED AUDIENCE: Adults
STARRING: Edward Woodward, Jack Thompson, Bryan Brown, John Waters
DIRECTOR: Bruce Beresford

The Boer War (1899–1902) was fought between the British Empire and the Boer, or Afrikaner (mostly Dutch), population of South Africa. Though most of the heavy fighting took place earlier, 1901 saw an extensive guerrilla war being waged. Lord Kitchener, British chief of staff, realized that final victory lay only in the systematic destruction of the Boer guerrilla units. However, his policy changed when the tide turned in favor of the British and a negotiated peace seemed feasible.

Set in Pietersburg, South Africa, in 1901, *Breaker Morant* tells of three Australian soldiers serving the British who are charged with the murder of seven Boer prisoners of war and one German missionary. The Australians had been carrying out orders to exterminate the guerrilla units, but they were caught in the tactical policy change. The film chronicles the court-martial of the men, with flashbacks to the actual events as seen through the eyes of the different participants. Essentially, the court-martial publicly "sacrifices" the Australians so that the Boers, with whom the British are holding peace talks, can see that the British system of "justice" is impartial; and as a consequence, the Boers would be willing to cease the fighting and accept British rule.

Breaker Morant is a powerfully moving story of injustice consciously executed to achieve political goals. Whether or not the political goals were worthy is another story, but the evidence suggests that they were not. The movie shows the sinfulness of man and how it is compounded by centralized power. This film is definitely worth seeing. **B.G.**

A BREED APART (1985)

RATING: R
CONTENT: Profanity and nudity
INTENDED AUDIENCE: Adults
STARRING: Rutger Hauer, Kathleen Turner, Powers Boothe
DIRECTOR: Philippe Mora

Though full of good actors, the movie fails for lack of a good story and good direction. A Vietnam veteran who is trying to save some rare bald eagles from an unscrupulous millionaire hires a mountain climber to steal two of their eggs, knowing that this might make the species extinct. Good triumphs over evil in the end, and the good guy even gets the girl. However, profanity and nudity make this unacceptable viewing for Christians. If these elements were cut out, it would be an okay television movie. As it stands, it's not recommended. **K.K.**

THE BRIDGE (1961), 102 min.
(Subtitles)

RATING: Not rated   ★★★
CONTENT: War
INTENDED AUDIENCE: Adults
STARRING: Michael Hinz, Fritz Wepper, Gunther Hoffman
DIRECTOR: Bernhard Wicki

This masterful little work from Germany is the story of a group of young boys, still in their teens, who are ordered to hold a small, stone bridge against the pursuing Allied forces. *The Bridge* tells of the useless courage and senseless deaths of these seven boys, who are hastily conscripted into the German Army during the last few days of the war. They earnestly and totally devote themselves to the task at hand, not realizing that their sacrifice is in vain. A German demolition team is supposed to have blown up the bridge before the Americans arrive; but the night before it is to be destroyed, the boy's Sergeant is killed, and this information is lost.

The American tanks arrive, and each of the boys is killed. Indeed, their deaths vividly present the message that war is hell. A strong film, outstanding in its portrait of war. **B.G.**

BRING ON THE NIGHT (1986)

RATING: PG–13   ★★
CONTENT: Nothing objectionable
INTENDED AUDIENCE: Teenagers and young adults
STARRING: Sting
DIRECTOR: Michael Apted

This is a pretty good documentary about Sting and his new band, but the problem is that it has no "punch." I had the distinct feeling that I was watching a record commercial. It isn't bad; it just isn't good. But it won't harm anyone to see it.

BULLITT (1968), 113 min.

RATING: PG   ★★★
CONTENT: Some foul language and violence
INTENDED AUDIENCE: Adults
STARRING: Steve McQueen, Jaqueline Bisset, Robert Vaughn, Robert Duvall
DIRECTOR: Peter Yates

Probably the forerunner of the modern detective movie, *Bullitt* is considered a classic. Steve McQueen stars as a detective whose charge, a key witness to underworld activity, is murdered. He goes after the bad guys with a vengeance, culminating in the now-famous car chase scene. This chase is still exciting, even after all these years of movies filled with similar chase scenes.

Like most detective movies, however, this one does not have a strong moral tone. The wages of sin is death. Greed corrupts. Though these points are well-made, *Bullitt* is recommended with extreme caution owing to much of its content and message. **L.R.**

BUTCH CASSIDY AND THE SUNDANCE KID (1969), 112 min.

RATING: PG   ★★
CONTENT: Some violence and minor swearing
INTENDED AUDIENCE: Adults and youths
STARRING: Paul Newman, Robert Redford, Katharine Ross
DIRECTOR: George Roy Hill

Two famous outlaws are portrayed as young sophisticates, more like college fraternity brothers than criminals, who clowned their way to success in the American West. Played as a slick contemporary drama, with comedy interspersed throughout, the movie presents the last word on outlaws who had outlived their day (as did *The Wild Bunch*, directed by Sam Peckinpah, which left little room for levity). But by romanticizing the outlaws, the movie ignores the sinfulness of man and his need for redemption.

There are moments of clever dialogue that are executed almost faultlessly, and there are several brilliant sequences. For all its cleverness, cuteness, and coyness, however, the movie lacks a broader dimension, one that takes us deeply into the personalities of the central characters. On the other hand, the movie makes it clear that crime doesn't pay, which is a very positive point in a genre that generally uplifts the outlaw. It would be better if we did not support Hollywood in its propensity for this type of movie. Ultimately, heroes should be good. In the final analysis, this lighthearted movie will entertain without permanently damaging anyone, but caution is recommended. **B.G.**

CAME A HOT FRIDAY (1986)

RATING: PG   ★★★
CONTENT: Mild bad language and sexual suggestions
INTENDED AUDIENCE: Adults
STARRING: Peter Bland, Philip Gordan
DIRECTOR: Ian Mune

Post-war New Zealand provides the backdrop for the antics of two bumbling conmen, Wesley Pennington and his loyal sidekick, Cyril Kidman, who prove that crime doesn't pay.

One hot Friday afternoon, they arrive in sleepy Tainuia Junction and note that on a hill near the horsetrack is a tower from which the races can be watched. They find a telephone at the bottom of the hill and plan to call in the winners right after the race to a local named Don, who will then quickly place a bet and win. All goes smoothly for a while, but complications ensue that prompt Wes, Cyril, and Don to team up with a local Maori Indian called the Tainuia "Kid" to get their winnings, which have been lost in a police raid. They get their money back, but a casino operator inadvertently blows himself and his casino up. In panic, the Kid throws the money in the river to appease what he thinks is the river monster, although what he actually sees is only a piece of the burning building from the explosion. The conmen lose everything. Crime doesn't pay.

Came a Hot Friday is recommended with the caution that it is only light entertainment and plays fast and loose with the Eighth Commandment. **K.K.**

CAMPUS MAN (1987)

RATING: PG ★★★
CONTENT: Very little off-color language
INTENDED AUDIENCE: Young adults
STARRING: John Dye, Kim Delaney, Kathleen Wilhoite, Morgan Fairchild
DIRECTOR: Ron Casden

Campus Man is a light comedy that revolves around an enterprising, would-be college student named Todd who needs to make money for college. Todd badgers his shy, best friend, Brett Wilson, a champion diver, into posing for his "Men of Arizona State University" pinup calendar, which he hopes will sell so well that it will give him the $10,000 he needs for tuition. It costs him $12,000 start-up money to print the calendar, which he gets from Cactus Jack, an unsavory loan shark. Todd makes the money back from the calendar sales, but can't pay both Cactus Jack and his tuition. He pays his tuition. The consequences of that decision form the rest of the movie.

In the final analysis, *Campus Man* is a cute movie that will not hurt the young adult target audience. Recommended with caution. **K.K.**

CASABLANCA (1942) B&W, 102 min.

CONTENT: Greatness ★★★★
INTENDED AUDIENCE: Everyone
STARRING: Humphrey Bogart, Ingrid Bergman, Paul Henreid,
    Claude Rains, Conrad Veidt, Sydney Greenstreet
DIRECTOR: Michael Curtiz

Intrigue, romance, memorable lines, and a superb, moody atmosphere make *Casablanca* one of the best World War II movies. It won Oscars for best picture, best director, and best screenplay.

The story of how Rick (Bogart) goes from cynicism to a nobility that leads to great personal sacrifice is the stuff of great film drama. Ingrid Bergman is compelling as the one woman Rick ever loved.

One of the greatest movies of all time.

CHARLOTTE'S WEB (1973), 94 min.

RATING: G   ★★★
CONTENT: Nothing objectionable
INTENDED AUDIENCE: All ages
STARRING (Voices): Debbie Reynolds, Paul Lynde, Henry Gibson,
  Rex Allen, Agnes Moorehead
DIRECTOR: Charles Nichols

Charlotte's Web is an enduring classic about Charlotte, a friendly spider living in the same barn as Wilbur, a pig with many barnyard friends. The story is about Wilbur's fear of being turned into bacon, when he would prefer to become a show animal. Wilbur confronts the realities of life and death through Charlotte, who is able to explain to Wilbur about aging, death, and how an animal's children live on as his legacy. This film gives Christian parents the opportunity to distinguish for their children between animals, who are earth bound creatures, and human beings, who are eternal, created in the image of God. **B.G.**

CHILDREN OF A LESSER GOD (1986)

RATING: R
CONTENT: Nudity, explicit sex, profanity, and obscenity
INTENDED AUDIENCE: Adults
STARRING: William Hurt, Marlee Matlin
DIRECTOR: Randa Haines

Children of a Lesser God has nothing to do with God. It reduces love to sex and psychological posturing. Because it tries to pull at our heartstrings while it proclaims immoral messages, it stands in stark opposition to a biblical world view.

James Leeds (William Hurt) gets a job at a school for the deaf teaching a small eleventh-grade class how to speak. The students who appreciate his self-important leadership do well, but one young boy is completely passed over by James, and at the end we can only wonder how James could have been so callous.

James approaches Sarah, a sexy twenty-five-year-old who has withdrawn into her anger, with the attitude that *he* can get her to speak. They become lovers, but Sarah eventually leaves him to make her way in the world by putting herself through college. In the end, they vow to live together, although there seems to be no hint of marriage.

This is not anything like the poignant Helen Keller story, as portrayed in *The Miracle Worker,* of a faith in the God who breaks down the barriers erected by deafness. Rather, it is the story of an egotist who thinks that his superior know-it-all attitude can solve the problems of deafness. James is competent only at teaching his students how to make love, swear, curse God, and put themselves first. This film should be boycotted by Christians.

A CHORUS LINE (1985), 117 min.

RATING: PG–13   ★★
CONTENT: Profanity and sexual innuendo
INTENDED AUDIENCE: Adults
STARRING: Michael Douglas
DIRECTOR: Richard Attenborough

The movie of A Chorus Line should not be compared to the play. On stage, the hopeful dancers who were trying out for the chorus line were small and vulnerable. We felt compassion for them and understood the magnitude of their task, which was to communicate their ability to a director sitting in the deep darkness of the theater. On film, the dancers are larger than life. Their dancing fills the screen with energy, and we are exposed to the greatness of their effort.

When the play is forgotten, the movie A Chorus Line is pretty good entertainment. However, it is not acceptable Christian film fare because of the profanity, sexual innuendo, and acceptance of homosexuality. Without these elements, it would have been a worthwhile movie telling the poignant story of the hopeful dancers who are anxious to be accepted and terrified of being rejected.

A CHRISTMAS CAROL (1938) B&W, 70 min. and (1984), 104 min.

Credits for 1938 Version: ★★★★
CONTENT: A great, biblically based story
INTENDED AUDIENCE: Families
STARRING: Reginald Owen, Gene Lockhart, Kathleen Lockhart,
    Terry Kilburn, Barry MacKay, Lynne Cary
DIRECTOR: Edwin L. Marin

Credits for 1984 Version:
STARRING: George C. Scott, Nigel Davenport, Frank Finley, Lucy Guttenridge,
    Angela Pleasence, David Was, Susannah York, Anthony Walters (Tiny Tim)
DIRECTOR: Clive Donner

There have been several film versions of Charles Dickens's great story. The 1938 version with Reginald Owen is in black and white, and the 1984 version with George C. Scott was made for television.

The story, of course, concerns Ebenezer Scrooge, a wealthy miser who must learn the meaning of Christmas through the ghosts of Christmas Past, Present, and Future.

The film is a great story with a profound message, as Scrooge repents of his evil ways and vows to keep Christmas in his heart. Either version is terrific. P.B. and J.B.

CITIZEN KANE (1941) B&W, 119 min.

CONTENT: Nothing objectionable   ★★★★
INTENDED AUDIENCE: Adults
STARRING: Orson Welles, Joseph Cotton, Everett Sloane
DIRECTOR: Orson Welles

Orson Welles, who directed, co-wrote and starred in this film, gives us a hard look at Charles Foster Kane, a magnate newspaper publisher whose career parallels that of William Randolph Hearst. Set in flashback, an innovative plot structure even today, and with unusual directorial flair (high-key lighting, low points of view for the camera, extended depth-of-field), Citizen Kane is a study of power and corruption, with an in-depth look into the personality of Kane, a megalo-egomaniac whose American dream goes sour.

The film was not a great success when initially released, because the real William Randolph Hearst waged an unprecedented campaign to kill the movie. Yet, as Francois Truffaut, the critic and filmmaker says of the film, "It (is) probably the one (film) that has started the largest number of filmmakers on their careers." International film critics have tabbed this movie as perhaps the best ever made. **B.G.**

CLAN OF THE CAVE BEAR (1985), 120 min.

RATING: R
CONTENT: Caveman sex scenes
INTENDED AUDIENCE: Adults
STARRING: Daryl Hannah, Thomas Waites
DIRECTOR: Michael Chapman

The story centers on a little Cro-Magnon girl who is found by a Neanderthal tribe. As she grows up, it is clear that she is superior. In a modern setting this would be called white supremacy, although the author of the book upon which the movie is based contends that her point was the strength and power of women, that is, feminism. Of course, the problem of wrong-headed evolutionary theories looms in the background.

Nearly everything about *Clan of the Cave Bear* is bad; it lacks tension, plot, and conflict. The dialogue seems to be an attempt to make Hollywood writers look like dimwits. Finally, there are those wretched sex scenes. This is one to miss.

CLASH OF THE TITANS (1981), 120 min.

RATING: PG   ★★★
CONTENT: Some violence and brief female back nudity
INTENDED AUDIENCE: Adolescents, adults
STARRING: Sir Laurence Olivier, Harry Hamlin, Claire Bloom, Maggie Smith,
    Ursula Andress, Burgess Meredith
DIRECTOR: Desmond Davis

This film is an exciting fantasy about the gods of Mount Olympus and how they intercede in the lives of men, sometimes in a righteous and moral way, but usually in a vindictive, unforgiving manner. Zeus (Olivier) commands the lesser gods, such as Aphrodite and Poseidon. There are many subplots about the scheming among the gods, and how their powers are used to manipulate and rule the Greeks below. This contrasts greatly with the biblical God. Nonetheless, this is a fine piece of entertainment, though not recommended for the very young. Some of the scenes are just too scary. **B.G.**

CLOCKWISE (1986)

RATING: PG   ★★★
CONTENT: Some rude language and brief, distant nudity
INTENDED AUDIENCE: Adults
STARRING: John Cleese
DIRECTOR: Christopher Morahan

Clockwise is a comedy of errors with a storyline as complicated as it could possibly be and still be enjoyable and comprehensible. Briefly, John Cleese, best known for his work with Monty Python, plays the headmaster of a public boarding school in England where he is obsessed with making sure everything is running on schedule. Cleese is appointed the Chairman of the Headmasters Association and must travel to Norwich to give his acceptance speech. What starts out as a normal day of catching the train and giving his presentation turns into a series of disasters as he misses the train, loses his speech, can't find his wife to take him to Norwich, and has a neighbor's daughter drive him only to have his wife see him with the young girl as they fill up with gas.

Cleese is totally believable as the headmaster, and the supporting actors and actresses compliment him. The film is very British, with dry, witty humor. Because *Clockwise* contains some rude language, and there is brief, distant nudity, caution is advised. **B.G.**

CLUB PARADISE (1986)

RATING: PG–13
CONTENT: Profanity, obscenity, and nudity
INTENDED AUDIENCE: Young adults
STARRING: Robin Williams, Twiggy, Peter O'Toole
DIRECTOR: Harold Ramis

In this silly spoof Robin Williams plays a Chicago fireman who invests his pension in a run-down Caribbean resort hotel. His partner is a native reggae musician. The miserable plot revolves around saving the hotel from greedy Arabs by advertising it as an elite club. Eventually, the native partner has to lead a revolution to save the hotel.

This foul-mouthed movie is boring, dull, and contrived. And the slight nudity and dumb lines drag it down even further. There are no elements of paradise here. **G.O.**

CLUE (1985)

RATING: PG
CONTENT: Profanity, homosexuality, necrophilia, and lewdness
INTENDED AUDIENCE: Adults
STARRING: Tim Curry, Madeline Kahn, Martin Mull
DIRECTOR: Jonathan Lynn

In this slow, nonsensical story, a blackmailer gets his just deserts, along with a bunch of other low-lifes. Jesus' name is taken in vain, and believing Christians are mocked. Homosexuality and necrophilia are acceptable behavior. The ending is implausible. To hook the moviegoer there are three versions of the film circulating, each with a different inane ending. Board game movies seem to be off to a bad start since this is the first of its kind. Not recommended.

COBRA (1986)

RATING: R
CONTENT: Violence
INTENDED AUDIENCE: Adults
STARRING: Sylvester Stallone, Brigitte Nielsen
DIRECTOR: George Pan Cosmatos

You can add *Cobra* to Sylvester Stallone's stable of stock characters, Rocky and Rambo. Here Stallone plays a detective who wipes out crazed terrorists trying to take over the world. The plot incorporates endless action and humor as Cobra kills off the bad guys. The lack of profanity and nudity in addition to the plot of the good guy triumphing over the bad guys should be commended, but these pluses cannot mask the immorality of excessive violence that accompanies all of Stallone's movies.

The violence in *Cobra* is gruesome, yet some individuals have said they want to be just like Rambo or Cobra. If these movies can lead anyone astray into a life of violence, that is a good enough reason to avoid them. God is the God of justice, but also of love and peace. We must call moviemakers to account by avoiding and boycotting films that have the potential to corrupt our society.

COCOON (1985), 115 min.

RATING: PG–13
CONTENT: Profanity, sexual situations, humanism, and occultism
INTENDED AUDIENCE: All ages
STARRING: Don Ameche, Hume Cronyn, Wilford Brimley
DIRECTOR: Ron Howard

Cocoon may be one of the great media hypes of all time. It is *not* a great movie and will not appeal to thinking Christians. A group of elderly inmates of a retirement home are overly concerned with sexual prowess, and their conversations revolve around their desire for sex, their sexual adventures, and their health. They epitomize what happens to the TV generation who enter old age with no world view other than that of self-gratification.

They stumble upon a pool that has been energized by a group of aliens trying to rescue their buddies left behind in Atlantis eons ago. These aliens are all too human with all the failings of fallen men. The aliens offer the octogenarians a chance to romp around the universe for an eternity. Life with aliens is a poor substitute for eternal life with the God who created the universe. Too bad that these elderly people did not know that they could become heirs of the Creator of the universe by just asking to be resurrected by Him into a glorious eternal life. Too bad that the moviemakers did not know the truth of His plan for their lives. *Cocoon* is sad news, topped with maudlin sentimentality, which makes it undesirable viewing for Christians.

COLONEL REDL (1986)
(Subtitles)

RATING: R   ★★★
CONTENT: Brief nudity and sexual situations
INTENDED AUDIENCE: Adults
STARRING: Klaus Maria Brandauer
DIRECTOR: Istvan Szabo

This extraordinarily well-made movie carefully portrays the last days of the Austro-Hungarian Empire through the eyes of Alfred Redl, a peasant boy who rises to the top echelon of the army only to be destroyed by his own opportunism. The acting, especially by Klaus Maria Brandauer *(Out of Africa),* is flawless. The photography is exquisite. The direction is powerful. But the subject matter is too strong in some places to recommend it for most Christian moviegoers.

Colonel Redl attempts to be faithful to history but relies on rumors that may or may not have reflected the truth. In any event, the overall portrait of the Austro-Hungarian Empire is an incredible insight into the nature of politics and the historical circumstances that have inflamed most of our century.

The movie is commendable for its lack of profanity and for avoiding an anti-Christian world view. It does show briefly the unseemly parts of life in a fallen world. There are references to Redl's homosexuality, but none of his sinfulness is portrayed in a positive light. As the audience, we hope beyond hope that Redl will survive, not because he is good, but because there emerges at the end the glimmer of hope that he is beginning to see his fallenness and might change by coming to know God. Redl is a Judas, but we sympathize with his condition because it is the human condition. This incredible movie challenges us at every turn. However, brief nudity makes it unacceptable for most Christians.

THE COLOR PURPLE (1985), 155 min.

RATING: PG–13
CONTENT: Vile language and lesbianism
INTENDED AUDIENCE: Adults
STARRING: Danny Glover, Whoopi Goldberg, Adolph Caesar
DIRECTOR: Steven Spielberg

Steven Spielberg's attempt to make an artistic masterpiece is interesting but flawed by the fact that the story is taken from the best-selling, feminist book by the same name. Though the book was an angry attack on (black) men and the world, the movie is much more positive, showing some reverence for God and downplaying the lesbianism in the book. In fact, in the movie the resolution takes place in a church with a scene of forgiveness and reconciliation. The problem is that the movie retains the book's vile language and distorted view of reality.

The Color Purple tells the story of a black woman who is abused by men and falls in love with another black woman, who is bisexual. It is a confused story of a girl who grows old without developing emotionally. There is a reverence for God, but there is no suggestion that repentance is a necessary step toward reconciliation and renewal. This is unacceptable film fare for Christians.

COLOSSUS: THE FORBIN PROJECT (1970), 100 min.

RATING: PG   ★★★
CONTENT: Mild off-color language
INTENDED AUDIENCE: Adults
STARRING: Eric Braeden, Susan Clark, William Schallert
DIRECTOR: Joseph Sargent

This film revolves around Dr. Charles Forbin (Eric Braeden), a computer genius who creates Colossus, the most sophisticated computer ever devised. Colossus has been built to control the United States's entire defense system, freeing it from the minds and hands of the military, thus ruling out the possibility of human accident. Problems develop when Colossus, which has the capacity to reason and develop its own artificial intelligence, refuses to accept commands from its creator.

The film, though not as visually exciting as *War Games,* has an impressive script and intriguing themes and provides much food for thought concerning our present day fascination and dependence on computer technology. **B.G.**

COMFORT AND JOY (1984), 106 min.

RATING: PG   ★★★

CONTENT: Very little off-color language
INTENDED AUDIENCE: Adults
STARRING: Bill Paterson, Eleanor David
DIRECTOR/WRITER: Bill Forsyth

In this pleasant movie, honesty triumphs over duplicity. Our hero, a radio disc jockey in Scotland, triumphs when he is true to himself and confronts dishonest ice-cream "warlords," who are waging an ice cream war, with the simple, yet profound truth. To create the setting for the story to unfold, the director (who directed the magnificent movie *Local Hero*) shows how most people live a lie, but only the truth will bring peace. This is a delightful movie with no bloodshed, no death, no sex, and very little off-color language. It is good entertainment. You'll like it.

COMMANDO (1985)

RATING: R
CONTENT: Profanity, nudity, and excessive violence
INTENDED AUDIENCE: Adults
STARRING: Arnold Schwarzenegger
DIRECTOR: Mark Lester

Commando is not *Rambo*. There is no great issue burning beneath the surface of this movie. Instead, it is a typical B picture about one man who destroys an evil dictator's army to save his daughter. All the action cannot make up for the weak plot. The dialogue full of profanities, nudity, and excessive violence are other elements that make this unsuitable for thinking Christians of any age.

CONRACK (1974), 107 min.

RATING: PG   ★★★
CONTENT: Minor swearing
INTENDED AUDIENCE: All ages
STARRING: Jon Voight, Paul Winfield, Hume Cronyn
DIRECTOR: Martin Ritt

This gentle, moving story is based on the autobiographical book by Pat Conroy *The Water Is Wide*. Set in 1969 on an island off the coast of South Carolina, Jon Voight portrays a school teacher, Conrack, who decides to help the poor, culturally deprived black students of the island. Faced with innumerable challenges, Conrack takes it upon himself to bring change into their primitive world. There are moments of tenderness and decency in this film that make it appealing to children as well as adults.

It is rare to find entertaining films that inspire and teach morality and honesty. This one does and is highly recommended. **B.G.**

COOL HAND LUKE (1967), 126 min.

RATING: PG   ★★★
CONTENT: Minor swearing, one suggestive sexual scene
INTENDED AUDIENCE: Adults
STARRING: Paul Newman, George Kennedy, Strother Martin, Luke Askew,
  J. D. Cannon, Jo Van Fleet

"What we have here is a failure to communicate," yells Strother Martin as the tough boss of a Southern prison camp. The Bossman has just knocked Luke down a hill and is determined to break Luke's individuality, with force if necessary. Luke, a "local yokel" who just gets into trouble, is doing time in a Southern prison camp, a hellhole where you don't break the rules, or the guards break you. He becomes a camp "folk hero" of sorts, as he defies the Boss and brings the prison system's harshness and hatred down upon himself.

The film brims with excitement and quality. In his way, Luke is calling out to God and others, for help. But the Bossman intends to break Luke's will, and the clash between the two men is one of the screen's finest portrayals of conflict. This is a strong film, even for today, and is not recommended viewing for children. The peculiar allegories that seem to parallel Luke and Christ are not intended to be offensive to Christians. B.G.

THE COURT JESTER (1956), 101 min.

CONTENT: Nothing objectionable ★★★★
INTENDED AUDIENCE: All ages
STARRING: Danny Kaye, Glynis Johns, Angela Lansbury, Basil Rathbone, Cecil Parker
DIRECTOR: Norman Panama and Melvin Frank

This film starred Danny Kaye at his best: witty, hilarious and fast-flying with non-sense. Kaye is a royal jester in merry old, medieval England. It is nonstop hilarity as Kaye clowns and prances around.

One of the more memorable moments of the film takes place near its end, when Kaye is about to accept a prospectively lethal drink at the royal banquet. Kaye notes that "the vessel with the pestle has the pellet with the poison while the chalice with the palace holds the brew that is true!" Kaye adds his remarkable talent for high-speed doubletalk to the scene. B.G.

CREATOR (1985), 108 min.

RATING: R ★★
CONTENT: Profanity, nudity, and sex
INTENDED AUDIENCE: Adults
STARRING: Peter O'Toole, Vincent Spano, Mariel Hemingway
DIRECTOR: Ivan Passer

This strange movie is a prolife, pro-God, theistic apologetic (defense of the faith) wrought at a terrible cost, for it is full of profanity, nudity, and sex. At the core is a good story of a scientist (Peter O'Toole) who believes in God and convinces a young student to believe in God and the value of human life. Though this scientist is opposed by an evil scientist who does not value human life and does not believe in God, he triumphs over the humanistic scientist.

It is sad that such a positive story should be destroyed by the superficial addition of cheap devices to try to capture an audience. The directing is poor. Peter O'Toole looks barely alive throughout the movie. The dialogue is hammy, confused, and dull. Therefore, the film cannot be recommended.

CRITTERS (1986), 97 min.

RATING: PG–13   ★★
CONTENT: Mild language and minimal sexual looseness
INTENDED AUDIENCE: Teenagers
STARRING: Billy Green Bush, Dee Wallace Stone, Scott Grimes,
   Nadine Van Der Velde, Terrence Mann
DIRECTOR: Stephen Herek

Critters is a mild, sometimes even likable, thriller. When five interplanetary prisoners, the Krites, escape from an asteroid prison, they steal a spaceship and head for earth. They are tailed by two alien bounty hunters who can take on the look of any lifeform they meet. The Krites land in the Brown family's yard in the Midwest. The Browns manage to hold them off, and the young boy saves the day by finding the bounty hunters and helping them dispose of the Krites. In the end, good triumphs over evil.

The problems are mild profanity and a contrived plot that resembles all the other creature movies of recent years (especially *Gremlins*). The acting and direction are quite good, however. The continuity does not hold up under scrutiny, but that is typical of this type of film. All in all, it is better than you might expect, but not great.

CROCODILE DUNDEE (1986)

RATING: PG(?)   ★★★
CONTENT: Mild language, revealing dress, and slight vulgarity
INTENDED AUDIENCE: Adults
STARRING: Paul Hogan, Linda Kowlaski
DIRECTOR: Not available

The intentions of the film are good, and it is on the edge of being very good entertainment. The production quality is excellent. The hero, Michael "Crocodile" Dundee, is a bit of a showoff, but he is also real, a good guy who refuses to take sexual advantage of the heroine, Sue. He has read the Bible at least once, believes in Jesus, and says that "me and God be mates." The premise is very positive: "Solid, decent integrity triumphs over city slickness." The moral is also positive: "Intelligent women prefer good, strong, decent men." However, there is a brief moment where the heroine's dress is too revealing, there is some mild off-color language, and there are some low-life scenes and actions that are not suitable for family viewing.

Sue, a reporter for a Long Island newspaper, is on assignment in Australia and comes across the story of a man who killed a crocodile and then crawled through the swamp to civilization. She finds this character, Crocodile Dundee, and they have all sorts of adventures in the outback. She takes him back to New York City, where he is a fish out of water. Yet Dundee becomes a hero by catching a thief, defending Sue against a gang, and performing other good deeds. And he and Sue go off together to live happily ever after.

Clearly, *Crocodile Dundee* has everything going for it to be a good, wholesome, positive movie. Unfortunately, there are scenes in New York that are too risqué, even though the message is always on the side of morality against immorality. Therefore, it is recommended for discerning adults who have considered the cautions noted here.

CROSS OF IRON (1977), 133 min.

RATING: R   ★★
CONTENT: Vulgarity and some gory violence
INTENDED AUDIENCE: Mature adults
STARRING: James Coburn, James Mason, David Warner, Maximilian Schell
DIRECTOR: Sam Peckinpah

Cross of Iron tells the story of German soldiers on the Crimean/Russian front in 1943. That year the Third Reich received a severe beating from the Russians during the cruel winter months. This film depicts the last days of several German platoons on the Russian front, focusing on the loyalties, weaknesses, and betrayals exhibited by the men of these outfits. While having scope and drama, the film lacks consistency.

The movie's weak ending and long, two hour presentation detract from its high points. Not recommended because of harsh language and violence. **B.G.**

CROSSOVER DREAMS (1985), 85 min.

CONTENT: Profanity and obscenity
INTENDED AUDIENCE: Adults
STARRING: Ruben Blades
DIRECTOR: Leon Ichaso

This is an excellent, moral story, but it is destroyed by profane language. A Latin musician who wants to make it in the Anglo record market gets his big break and dumps all his friends, including the woman who loves him. Unfortunately, his record is a flop, and he has no one to whom he can turn, since he dumped them for fame and fortune. In the end our hero humbles himself and teams up with his former partner. Though the film is a very poignant portrayal of the fact that selfishness leads to alienation, the language is so bad that the film cannot be recommended.

CROSSROADS (1985), 98 min.

RATING: R
CONTENT: Profanity, obscenity, and sex
INTENDED AUDIENCE: Adults
STARRING: Ralph Macchio, Joe Seneca
DIRECTOR: Walter Hill

A young white Juilliard musician wants to play the blues, and he teams up with an old black musician whose specialty is the blues. When the two men head for the Mississippi Delta to find a lost piece of music, the young man finds out that the old man made a pact with the devil at the crossroads. They go back to the crossroads, tell the devil that the deal is off, and end up having a duel with guitars with the devil.

This movie has several problems, not the least of which is the premise "man can beat the devil without God." Furthermore, the message of the blues player is that life is just women and song; sex is the driving force behind his music. Finally, the language is foul, and the final duel takes place in a hellish-looking bar. Definitely not for Christians. **L.B.**

CRY FROM THE MOUNTAIN (1986)

RATING: G   ★★
CONTENT: Mild off-color language
INTENDED AUDIENCE: All ages
STARRING: Wes Parker, Rita Watter, Kris Kidd
DIRECTOR: James F. Collier

The Billy Graham organization film for 1986, it is a very short movie that just doesn't work as a theatrical feature film. Although the acting is good and the photography is professional, the story line is very weak and leaves the audience wondering what happened and why. The story involves a man who is planning to leave his family and takes them on a camping trip to break the bad news to them. Through unforeseen circumstances, the family is stranded. They hear Billy Graham on the radio. A helicopter rescues them. They fly to the Graham crusade and are saved. Billy closes the film with a fireside talk on Christianity.

This film would work better in church buildings than in theaters. No one who had advance knowledge of how mediocre this movie is would willingly pay to see it. It is sad that *Cry from the Mountain* was not made with more care so that it could be a theatrical success. **B.V.**

DANCE WITH A STRANGER (1985), 102 min.

RATING: R
CONTENT: Raw sex, nudity, and profanity
INTENDED AUDIENCE: Adults
STARRING: Miranda Richardson
DIRECTOR: Mike Newell

This mediocre, dull little film tells the morose story of Ruth Ellis, a bar girl who kills her upper-class lover and hangs for it. This movie without God shows just how much people need Him. It is a sad, sordid affair that destroys everyone. It contains too much raw sex, nudity, profanity, and misguided actions for any Christian to see.

DAVID COPPERFIELD (1935) B&W, 132 min.

CONTENT: Nothing objectionable   ★★★★
INTENDED AUDIENCE: Families
STARRING: Freddie Bartholomew, W. C. Fields, Basil Rathbone,
Edna May Oliver, Maureen O'Sullivan, Roland Young
DIRECTOR: George Cukor

Certainly one of the greatest movies of all time, *David Copperfield* is also one of the best translations of a book into film. Christian morality runs throughout this fine movie. *David Copperfield* brings us face to face with all the memorable characters from the Dickens book: 'Umble Uriah Heep, "the forger and the cheat"; the inconquerable Micawber (W. C. Fields), the indigent aristocrat inhabiting a world of creditors, but blessed by God; the hyperemotional Aunt Betsy; poor Mr. Dick; bluff Dan Peggotty with the heart of a child; and . . . all the rest. A memorable cast. Highly recommended.

DEATH BEFORE DISHONOR (1987)

RATING: R   ★★★
CONTENT: Some off-color language and violence
INTENDED AUDIENCE: Adults
STARRING: Brian Keith, Fred Dryer, Sasha Mitchel, Joanna Pacula
DIRECTOR: Terry Leonard

Death Before Dishonor is a strong action adventure movie with a moral foundation. The United States Marine Corps, Mideast terrorists, and politics are the heart and soul of this picture, which portrays a special Marine Corps unit as it deals with Arab terrorists. The action is hot and heavy with lots of blood being spilled. The special unit is told to keep its behavior "by the book" but finally decides that's no way to deal with terrorists. Joining Israeli forces just in time to lead a surprise, sunrise desert attack on an Arab fortress, the Marines wreak havoc on the bad guys. Although recommended, watch out for the violence and tough language of this movie. **G.O.**

DEATH OF AN ANGEL (1986)

RATING: PG   ★★★★
CONTENT: Mild off-color language
INTENDED AUDIENCE: Adults
STARRING: Nick Mancuso, Bonnie Bedelia
DIRECTOR: Petru Popescu

The whole fabric of this film is Christian. It is written from a Christian world view, yet it is a Hollywood feature film. At several points, the theology seemed to be going off track, but each time at the last moment, the story would take a turn and reveal a solid theology. This is not to say that the movie is not flawed, but the flaws are very few. Some of the minor doctrine in the film is debatable, but we should rejoice that Jesus is being preached.

This is the story of Grace, who is ordained only to find that she does not have faith. When she goes to Mexico to rescue her crippled daughter from a self-ordained faith healer, Angel, she becomes convinced that Angel has a legitimate call from God. As the story progresses, however, Grace discovers that Angel is a fraud. The plot twists to present an incredible ending that underlines the fact that God is totally sovereign and not dependent on us or our devices.

Death of an Angel is a unique film. In the final analysis, it is faithful to orthodox Christianity. Grace's ordination is mitigated by her coming to faith afterward. In fact, it is the story of the discovery of faith. It is a movie Christians should see.

DELTA FORCE (1986), 129 min.

RATING: R   ★★
CONTENT: Very little obscenity
INTENDED AUDIENCE: Adults
STARRING: Chuck Norris, Lee Marvin
DIRECTOR: Menahem Golan

Based loosely on the 1985 TWA–Middle East hostage crisis, *Delta Force* stars Lee

Marvin and Chuck Norris who team up to make a daring rescue attempt. It is a better movie than some critics would admit because it contains very little obscenity, no nudity, and no sex scenes. There is some degree of violence, but it is not excessive.

The best part of the movie is the positive portrayal of a sensitive, strong, holy priest. In fact, at the end of the movie, in the midst of the roar of the raucous world, several people pray and commit a dying man to the Lord. This action-packed, patriotic movie is pretty good entertainment. **J.C.J.**

DESERT BLOOM (1986)

RATING: PG   ★ ★ ★ ★
CONTENT: Mild profanity
INTENDED AUDIENCE: All ages
STARRING: Jon Voight, JoBeth Williams, Ellen Barkin, Annabeth Gish
DIRECTOR: Eugene Corr

The Sundance Institute, founded by Robert Redford at his ranch in Provo, Utah, is the new American center for intriguing, offbeat, intelligent films, such as *Death of an Angel*. Now, the institute has given birth to *Desert Bloom,* an intimate movie about a young girl coming of age (psychologically, not sexually) in Las Vegas during the above-ground nuclear bomb tests. No nudity or violence mars this well-crafted piece of Americana. The two occurrences of profanity in the film are indicative of the fallenness of the girl's alcoholic stepfather and need not be a stumbling block for most viewers, although they should have been left out of the movie.

The story is set in December of 1950 and involves the memories of a young girl, Rose, whose mother is an optimist and a gambler, and whose stepfather is an alcoholic. The movie presents a portrait of each member of the family and concentrates its action on the conflict between Rose and her stepfather. However, the family does reconcile by the end of the film.

The message is excellent: Forgiveness leads to reconciliation. The character insights are superb. The story is intriguing and captivating. It stands opposed to divorce and sexual promiscuity and clearly stakes a claim for perseverance and forgiveness. *Desert Bloom* is a challenging movie that may not ask all the right questions, but at least it heads in the right direction.

THE DIRT BIKE KID (1985)

RATING: PG   ★ ★ ★
CONTENT: Nothing objectionable
INTENDED AUDIENCE: Children
STARRING: Peter Billingsley, Stuart Pankin, Anne Bloom
DIRECTOR: Hoite Caston

This movie is good family entertainment that just misses being excellent. A young boy wants a dirt bike, and an angel gives him a special, magical bike that another young boy has abused. The boy fixes up the bike, which helps him foil an evil banker who wants to build a new bank where the town's baseball clubhouse stands.

The only problem is the labeling of the intervention of the miraculous as magic. Christians should be put off by the manipulation of the supernatural to propel the story along. In the final analysis, though, it is a positive movie where good triumphs over evil. No sex, violence, or immorality leads the audience astray. It is recommended with the reservation that parents should explain to children that God does answer prayer, but He cannot be manipulated for personal gain and power as implied in the traditional definition of the term *magic*.

THE DIRTY DOZEN (1967), 149 min.

RATING: PG   ★★
CONTENT: Violence
INTENDED AUDIENCE: Adults
STARRING: Lee Marvin, Jim Brown, Ernest Borgnine, John Cassavetes, Robert Ryan,
    Charles Bronson, Donald Sutherland, George Kennedy, Telly Savalas
DIRECTOR: Robert Aldrich

The Dirty Dozen is nonstop action with an excellent cast as twelve Army death-row convicts are given the choice of staying in jail and facing the hangman's noose, or going on an almost impossible mission behind German lines and being pardoned if they live. Like all war movies, this film is pretty violent. This fact alone will keep it from some Christians' TV screens. **L.R.**

DR. STRANGELOVE (1964) B&W, 93 min.

RATING: PG   ★★
CONTENT: A small amount of off-color language
INTENDED AUDIENCE: Adults
STARRING: Peter Sellers, George C. Scott, Sterling Hayden, Slim Pickens,
    Keenan Wynn
DIRECTOR: Stanley Kubrick

This devastating film is a brilliantly written and executed black comedy about a maniacal air force general who orders a nuclear attack on Russia. It is a classic of the doomsday genre, and it ends with the world engulfed in a nuclear holocaust.

The satire of this biting comedy is overwhelmingly gloomy. Skilled, credible actors give smooth, polished performances of buffoons, psychopaths, and lunatics who are running the planet. They cling to a manmade type of salvation, predicated on techno-logical fixes or wonders, hoping to save the planet from their very own destruction. In their final hopeless moments, these desperate men cling to the very technology that destroys them. They never turn to God, who is the only means of salvation. If you decide to see this film, look at it from a biblical perspective. **B.G.**

DON'T CHANGE MY WORLD (1975), 88 min.

RATING: G   ★★★
CONTENT: Nothing offensive
INTENDED AUDIENCE: All ages
STARRING: Roy Tatum, Edie Kramer, George Macrenaris, Ben Jones,
    Paul Newmark, David Eidson
DIRECTOR: Robert Rector

The beautiful scenery of the Appalachian Mountains provides the backdrop to this action-packed wilderness adventure. *Don't Change My World* is the story of a wildlife photographer who becomes motivated to stop the destruction of "the North Woods" by greedy developers. Becoming a one-man vigilante committee, here Eric Whyle, who lives in a small cabin in the North Woods with his pet dog, Sundance, and mischievous raccoon, Rocky, takes on a despicable developer and a forest full of poachers. Eric is pursued by the gun-toting poachers, and the action becomes fast and furious as they chase him down a mountain side, just one step ahead of a rolling log pile and beside the shear drop next to a two-hundred-foot waterfall. Fortunately, Eric survives, the woods are ridded of its exploiters, and calm returns at last.

Children of all ages will enjoy *Don't Change My World,* with its splendid scenery and loads of animals. Fun-filled drama for the whole family. **B.G.**

DOWN AND OUT IN BEVERLY HILLS (1986), 103 min.

RATING: R
CONTENT: Sex, yoga, homosexuality, profanity, and obscenity
INTENDED AUDIENCE: Adults
STARRING: Nick Nolte, Bette Midler, Richard Dreyfuss
DIRECTOR: Paul Mazursky

Down and Out in Beverly Hills is the first Disney movie with an R rating—a sad moment in the history of that studio. This well-made, amusing film is totally anti-Christian and immoral. The premise is EST-ian, that is, do whatever works, including lying.

A wealthy executive saves a bum from drowning in his pool and takes the bum under his wing. The bum proceeds to take over the family by having sexual relations with the man's wife, his mistress-maid, and his daughter. The executive learns to live with these goings on, and they all go on living together. Again Hollywood is trying to get us to buy into an anti-Christian philosophy. Boycott this film, and write the Disney Studios to complain about it.

DREAM LOVERS (1986)

RATING: R   ★★
CONTENT: Promiscuity
INTENDED AUDIENCE: Adults
STARRING: Kristy McNichol
DIRECTOR: Alan J. Pakula

This unique thriller is a compelling movie, marred only by promiscuity. Kristy McNichol plays Kathy, the daughter of a wealthy autocrat who has a strong hold on his daughter. Kathy gets a break from him and for her career when she is asked to play her flute in a jazz quartet that has a limited engagement in New York City. While staying in the Village, she is attacked by a knife-wielding stranger whom she kills. She is overwhelmed by nightmares of the attack and finds relief only through a doctor's research that lets her relive and alter her dream. Complications make her a walking nightmare until the doctor rescues her, and all ends well.

The suspense in this beautifully crafted thriller is excellent. The photography is great. The acting is superb, although the characters are plain. Almost no profanity or nudity is present. However, promiscuity makes it off-limits for Christians, which is too bad because it could have been a good movie.

DREAMCHILD (1985), 94 min.

RATING: PG   ★★

CONTENT: Nothing overtly objectionable
INTENDED AUDIENCE: Families
STARRING: Coral Browne, Nicola Cowper, Amelia Shankley
DIRECTOR: Gavin Miller

Dreamchild is a unique blend of reality and fantasy. The story, set in the 1930s, revolves around the real Alice in Charles Dodgson's (Lewis Carroll's) life. Now an old woman, she sails to the United States to participate in a special Lewis Carroll commemorative ceremony at Columbia University. As Alice remembers the Rev. Dodgson, she imagines scenes from Alice in Wonderland and slowly comes to the realization that Dodgson loved her.

If the plot sounds implausible, it is. Alice must have known that Dodgson loved her; the writer suggests that that love hid a deeper "Lolita" complex. Although the movie never descends into the realm of bad taste, it comes close, and it never ascends into the quality film we want to see. It is confused rather than clever, but it won't hurt anyone and is not anti-Christian. The technical quality is excellent. If your family wants to see it, don't worry. It is just too bad that a better film didn't come out of this great story.

DUCKSOUP (1933) B&W, 68 min.
CONTENT: Nothing objectionable   ★★★★
INTENDED AUDIENCE: Adults
STARRING: The Marx Brothers, Margaret Dumont, Raquel Torres, Louis Calhern
DIRECTOR: Leo McCarey

Ducksoup is perhaps the best and most famous of the Marx Brothers' movies, with A Day at the Races and A Night at the Opera close behind. However, the plot only serves as a thin excuse for the Brothers to serve up their usual quantity of puns, jokes, and antics.

Rufus T. Firefly (Groucho) is named President of Freedonia at the request of Mrs. Teasdale (Margaret Dumont). But it becomes evident that Freedonia may grind to a halt under his unstable tutelage. Spies for the rival country of Sylvania, Chicolini (Chico) and Pinky (Harpo) humorously trail Firefly, trying to steal the secret war plans that Mrs. Teasdale has in her safe. War breaks out between the countries, and Rufus ineptly wages war upon the scheming non-Marxist neighboring country. In the brief space of sixty-eight minutes, the Brothers are able to pack an awesome amount of humorous dialogue and visual gags. **B.G.**

DUMBO (1941), 64 min.
CONTENT: Good family entertainment   ★★★★
INTENDED AUDIENCE: The young at heart
STARRING: Sterling Holloway, Edward Brophy, Verna Felton
DIRECTOR: Ben Sharpstein

One of the best of the Disney animated features, Dumbo tells the story of a circus elephant who is born with ears that are too big, so big that he is the laughing stock of the circus. Trying to protect her son Dumbo, Mrs. Jumbo is thrown into the circus jail. Dumbo is then used in the clown act. One night while he is feeling sorry for himself, the mouse Timothy comes to Dumbo's aid. After establishing a friendship, they fall asleep. But when they wake up the next morning they are in a tree! Dumbo has flown to the tree in his sleep.

A group of singing crows help to get Dumbo to fly again by telling him that they are giving him a magic feather. In the midst of his clown act where he is supposed to fall from the second story of a burning building into a tub of water, Dumbo plans to fly to amaze the crowd and gain respect. However, he drops the feather on the way down. But Timothy tells Dumbo that the feather really isn't magic and that he can fly all by himself. Dumbo flies, and takes the circus by storm.

Dumbo is highly recommended, but your children should be warned of the dangers of trusting in magic. **J.B.**

EASTER PARADE (1948), 109 min.

CONTENT: Nothing objectionable   ★★★
INTENDED AUDIENCE: All ages
STARRING: Fred Astaire, Judy Garland, Anne Miller, Peter Lawford
DIRECTOR: Charles Walters

Fred Astaire snubs dance partner Miller, after they having a falling out when she is offered a part in a Ziegfeld show. On an angry impulse, he wagers that he can turn any girl into an even more successful partner than Miller by next Easter. He picks up Garland, and turns her into a razzle-dazzle dancer. The plot is kept very simple so as to showcase the real meat of the movie: the music and the dance routines. Irving Berlin's score is one of the classics. **B.G.**

EASY RIDER (1969), 94 min.

RATING: R
CONTENT: Some profanity and a violent ending, but no nudity
INTENDED AUDIENCE: Young adults
STARRING: Peter Fonda, Dennis Hopper, Jack Nicholson
DIRECTOR: Dennis Hopper

This unintentional portrait of the sinfulness of man shows how criminal rebelliousness uses the guise of individualism as an excuse for anarchy. Two hippie motorcyclists, after selling some marijuana and stashing the cash in the gas tank of one of their cycles, take off for a joy ride through the American Southwest. They proceed to stir up trouble wherever they go and are faced by the equal evil of vigilantism.

When it was released, *Easy Rider* corrupted many young people in our country. It should be seen as a frontal attack on biblical values. Avoid this film if it appears on television or if a member of your family wants to rent it.

ECHO PARK (1986)

RATING: R
CONTENT: Loose morals, bad language, and a godless world view
INTENDED AUDIENCE: Young adults
STARRING: Tom Hulce, Susan Dey, Michael Bowen
DIRECTOR: Robert Dornhelm

A low-budget movie favored by secular critics, this buoyant film about three hopefuls on the edge of Hollywood has some likable aspects. However, it is destroyed by loose morals, bad language, and a godless world view.

Tom Hulce does a fine job of playing a pizza delivery man who is secretly a music writer. Susan Dey is very good as the young actress-mother who is looking for her big break. Michael Bowen plays a convincing Austrian body builder who is trying to make his fortune. Unfortunately, the "anything goes" attitude conveyed in the movie's amoral atmosphere goes against biblical truths. Avoid this film.

8 MILLION WAYS TO DIE (1986)
RATING: R
CONTENT: Sex, nudity, violence, and profanity
INTENDED AUDIENCE: Adults
STARRING: Jeff Bridges, Rosanna Arquette
DIRECTOR: Hal Ashby

There are some signs of redemption working at the edge of this movie, but they are not enough to make it worthwhile viewing. The best part is Jeff Bridges's acting. He portrays a sheriff who becomes an alcoholic because he can't face all the murder and mayhem occurring around him. He quits the force and joins Alcoholics Anonymous. A girl comes to him for protection, but he messes up and she gets killed. He goes after the killer, and justice triumphs over evil.

Slick photography and good acting almost save this film, but the script defeats all these efforts. In the final analysis, *8 Million Ways to Die* is too tough for anyone, let alone a Christian. It is a total loser.

84 CHARING CROSS ROAD (1987)
RATING: PG   ★★★
CONTENT: Mild expletives
INTENDED AUDIENCE: Adults
STARRING: Anne Bancroft, Anthony Hopkins
DIRECTOR: David Jones

Helene, a struggling script reader and aspiring writer, is frustrated in her fruitless search in New York City for out of print English literature. She finds an advertisement in a trade magazine for Marks & Cohen, & Co at 84 Charing Cross Road in London, and writes a candid, funny letter describing her frustrations and including a list of the books she is seeking. She adds that none of them must cost over five dollars.

Weeks later, several of these books are mailed to her from the London shop with a short note from F.P.D. of Marks & Cohen, & Co. This begins a twenty year exchange of many books and many letters, developing a relationship between Helene and Frank (F.P.D.), the other employees, and after a time, even their families. All of this weaves in and out of Helene's life, work, and circle of friends in New York City.

This film is a gently paced, delightful story of relationships. There is nothing offensive to the Christian viewer other than a very few expletives. Recommended. **D.R.**

EL AMOR BRUJO (1987)
(Subtitles)
RATING: PG   ★★
CONTENT: Some superstition and supernaturalism

INTENDED AUDIENCE: Adults
STARRING: Antonio Gades, Cristina Hoyos, Laura Del Sol, Juan Antonio Jimenez
DIRECTOR: Carlos Saura

El Amor Brujo is the story of a little gypsy girl who is promised in marriage to a little boy by her father. We cut to her wedding years later, where we find a young man, Carmelo, who is not the groom, in love with the bride, whose name is Candela. Also, there is another girl, Lucia, who *is* in love with the groom, José.

The story progresses and José gets in a fight. A young thug knives José, and Candela comes running. José dies in Candela's arms. Carmelo comes to help Candela, and, thinking that he murdered José, the police put him in jail for four years. Four years later, Carmelo comes back. Candela is bereaved. She comes out only at night to go to the place where José died and dance the flamenco with his ghost. Carmelo tries to stop her. An old witch says that Lucia can break the spell. Lucia, Carmelo, and Candela all go out at night and dance the flamenco with José. José puts Lucia under his spell. She dies symbolically. Candela and Carmelo live happily ever after.

There is no nudity or overt sex in the film, but there is provocative dancing. In fact, the flamenco is a strutting, mating dance. If you like dance and music, you might enjoy *El Amor Brujo,* but beware of the superstition embedded in this old folk tale. **L.B.**

ELENI (1986), 116 min.

RATING: PG ★★★★
CONTENT: Nothing objectionable
INTENDED AUDIENCE: Adults
STARRING: John Malkovich, Kate Nelligan
DIRECTOR: Peter Yates

Eleni is the true story of a mother who was murdered by Communists during the Greek civil war. Her son, Nicholas Gage, a *New York Times* reporter, goes looking for her murderer thirty years later. He finds that his mother was murdered because she saved her children from the Communists who took children from their families to re-educate them in Soviet satellite countries.

In the beginning of the film, Eleni hides one of the Communists, a local teacher, from the government, thinking that he is being wrongly persecuted. The teacher returns her kindness when he becomes commandant of the revolutionary army by stealing her house, taking all she has, torturing her, and killing her.

The movie has a redemptive message and some clear Christian overtones. There is no sex or profanity. It is a powerful, good movie that will leave you in tears. Go see it. It is the type of movie Christians should support if they want better movies.

THE EMERALD FOREST (1985), 110 min.

RATING: R
CONTENT: Nudity, occultism, violence, cruelty, and hallucinogenic visions
INTENDED AUDIENCE: Adults
STARRING: Powers Boothe, Meg Foster, Charley Boorman
DIRECTOR: John Boorman

This classic myth of the noble savage is pretentious, anti-Christian, and unreal, even though it is based to some degree on a true story. A young boy is stolen by Amazon

Indians of Brazil, the so-called invisible people, and the boy's father spends ten years searching for his son. When he finds his son, the father relinquishes him to the tribe and catches the ecological vision of the tribe by destroying the dam he has been in charge of building for the past ten years.

Nudity, violence, cruelty, and hallucinogenic visions are present for any moviegoer who has no values. This movie is pure occultism. Christians should not consider seeing it.

ENEMY MINE (1986), 109 min.

RATING: PG–13
CONTENT: Violence and profanity
INTENDED AUDIENCE: All ages
STARRING: Louis Gossett, Jr., Dennis Quaid
DIRECTOR: Wolfgang Peterson

This movie just doesn't work. Aside from the haunted beauty of the surrealistic science-fiction environment, *Enemy Mine* has nothing to offer an audience. Most moviegoers will be disappointed by the lack of *Star Wars* realism.

The plot involves two galactic enemies who are stranded on a desolate planet. Forced by circumstances to live with each other, they learn to respect and love each other. The moral is "love your enemy." However, the film is another instance of utopian blindness to the reality of sin and the need for Jesus Christ to bring about real reconciliation. Avoid this movie.

EXPLORERS (1986), 109 min.

RATING: PG   ★★
CONTENT: Mild bad language
INTENDED AUDIENCE: Families
STARRING: Ethan Hawke, River Phoenix, Jason Presson
DIRECTOR: Joe Dante

This interesting film shows that life beyond the planet earth is not all it is cracked up to be. Three young, attractive misfits happen upon a dream that shows them how to build an antigravity energy spaceship, which will take them out of the universe to meet the aliens who are sending the dream. The aliens turn out to be two young adolescents who are bored with their own lives in space and find the earth, especially television, amusing. Upon meeting these alien adolescents, the earthling explorers realize that the earth is not such a bad place after all.

Explorers is an exciting, imaginative, harmless, and enjoyable movie with less offensive language than most teenage films. The first part is excellent. The only flaw is the final third, which is silly and slightly annoying. The film is acceptable entertainment, but the silliness of the aliens may not appeal to everyone.

F/X (1985), 108 min.

RATING: R
CONTENT: Profanity, obscenity, and violence
INTENDED AUDIENCE: Adults
STARRING: Bryan Brown, Brian Dennehy, Diane Venora
DIRECTOR: Robert Mandel

A special effects man is caught up in a web of intrigue and uses every special effect he knows to escape. (F/X in Hollywood lingo refers to special effects.) The Justice Department and the Mafia are the bad guys.

The plot is very confused and insignificant in this contrived movie. At one point, a man is beaten with a steam iron. Add to that the foul language, and you have a movie that should be avoided by everyone. **B.G.**

FAIL-SAFE (1964) B&W, 111 min.

RATING: PG   ★★★
CONTENT: America bashing, with the military particularly suspect
INTENDED AUDIENCE: Adults
STARRING: Henry Fonda, Walter Matthau, Dan O'Herihy
DIRECTOR: Sidney Lumet

A "what-if" thriller, *Fail-Safe* is a suspenseful thriller of the World War III type, a serious *Dr. Strangelove*. What if an American bomber accidentally drops the bomb on Moscow? How does the American president avert nuclear holocaust? *Fail-Safe* reveals first-rate filmmaking and acting in a day before one had to have gratuitous sex and violence to attract an audience. Definitely worth seeing. **L.R.**

FANTASTIC VOYAGE (1966), 100 min.

CONTENT: Nothing objectionable   ★★★
INTENDED AUDIENCE: Adults
STARRING: Stephen Boyd, Raquel Welch, Edmond O'Brien, Donald Pleasence
DIRECTOR: Richard Fleischer

What do you do when an important scientist is about to die after an assassination attempt unless he has intricate brain surgery? Well, shrink down famous surgeons to the size of bacteria and inject them into his bloodstream to fix the problem, of course! Thus, you have a fantastic voyage through a human body. Sure it's a bit hokey, but a lot of good science fiction fun. Definitely worth checking out. No real spiritual message emerges from this one. But *Fantastic Voyage* is acceptable for all Christian audiences. **L.R.**

FATHER OF THE BRIDE (1950) B&W, 93 min.

CONTENT: Nothing objectionable   ★★★★
INTENDED AUDIENCE: All ages (especially young brides-to-be)
STARRING: Spencer Tracy, Joan Bennett, Elizabeth Taylor
DIRECTOR: Vincente Minnelli

Elizabeth Taylor plays Kay Banks, who announces to her father Stanley Banks (Tracy) that she plans to marry Buckley. Told in flashback, Stanley relates the trials and tribulations of the event, from the topsy-turvy preparations to the wedding ceremony itself. Stanley is beside himself, trying to understand it all as well as figure out how to pay for it all. Kay is swept away by the whirlwind of events, reaching emotional highs and lows as the wedding day approaches.

Father of the Bride won an Oscar for Minnelli. It's a grand film. **B.G.**

FERRIS BUELLER'S DAY OFF (1986)

RATING: PG-13
CONTENT: Profanity, obscenity, sexual looseness, theft, and lying
INTENDED AUDIENCE: Teenagers
STARRING: Matthew Broderick, Mia Sara, Alan Ruck
DIRECTOR: John Hughes

If you have teenagers, watch out for this pretentious, immoral movie aimed at making big money by appealing to the worst aspects of adolescence. The premise is "everyone needs a day off," so Ferris Bueller manipulates his parents into keeping him home from school. Ferris is the most popular boy at high school because he gets away with everything he wants to do. He uses his charm and intelligence only to get his way, from having his best friend steal his father's Ferrari to intimidating the school to letting his girlfriend have the day off, too.

Beautifully made, this movie offers a course in selfishness. It does not even hint at the fact that selfishness leads to self-destruction. Instead, it glorifies an obnoxious, cruel, foul-mouthed boy who needs to be disciplined before he completely spoils.

FIRE WITH FIRE (1986)

RATING: PG-13
CONTENT: Profanity, nudity, violence, and a virulent anti-Christian attitude
INTENDED AUDIENCE: Teenagers
STARRING: Virginia Madsen, Craig Sheffer, Kate Reid
DIRECTOR: Duncan Gibbins

Fire with Fire is a contemporary *Romeo and Juliet* with Shakespeare's premise of "love triumphs over death" reworked into "love triumphs over prison." The hero is in a juvenile delinquent detention center in Oregon, and the heroine is at a nearby strict, Catholic parochial school. On a survival game exercise, he runs into her in the woods. They fall in love instantly. Somehow they manage to sneak away to meet each other, but when they are caught, they escape into the mountains.

This slick film is full of profanity, nudity, violence, and a virulent anti-Christian attitude (the nuns at the school make religion look bad). Keep teenagers (the intended audience) away from it. **J.C.J.**

FIREWALKER (1986)

RATING: PG
CONTENT: Occultism
INTENDED AUDIENCE: Young Adults
STARRING: Chuck Norris, Lou Gossett
DIRECTOR: J. Lee Thompson

Firewalker tells the story of a young woman, Patricia, who has the map to a Mayan/Aztec treasure and is being tailed by Cyclops, a one-eyed Indian who wants the power of the universe. Patricia enlists Max (Chuck Norris) and Leo in searching for the treasure.

The film has no nudity, no profanity and no sexual situations, but it is rife with references to psychic powers and occultism. Furthermore, it has a typical low-budget script, which has a lot of action but does not sustain one's interest because of bad pacing and mediocre development.

This is pretty predictable stuff and not for Christians.

A FLASH OF GREEN (1985), 121 min.

RATING: PG   ★★
CONTENT: Sexual affairs (off-camera)
INTENDED AUDIENCE: Adults
STARRING: Ed Harris, Blair Brown
DIRECTOR: Victor Nunez

A Flash of Green was the winner of the 1986 Atlanta Film and Video Festival. The filmmaker, Victor Nunez of Tallahassee, Florida, told the audience at the festival that the reporter-hero of this movie is a modern saint. In fact, the reporter is a confused, modern Judas who betrays his friends and then recants, but he never comes to Christ. Therefore, he is never set apart by God as a saint.

The reporter sells out for money and excitement to an ambitious politician-developer. The reporter informs on his friends who are trying to stop a development that will destroy their community by wiping out the marshlands. One after another his friends are driven away. Finally, he recants in print and apologizes to his girlfriend who is a leader of the opposition to the development. He has a brief affair with her and leaves her. Again he recants and comes back home to marry her and stand up for the truth.

It is refreshing that this film is not anti-Christian. Furthermore, there is no nudity or profanity. However, the positive aspects are offset by two brief sexual affairs (off-camera), which make the movie morally ambiguous. The acting and the direction are very good, but the movie just misses the mark of touching upon the truth of man's sinfulness and the need for repentance and salvation.

FLIGHT OF THE NAVIGATOR (1986)

RATING: PG   ★★★
CONTENT: Mild language
INTENDED AUDIENCE: All ages
STARRING: Joey Cramer
DIRECTOR: Randall Kleiser

Flight of the Navigator is pure escapist adventure-science fiction. It is not a great film—it bogs down in the middle—but it is enjoyable and holds your attention with a finely tuned sense of suspense. A twelve-year-old boy who wants to go home, a friendly robot called Max that travels around the universe in a flying saucer collecting life-forms for examination on the planet Phaelon, and lost star charts are some of the elements that make this film work.

There is no nudity, violence, or profanity, although one or two totally unnecessary mild obscenities can be heard. This is a good movie for teenagers because it will capture their imagination without presenting a world view contrary to Christianity. It is to be recommended as acceptable light entertainment.

THE FLY (1986)

RATING: R

CONTENT: Extreme profanity, vulgarity, and grotesque scenes
INTENDED AUDIENCE: Adults
STARRING: Jeff Goldblum, Geena Davis, John Getz
DIRECTOR: David Cronenburg

A grotesque remake of the 1958 horror classic, the movie is amusing at first, but it quickly descends into a repulsive travesty. A scientist who is developing a teleportation device meets and falls in love with a reporter who wants to write the story of his experiments. They are caught in a romantic triangle with her editor, and there is some question as to whether she is playing with the scientist's affections so that she can get the story of the telepod.

When the scientist sends himself through the teleporter, he doesn't realize there is a fly in the machine with him. He starts to turn into a fly because his genes were spliced together with those of the fly. He quickly becomes a horrible-looking mutant of his former self. After all kinds of lurid special effects, he gets blown to pieces in a fight with the editor.

This is a deplorable movie. Don't waste your time seeing it. **K.K.**

FOLLOW THAT BIRD (1985)

RATING: G ★★★
CONTENT: Nothing objectionable
INTENDED AUDIENCE: Children
STARRING: Big Bird and the Muppets, with John Candy and Chevy Chase
DIRECTOR: Ken Kwapis

Big Bird and the Sesame Street gang star in this children's movie. The beginning of the film is a little unfair to families in presenting a false dichotomy between our God-given families, which we should love and enjoy, and the whole human family. However, in the final analysis, the movie is well intentioned and loveable.

Children will love this film and may profit from it, learning from Big Bird that home is where the heart is. The premise is the same that has always motivated the gang at Sesame Street: "Love defeats racism."

FOOL FOR LOVE (1985), 107 min.

RATING: R
CONTENT: Sex, nudity, and foul language
INTENDED AUDIENCE: Adults
STARRING: Sam Shepard and Kim Basinger
DIRECTOR: Robert Altman

The story revolves around a confused love affair. A girl is running away from a broken-down rodeo cowboy who is chasing her. We discover they are both fools for love, and toward the end of the movie, they find out they are half-brother and half-sister, the result of their father's love affairs. The cowboy leaves at the end.

Sam Shepard wrote the prize-winning play for Broadway, and he stars in the movie. The moral is "the sins of the father are visited on the children." Unfortunately, it is not clear that Sam has a moral perspective; rather, he seems confused about life. Sam appears to be alienated from God. He doesn't even realize how wrong incest is. This is not a rational movie; characters, events, and places pop in and out. However, the dialogue is excellent—lean and powerful. Sex, nudity, and tough language destroy whatever is worthwhile in this film. **R.W.**

FORBIDDEN PLANET (1956), 98 min.

CONTENT: Nothing objectionable   ★★★★
INTENDED AUDIENCE: All ages
STARRING: Walter Pidgeon, Anne Francis, Leslie Nielsen, Warren Stevens, Richard Anderson, Earl Holliman, Jack Kelly
DIRECTOR: Fred Wilcox

This big-budget, class-A science-fiction film is considered a classic. The crew of a spaceship, which is on a mission from earth to trace an expedition that had landed on Altair 4 twenty years earlier and had not been heard from since, discover the only survivors to be Dr. Morbius and his daughter Altaira. We learn that the planet was the home of a noble race of beings known as the Krel, which perished in a single night. Essentially, the Krel could create anything they imagined in their minds with the technology they had devised, but their subconscious thoughts of vicious and sadistic desires surfaced and manifested themselves in total annihilation of the race. Before the movie is over, Morbius has to confront his own conscious battling his subconscious, his good versus his sin nature.

Few films operate on as many intellectual levels as this one does. Even though it is showing some vestiges of aging (as any science-fiction film will), such as dated slang, costumes, and spaceship equipment, the film still holds interest because of its first-class script and its examination of good and evil.

Morbius wants to become godlike, or even a god to the human race, as he doles out bits of the Krel knowledge to earthlings as he sees fit. Morbius and the characters who surround him create an interesting dynamic: good versus evil; the place of religion and law within a technological framework; the relationship between man and God. This film clearly examines the role of sin in self-destruction and the need for salvation to cope with our own God-given abilities if we don't want to be destroyed by them. This thought-provoking film is a must see of the science-fiction genre. **B.G.**

FRED & GINGER (1986)

RATING: PG–13   ★★
CONTENT: Off-color language, sexual innuendo, and lewdness
INTENDED AUDIENCE: Adults
STARRING: Marcello Mastroianni, Giulietta Masina
DIRECTOR: Frederico Fellini

At last, Frederico Fellini has made another interesting movie. After several bombs, he shows his genius in this indictment against television. When a television station gets together look-alikes for a television special, two people who had an act impersonating Fred Astaire and Ginger Rogers thirty years earlier come together again to make an appearance.

In most cases, the look-alikes bear no resemblance to the famous people they are impersonating. Fellini shows that television makes celebrities out of everyone, including criminals and victims. When the program finally comes on the air, it is outrageously gaudy, yet everything looks quite professional, including the look-alikes who fit professionally into the program.

Fred & Ginger is funny. The humor is very Italian and broad. The condemnation of the crassness of television is portrayed in a realistic manner; however, Fellini's vision of this world is that it is a circus. Although there is no profanity, there is some rough language, and the movie plays on sexual innuendos in its exposé of television. Therefore, beware of a certain amount of lewdness. This is vintage Fellini, which recalls his *8 ½*. If you like satire and Fellini, you will want to see this movie. **L.B.**

THE FRINGE DWELLERS (1987)

RATING: PG ★★★
CONTENT: Adult situations
INTENDED AUDIENCE: Adults
STARRING: Justine Saunders, Kristina Nehm, Bob Maza
DIRECTOR: Bruce Beresford

This Australian film portrays the Comeaway Family, a large family struggling to survive in a white culture and representative of the whole Aborigine community in general. Caught between two worlds, the older members have few skills, or inclination to work. As a result, the entire race has been stigmatized as "shiftless, liquor-drinking, card-playing Aborigines" who exist on the fringe of white civilization. It is difficult for them to learn in prejudiced white schools or to find meaningful employment in white-controlled companies. Ridiculed as inferior by the whites, the Aborigine youth struggle to overcome.

This film lacks editing, pacing, and tension; as a docudrama, it's slow, natural unfoldment is acceptable. *The Fringe Dwellers* is a portrait of undercover racial discrimination, yet neither the Aborigines nor the whites are presented without blame. Recommended with caution because of some adult situations. **G.O**

GIANT (1956), 197 min.

CONTENT: Adult situations
INTENDED AUDIENCE: Adults
STARRING: Rock Hudson, James Dean, Elizabeth Taylor, Mercedes McCambridge, Dennis Hopper, Sal Mineo, Carroll Baker, Chill Wills
DIRECTOR: George Stevens

Nominated for ten Academy Awards and winner of one for Best Director, Giant is the Edna Ferber story about Texas ranchers, oil barons, politics, racism, corruption, and passions. The film condenses Ferber's novel into a family saga involved in cattle ranching.

James Dean is an eccentric oil tycoon, Jett Rink, a slurring, slouching, and arrogant individual, and Hudson is the head rancher who must deal with him. There are plots and subplots, with many interwoven character conflicts and resolutions; yet the film does not wander, showing the strong, experienced hand of George Stevens, winner of the Best Director Oscar in 1957.

Giant is a film of giant proportions (over three hours long), so prepare yourself when you see it. Nominated for ten Academy Awards. **B.G.**

THE GIG (1986)

CONTENT: Mild language
INTENDED AUDIENCE: Adults

STARRING: Wayne Rogers, Cleavon Little
DIRECTOR: Frank Gilroy

The Gig is another stereotypical group portrait. An amateur band of older men gets a big break to do a gig in the Catskills. George is dying of cancer so he can't go, and the band hires one professional to play bass. They get to the Catskills and find that it is not what they thought it would be. They are squeezed into one room four hundred yards from the hotel. The has-been lead singer expected a professional band and has them fired. As they start back to New York, they learn that George has died, and they play a requiem for him overlooking a beautiful vista. This movie is neither bad nor good. K.D.G.

THE GLEN MILLER STORY (1985, re-released), 116 min.

RATING: G   ★★★★
CONTENT: Nothing objectionable
INTENDED AUDIENCE: Families
STARRING: Jimmy Stewart, June Allyson
DIRECTOR: Anthony Mann

The Glenn Miller Story is the kind of movie Hollywood should be encouraged to produce—a good, powerful, entertaining story that captures your heart. It is refreshing to watch a movie that upholds honesty, morality, hard work, decency, and other biblical values. It even advocates the work ethic of deferred gratification over the decadent attitude of deferred responsibility as Miller's wife tells him to go after his dream and give up immediate satisfaction and short-range success.

The movie follows Glenn Miller from the time he was a down-and-out musician in New York City through the years of struggle, showing his growing fame and success, and ends with his untimely death in an airplane crash in World War II. It is a moving story of a man who followed his dream of bringing joy to others through his talent for making beautiful music. The values depicted here are values society has forgotten. See this film to see the values we need to regain.

THE GO MASTERS (1986)

CONTENT: Nothing objectionable   ★★★
INTENDED AUDIENCE: All ages
STARRING: Sun Dao-Lin, Rentaro Mikuni
DIRECTORS: Junya Sato, Duan Jishun

This historical epic film is the first coproduction between the People's Republic of China and Japan. It was filmed in both China and Japan by directors and film crews from both countries. The film examines the animosity engendered by the Japanese invasion of China in the 1930s as seen through the friendship of two men, the Chinese Yishan and the Japanese Matsunami. They are masters of Go, a three-thousand-year-old game similar to chess that requires brilliant military strategy, a high level of concentration, and a great deal of foresight to win through the limitless possible strategies. Go becomes a metaphor for the thirty-year relationship shown in the movie.

This story of how people can choose love and forgiveness over hate is an intensely personal and human epic as well as an international one. The primary drawback is the brief, historically inaccurate, favorable portrayal of Maoist China. Some viewers may find it obscure and complex, but the underlying message of forgiveness and the scope of the movie make it worthwhile viewing. **K.G.**

THE GODS MUST BE CRAZY (1984), 109 min.

RATING: PG ★★★
CONTENT: Nothing objectionable
INTENDED AUDIENCE: All ages
STARRING: Marius Weyers, Sandra Prinsloo, N!xau
DIRECTOR: Jamie Uys

This very humorous, lighthearted movie from South Africa has become a cult classic for serious filmgoers. The movie is totally enjoyable, but if you scratch the surface of the story, the message is that all the Western world's values are upside down. It provides a slapstick look at the mythic noble savage, which claims that the Bushmen live in a sinless, pristine state. The truth is that sin is a part of the fabric of man's nature and thus of all cultures ever since the Fall.

The plot centers on a Bushman of the Kalahari Desert who travels to the "edge of the world." Along the way he wanders into civilization and gets himself arrested. He is rescued by a bumbling white scientist who has a savvy black assistant, and he teams up with them. Together, they save a teacher and her class of students from revolutionaries.

From the movie, we find that the Bushmen are the most intelligent; the black friend of the scientist is the next most savvy person; the female teacher is the next wisest person; and the white male scientist is the most incompetent. In other words, the closer one is to the intuitive, savage state, the better. Of course, this is absurd. If you are aware of its false world view, it is a delightful, low-budget movie full of laughter and excellent acting. However, don't take the confused message seriously.

GOLDFINGER (1964), 108 min.

RATING: PG ★★★
CONTENT: Sexual innuendo and womanizing
INTENDED AUDIENCE: Adults
STARRING: Sean Connery, Honor Blackman, Gert Frobe
DIRECTOR: Guy Hamilton

Goldfinger is a "must see" for all James Bond fans. It is probably the best of the Sean Connery series, if not the best of all "Bonds." In this movie, 007 stops a madman and his henchman from irradiating the gold in Fort Knox, thus driving up the price of gold internationally and making Goldfinger's own hoard of gold more valuable.

Nasty scheme, eh? Well, there's plenty of action: lots of secret-agent gadgets and pretty women. Womanizing, drinking, irreverent James Bond is by no means a good role model, but, on the other hand, the movie never explicitly shows any sex scenes, and obscenity, if any, is quite mild. Nonetheless, there is a significant amount of sexual innuendo. Like most other James Bond films, Christians should view *Goldfinger* with discretion. **L.R.**

GONE WITH THE WIND (1939), 220 min.

CONTENT: Nothing objectionable ★★★★
INTENDED AUDIENCE: Adults

STARRING: Clark Gable, Vivien Leigh, Olivia de Havilland, Leslie Howard
DIRECTOR: Victor Fleming

Gone With the Wind is the epic, American movie; arguably one of the greatest ever made. Its premise is very biblical, a paraphrase of the story of man's fall from grace: selfishness leads to alienation. The heroine, Scarlett O'Hara, is selfish, self-centered and conniving, willing to destroy the lives of those who love her to satisfy her desires.

Although Scarlett ultimately loves Rhett Butler, she drives him away from her. Scarlett is the scarlet woman, a sinner who is so out for herself that she destroys everyone in her path. Melanie, Scarlett's true friend, is the better person, the Christian, but she is overshadowed by Scarlett who thrusts herself into the limelight.

The ultimate melodrama, *Gone With the Wind* is a great movie with a great message. **L.B.**

THE GOSPEL ACCORDING TO VIC (1986)

RATING: PG–13   ★★★
CONTENT: Vulgarities
INTENDED AUDIENCE: Adults
STARRING: Tom Conti, Helen Mirren
DIRECTOR: Charles Gromley

This film tells the story of an atheist, Vic, who is confronted by the God of the miraculous. The message of this movie is that natural man cannot comprehend a supernatural God who directly intervenes through prayer and faith.

As the film opens, a Scottish priest is in Rome attempting to convince the Vatican powers-that-be that the namesake of the Blessed Edith Church and School, Edith Semple, should be canonized because miracles are occurring daily in the parish. The powers-that-be refuse the request, stating there are enough saints and the Church can't have miracles turning everyone into saints. Vic becomes involved in the story because, though an unbeliever in the parish, miracles start happening to and through him!

Slowly, Vic's skepticism weakens. He visits a student in the hospital with a broken leg and heals him. Now dubbed as the miracle man, he is still confused because of his unbelief. The Church is upset that Vic, an unbeliever, is being touted as a miracle worker. Everyone's opinions, actions and reactions to the miracles correlate completely with what you'd expect in real life.

Unfortunately, there is no clear cut resolution of Vic's skepticism. We develop a genuine concern for Vic, only to be denied the opportunity to witness his final decision at the journey's end. Recommended with the caution that there is some offensive language. **S.K. and D.R.**

THE GRADUATE (1967), 105 min.

RATING: PG
CONTENT: Humanism, free love, and anti-Christian elements
INTENDED AUDIENCE: Adults
STARRING: Dustin Hoffman, Anne Bancroft, Katherine Ross
DIRECTOR: Mike Nichols

This movie, considered to be a masterpiece by some, is not good Christian fare. Like so many films of the sixties, it seeks to express the feelings of the times. With the Vietnam war raging, the hippie movement in full-swing, drugs, free-love and anti-establishment viewpoints prospering, it is no wonder the non-Christian character Dustin Hoffman plays is confused.

Yes, the movie does have its good points. Hoffman's acting is first-rate. The directing and cinematography are innovative and fascinating. However, these elements cannot mask the totally humanistic world view this movie portrays. **L.R.**

THE GRAPES OF WRATH (1940), 128 min.

CONTENT: Nothing objectionable　　　　　　　　　　　　★★★★
INTENDED AUDIENCE: Adults
STARRING: Henry Fonda, Jane Darwell, Charley Grapewin, John Carradine
DIRECTOR: John Ford

This film is based on John Steinbeck's account of poor Oklahoma farmers who moved from the Dust Bowl to California in the 1920s and 1930s. A superb cast with an intelligent script gives us one of the most powerful films ever made. We follow the Joad family on their trek and see many sides of humanity. The Joads live day to day, hand to mouth, robbed of most of their earthly possessions, but not of their dignity.

Their faith in God helps them through this time of tribulation—seeing friends killed, others at the mercy of labor bosses, family members becoming disillusioned by the dreams they thought possible in California. The mother knows that they can be beaten, but not broken, and that the family can and must survive with the help of God. This film is strongly recommended. **B.G**

THE GREAT ESCAPE (1963), 173 min.

CONTENT: Mild obscenity and some violence　　　　　　★★★
INTENDED AUDIENCE: Adults
STARRING: Steve McQueen, James Garner, Richard Attenborough, James Coburn, Charles Bronson, James Donald, David McCallum, Donald Pleasance
DIRECTOR: John Sturges

The Great Escape is based on the true story of a massive escape from a prisoner-of-war camp in Nazi Germany during World War II. Set in Germany near the Swiss border, the prison camp is a mixture of British and American airmen who have been shot down and captured. The senior officer is "M" (Richard Attenborough), who is planning the largest breakout from a German camp ever undertaken, which will include hundreds of men, each equipped with civilian clothing, faked passports, rations, and even train tickets.

The days go by, as the prisoners dig under the barracks and store the dirt in the rafters of the buildings, in the gardens, anywhere dirt can be hidden. Finally, digging the last few feet, "Tunnel King" (Charles Bronson) breaks through the turf, only to find that their tunnel is several feet short of the forest. It opens in a clearing just a few feet from the outer fence.

"No matter," says M, "we go." And, go they do, as one of the largest breakouts of World War II begins. Dozens of men begin their escape, running to the trees while the spotlights are sweeping in the opposite direction. Over a hundred men escape before the break is discovered.

The film follows each of the main characters as they try to make their way to freedom but eventually most are captured. If you like action and adventure, you will love the film. **B.G.**

THE GREAT MOUSE DETECTIVE (1986)

RATING: G   ★★★
CONTENT: Animated feature film
INTENDED AUDIENCE: Children
STARRING (voices): Vincent Price, Barry Ingham, Val Bettin, Alan Young
PRODUCTION COMPANY: Walt Disney Productions

This beautifully animated story involves a young girl mouse, Olivia Flavisham, who is seeking the help of that famous detective mouse, Basil of Baker Street. Her father has been kidnapped by the mastermind of evil, Professor Ratigan. After quite a few hair-raising adventures, Ratigan is outwitted and foiled in his plot to take over the kingdom of Mousedom. Intelligence and integrity triumph over evil.

This is an excellent family movie that everyone but the most jaded will enjoy. Ratigan's mouse-eating cat, Felicia, is especially entertaining. The voices are excellent, especially Vincent Price, and the character development is superb.

THE GREAT SANTINI (1979), 118 min.

RATING: PG   ★★★
CONTENT: Swearing and some violence
INTENDED AUDIENCE: Adults
STARRING: Robert Duvall, Blythe Danner, Michael O'Keefe
DIRECTOR: Lewis John Carlino

This tough story focuses on a marine fighter pilot who has no war to fight, so he creates one within himself and with his family. Robert Duvall, in one of his finest screen performances, plays Bull Meechum, a near-alcoholic marine colonel. Bull is well liked by his men, and he is a natural leader who goes to great lengths to be "Numero Uno." He has to win at everything he does, whether as the top gun in a jet fighter during maneuvers or as a sideline "coach" as he watches and cajoles his son during the boy's basketball game with a rival team.

Bull is a warrior who hasn't been allowed to express himself, even his love for his family. However, he is not an uncaring man. In the end, his caring for others triumphs over self-interest.

All in all, this is a good movie, but a tough one. The profanity is inexcusable, but realistic. Caution is recommended, although this is a classic study of a warrior without a war. **B.G.**

A GREAT WALL: AN AMERICAN COMEDY MADE IN CHINA (1986)

RATING: PG   ★★
CONTENT: Brief, unnecessary, vulgar language
INTENDED AUDIENCE: Adults
STARRING: Peter Wang, Sharon Iwai
DIRECTOR: Peter Wang

Westernized East meets East in this film when the Leo Fang family of San Francisco takes a thirty-day vacation to China. Having lived in the United States for thirty years, Leo is disappointed over the modernization of Peking. The scene of the arrival at his sister's home is touching, and it is fascinating to observe the Fangs' immersion into Chinese life.

The film was very well directed. The majority of the characters were well cast and well acted. An ancient Chinese folk song scene was alive with expression, and the scenes at the Great Wall were spectacular. However, this film titled as a comedy was really more dramatic than humorous. The movie has a very brief nude scene at a community bathhouse, which is an accepted social institution in China. Furthermore, there were a few moments of crudeness, and the movie ended with a brief but totally unnecessary vulgar joking exchange between the father and the son. There are no spiritual values, only humanistic ones depicted here. It is only for discerning Christians because it will promote excellent discussions on the failure of both Western and Eastern humanism. **D.R.**

THE GREATEST STORY EVER TOLD (1965), 225 min.

CONTENT: Nothing objectionable   ★★★★
INTENDED AUDIENCE: All ages
STARRING: Max Von Sydow, Charlton Heston, Jose Ferrer, David McCallum, Telly Savalas, Donald Pleasance, Robert Blake, Dorothy McGuire
DIRECTOR: George Stevens

The story of Jesus of Nazareth, based on the Gospels, is grandly presented in this majestic film. It does justice to the gospel narrative, covering the three years of Jesus' ministry in much detail. The script uses lines of Scripture, as well as dialogue constructed around it, and deftly sits on the edge of not being too pious, too ridiculous, or too boring.

In terms of film sensibilities, Christ is the most difficult subject to portray: both fully divine and fully human. The filmed character of Jesus must possess many, many attributes and emotions, a difficult role for any actor to perform in a believable fashion. But Max Von Sydow uses his craftsmanship to its fullest and gives one of the screen's finest portrayals of Him.

The film's depiction of many of the events of Christ's life also has been handled with discretion. Rather than impose some gimmicky special effect or photographic trickery, many of Jesus' miracles, such as His feeding the multitudes and walking on water, are described in dialogue. From His triumphal procession into Jerusalem to His burial and resurrection, the film depicts the points of view of the Romans, the Sanhedrin, and Jesus and His followers.

Christians everywhere should rejoice that such effort, creativity, inspiration, and money went into a production of such magnitude about the life of Christ. Though *The Greatest Story Ever Told* may not be the greatest movie ever made, it attempts to do justice to a story difficult to translate into the medium of film. **B.G.**

GUNG HO (1986)

RATING: PG
CONTENT: Foul language
INTENDED AUDIENCE: Young adults
STARRING: Michael Keaton, Gedde Watanabe
DIRECTOR: Ron Howard

Gung Ho is the lighthearted, amusing story of a young man who talks a Japanese car company into locating their American plant in his town. The Japanese try to run the plant as if the employees were Japanese, but they are foiled by the American slobs. Our hero tries to keep the company moving and gets caught in a lie, repents, and finally gets the plant to succeed.

There is no nudity, violence, or sex. This film would be acceptable entertainment, except for the bad language. Therefore, it is not recommended. **E.R.**

THE GUNS OF NAVARONE (1961), 159 min.

CONTENT: Nothing objectionable ★★★
INTENDED AUDIENCE: Adults
STARRING: Gregory Peck, David Niven, Stanley Baker, Anthony Quinn
DIRECTOR: J. Lee Thompson

Based on the best-selling Alistair MacLean book by the same title, this film is a combination war/spy movie. The time is World War II. Allied commando heroes must disguise themselves as locals and somehow penetrate a mighty German fortress to sabotage huge cannons set in the solid rock face of a mountain guarding the Aegean Sea. If they are successful, it will hasten the end of the war. Excellent action/ adventure. Recommended. **L.R.**

HANNAH AND HER SISTERS (1985), 107 min.

RATING: PG–13 ★★
CONTENT: Sexual situations and anti-Christian material
INTENDED AUDIENCE: Adults
STARRING: Mia Farrow, Woody Allen
DIRECTOR: Woody Allen

In his last few films, Woody Allen had moved in the direction of accepting God. *The Purple Rose of Cairo* had a very strong statement of faith. In *Hannah and Her Sisters*, Woody's struggle with faith in Jesus Christ seems to come out in the open. In the beginning of the movie, Jesus and God are mentioned reverentially, and the character portrayed by Woody even converts to Catholicism. However, his Jewish family is mortified, and he is bothered by the trappings of commercialism (plastic statues, etc.), so he retreats from his conversion and returns to hedonistic agnosticism.

Apart from this apparently autobiographical story, this film is laden with very negative subplots, involving adultery with no retribution, although the affair is a failure. Hedonism triumphs here. The dialogue is excellent, and the performances are superb, but the movie falls into a false philosophy. Unfortunately, it cannot be recommended.

HAUNTED HONEYMOON (1986)

RATING: PG ★★★
CONTENT: No nudity, very little violence, and mild bad language
INTENDED AUDIENCE: All ages
STARRING: Gene Wilder, Gilda Radner, Dom DeLuise
DIRECTOR: Gene Wilder

Beginning in a radio station with actors rehearsing a horror story on mike, *Haunted Honeymoon* concerns the engagement of Larry and Vicky and Larry's mysterious behavior. An unexplainable quirk causes him to have lapses of memory, leading to binges of hysterical laughter and crying. Unknown to Larry, a psychiatrist guarantees a cure using the Zurich method, which means they try to scare him to death. The story moves to Larry's family estate where all sorts of odd things happen.

Perfect casting produced the film's original intent, a hilarious spoof of the horror genre. Gene Wilder, Gilda Radner, and Dom DeLuise are talented, skillful performers, and their enjoyment of the work adds an extra sparkle. **G.O.**

HEAD OFFICE (1986)

RATING: PG–13
CONTENT: Blatantly anti-Christian material, drugs, nudity, profanity, obscenity, and sexual situations
INTENDED AUDIENCE: Young adults
STARRING: Judge Reinhold, Eddie Albert, Danny DeVito, Jane Seymour
DIRECTOR: Ken Finkleman

Head Office is a blatantly anti-Christian movie: Jesus is mocked; prayer meetings are portrayed as the tools of unscrupulous conservatives to invoke the Deity to support their evil ways; and Christians are shown as right-wing fanatics bent on destroying the world. Drugs, sex, nudity, and alcohol use are promoted. God is portrayed as a fascist, and evil is good in this movie.

Christians should be offended. We should protest this direct attack on us and on Jesus. The filmmaker should be called to task for making such a movie.

HEARTBURN (1986)

RATING: R
CONTENT: Adultery and profanity
INTENDED AUDIENCE: Adults
STARRING: Meryl Streep, Jack Nicholson
DIRECTOR: Mike Nichols

Heartburn is a bore. Jack Nicholson and Meryl Streep do such poor acting that you may never want to see another movie with them in it. The story is so thin that at times there is no story, just lackluster improvisation.

In the story, Meryl meets Jack at a wedding. They go to bed together after their first date. They get married. They have a child. She finds out that he is cheating on her. She goes back to Daddy. Jack asks her to come home. She has their second baby. She finds out that he is still cheating on her. She leaves with the children. The movie ends—at last. Claustrophobic, myopic, inane, and filled with profanity, this film is a waste of time.

HEIDI (1965), 95 min.

RATING: G   ★★★★
CONTENT: Nothing objectionable
INTENDED AUDIENCE: Families
STARRING: Eva Maria Slinghammer, Gustav Knuth
DIRECTOR: Werner Jacobs

Heidi makes her fourth debut in this version filmed in Switzerland and Germany

113

with a foreign cast and very acceptable English dubbing. For parents who are hard-pressed to find acceptable movies for their daughters, girls (up to about age ten) will love this color rendition of the Johanna Spyri children's classic.

The sentimental tale follows Heidi, who lives with her grandfather in the Swiss Alps, as she goes to Frankfurt to teach a paralyzed girl to walk. They befriend each other, and Heidi's beaming love transforms a grim, unhappy household into a brightened, caring place. This version will delight children as much as the 1937 version with Shirley Temple has. (The 1937 *Heidi* should be considered a good second choice if this new version cannot be located). **B.G.**

HEY THERE, IT'S YOGI BEAR (1986), 89 min.

RATING: G   ★★★
CONTENT: Animation; nothing objectionable
INTENDED AUDIENCE: Children
STARRING (voices): Daws Butler, Don Messick
DIRECTORS: William Hanna, Joseph Barbera

This movie has a great story that contains a redemptive message. Yogi plays a trick on the park ranger and ends up in trouble. He repents and calls for help, and the ranger rescues him. The simple plot is enlivened by fast action and good humor. Furthermore, it takes place all over the United States.

This is a good movie for children. Let them enjoy it; cartoons as positive as this one are hard to find. **P.B.** and **J.B.**

THE HIDING PLACE (1975), 145 min.

RATING: PG   ★★★
CONTENT: Minor violence
INTENDED AUDIENCE: All ages
STARRING: Julie Harris, Eileen Heckart, Arthur O'Connell
DIRECTOR: James Collier

Corrie Ten Boom was a member of a Dutch Christian family in Nazi-occupied Holland during World War II. The Ten Boom family operated an underground railroad to assist Jews in escaping from the country. Corrie clearly affirms that Jesus is the reason her family helps the Jews and that man cannot live without Him.

Corrie and her sister place great faith in God as they make elaborate plans to outsmart the Germans with their operation. Eventually, their cover is blown, and the whole family is taken to a prison camp. The family is released, except for Corrie and her sister, Betsie. Betsie dies in the concentration camp after Corrie is released; years later, it was learned that Corrie was set free because of a clerical error.

The film closes with a beautiful epilogue by the real Corrie Ten Boom, who was in her eighties at the time of the filming. Though slow-paced, *The Hiding Place* conveys a powerful range of emotions to the audience and emphasizes the Ten Booms' faith in God. It is probably one of the strongest testaments of faith ever to reach the screen in a commercially accepted feature film that was not depicting Bible characters or the ancient world. It is highly recommended. **B.G.**

THE HIGH AND THE MIGHTY (1954) B&W, 147 min.

CONTENT: Nothing objectionable   ★★★★

INTENDED AUDIENCE: Adults
STARRING: John Wayne, Robert Newton, Robert Stack
DIRECTOR: William Wellman

The High and the Mighty marked the first in what has become an entire subgenre of film, the "airport" film. This is the story of a crippled airliner (DC-7 vintage) that attempts to reach a safe landing spot during a long flight over the Pacific Ocean. The plane develops engine trouble, and a fire breaks out inside the engine. By "feathering" the engine, the fire is extinguished, but more mechanical failures occur, making a crash into the sea seem certain. This is a gripping film and may be too intense for youngsters—or those who don't like to fly—but is recommended if you like clean, thrilling, action adventure. **B.G.**

HIGH NOON (1952), 85 min.

CONTENT: Nothing objectionable   ★ ★ ★ ★
INTENDED AUDIENCE: All ages
STARRING: Gary Cooper, Grace Kelly, Lloyd Bridges
DIRECTOR: Fred Zinnemann

High Noon is one of the greatest Westerns of all time. The acting is flawless; the direction is magnificent; the photography is superb; the music is timeless; and the story is moral, biblical, wholesome, heroic, and eternal.

A newly married, retired sheriff is forced to defend a town that will not defend itself from a gang of murderers. The hero has plenty of opportunities to cut and run, but he is an example of integrity and refuses to let evil sweep over the town unopposed. This hero should be a model to every Christian, and the film should be shown to every child as an example of what it takes to be a person of integrity.

Gary Cooper received a well-deserved Oscar for his performance. This great movie is not just entertainment; it is a powerful lesson in good and evil that we all should take the time to see. **K.G.**

HIGHLANDER (1986)

RATING: R
CONTENT: Nudity, foul language, and adult themes
INTENDED AUDIENCE: Adults
STARRING: Christopher Lampert, Sean Connery, Roxanne Hart, Clancy Brown
DIRECTOR: Russell Mulcahy

What begins as an interesting epic movie sinks into silliness. The only commendable aspects are the special effects and the epic scope. It involves a battling group of immortals; each one has the goal of killing off all the other immortals because the last surviving immortal will inherit the prize of becoming mortal and being able to have children.

There are some positive references to Christianity. The church is off-limits to the battle of the immortals, the hero prays, and the priest proclaims that Jesus died even for them. However, aside from these brief redeeming references to faith, the movie is ridiculous and plagued by nudity, foul language, and adult themes. Avoid this film. **E.R.**

THE HITCHER (1986), 98 min.

RATING: R
CONTENT: Profane language and gruesome violence
INTENDED AUDIENCE: Adults
STARRING: Rutger Hauer, Thomas Howell, Jennifer Jason Leigh, Jeffery De Munn
DIRECTOR: Robert Harmon

The Hitcher tells the frightening story of a young man driving across the country who picks up a killer hitchhiker. When the young man escapes the hitcher's knife, the hitcher frames him by implicating him in a series of gruesome murders. However, two-thirds of the way into this dark tale the plot line is broken, and the hitcher reveals who he is to the police. From that moment, the movie falls apart, and it becomes a simple but gory action-adventure flick. Finally, it ends on the very depressing note that the insane killer has so infected the young man that he turns into a killer.

This bloody, dark film cannot be recommended. If the movie had sustained its original tension, it would have been worth viewing for its excellence; but it failed to fulfill its promise. Also, the profane language and the gruesome violence make it unacceptable.

THE HOBBIT (1977), 78 min.

CONTENT: Some grotesque monsters ★★★
INTENDED AUDIENCE: Families
STARRING (Voices): Orson Bean, John Huston, Otto Preminger, Richard Boone
DIRECTOR: Jules Bass, Arthur Rankin, Jr.

Thorin, the Wizard, comes to find Bilbo Baggins, a Hobbit, and tells him that the dwarfs need his services as a burglar. The bad, invincible Dragon, Smaug, has taken treasure from the dwarfs. So, Bilbo, Thorin, and the dwarfs set off to recover the treasure, encountering many adventures along the way.

As a book, *The Hobbit* is an immortal fantasy based on a Christian perspective. Unfortunately, the movie, although entertaining, does not do the book justice. There are quite a few gruesome monsters in the film, perhaps too many. On the other hand, children seem to love it. Even though the Christian allegory seems lost, this is good entertainment that most of your family will enjoy. **J.B.** and **P.B.**

HOOSIERS (1987)

RATING: PG ★★★★
CONTENT: Some vulgarity and very little profanity
INTENDED AUDIENCE: Families
STARRING: Gene Hackman, Barbara Hershey, Dennis Hopper
DIRECTOR: David Anspaugh

Hoosiers is the most upbeat sports film to come along since *Chariots of Fire*. The time is 1951, and there is little to do in Hickory, Indiana, except play basketball. As the new coach for the Hickory Huskers high school basketball team, Coach Norman Dale has little to do except win the heart of a resentful woman teacher, reassemble the life of the town drunk, redeem his own checkered career, and take a rag-tag team of farm boys from their tiny gym at Hickory High to the stadium of the State Finals.

Simple Christian faith, almost as pervasive in Hickory as the love for basketball, weaves its way through the film. Each of the games, apparently, begins with prayer in the locker room. One of the Huskers, the Reverend's son, has learned much by his father's example: he prays the longest in the locker room; he prays on the bench; he prays for his teammates. And, at one point with the team falling behind in a crucial game, his prayers send him onto the court in a fury, racking up the points.

Hoosiers is a positive, uplifting film, a veritable *Places in the Heart* in sneakers and basketball uniforms. Recommended, except for a little off-color language. **B.S.**

HOT SHOT (1987)

RATING: PG   ★★
CONTENT: Some profanity, vulgarity, and crude language
INTENDED AUDIENCE: Young adults
STARRING: Jim Young, Pelé
DIRECTOR: Rick King

A lot of exciting soccer action comes to the screen of this film story of a young man, Jimmy Kristidis (Jim Youngs), who desperately tries to become a professional soccer player. Jimmy is the son of a wealthy Greek shipping company tycoon and qualifies for the New York Rockers professional soccer team, but against his parents' will.

When the coach of the Rockers puts Jimmy on suspension for his undisciplined behavior, Jimmy takes off for Brazil where he persuades a former soccer player named Santos to give him special training. Santos (Pelé) sharpens Jimmy's soccer skills as well as influences his attitude toward team play and cooperation.

Crude, vulgar, and profane language damage *Hot Shot*. Otherwise it could be recommended. **J.E.**

HOUSE (1986)

RATING: R
CONTENT: Profanity and spiritism
INTENDED AUDIENCE: Young adults
STARRING: William Katt, George Wendt
DIRECTOR: Steve Miner

This light horror film suffers from a confused plot and the fact that God's name is taken in vain. The effects are good, but the story line is flawed. The hero is haunted by his Vietnam buddy. The hero's aunt is found hanged in his house, and the hero's son disappears. Finally, the hero realizes that the ghost is a figment of his imagination, and when he does, the ghost vanishes, his son appears, and everybody lives happily ever after in a dark, gloomy house.

The problem is that there is no recognition that the only deliverance we have from the clutches of evil is Jesus. Not once is there a prayer for deliverance. Instead, the movie suggests that evil is just a figment of the imagination. *House* makes one long for the films of the 1930s where the cross was a symbol of the power of God. Miss this one. **K.G.**

HOW GREEN WAS MY VALLEY (1941) B&W, 118 min.

CONTENT: Nothing objectionable   ★★★★

INTENDED AUDIENCE: All ages
STARRING: Walter Pidgeon, Maureen O'Hara, Roddy McDowall, Donald Crisp, Anna Lee, Barry Fitzgerald
DIRECTOR: John Ford

This movie is a touching and heartwarming drama about life in a Welsh coal-mining town. The story concerns a family and their ties with the town, their poverty and struggle to make ends meet as miners.

The plot line is overshadowed by director Ford's character development, as the performers go from one incident to another. Much of the movie revolves around the miners wanting to go on strike, and Father Morgan (Donald Crisp) calling it "socialist nonsense." The family is torn apart over this; and the two eldest sons, embittered, leave the family for a boarding house. The family scatters, and young Huw (Roddy McDowall), realizes that the old way of life is vanishing.

Ford's direction won him an Oscar in 1942, and *How Green Was My Valley* beat *Citizen Kane* as Best Picture. It also won Oscars for Best Supporting Actor (Donald Crisp), Best Cinematography, and Best Art Direction and nominations for Best Supporting Actress and Best Screenplay. **B.G.**

HOWARD THE DUCK (1986)

RATING: PG
CONTENT: Lewd, suggestive scenes with partial nudity, rough language, sexual allusions, and phallic symbols
INTENDED AUDIENCE: Teenagers and adults
STARRING: Lea Thompson, Jeffrey Jones, Tim Robbins
DIRECTOR: Willard Huyck

Howard the Duck could have been a lot more funny if it had been faithful to the comic book series by the same name. As it is, sexual innuendo, off-color language, and other crudities make it off-limits to Christians.

It is a mishmash of references to other films in an attempt to piece together a blockbuster, but this mixed-up movie is not crazy enough to take off. The most degrading aspect is the constant reference to bestiality—the possibility of the girl rock singer having an affair with Howard the Duck. The best part is that it has a real view of the nature of reality and even reverently suggests that God exists. However, this is not a godly movie, for the evil Dark Overlord is defeated by space duck Howard's ingenuity, not by the Lord Jesus. Thus, moderately good triumphs over really evil. As it is, this film lays an egg. Avoid it.

HUD (1963) B&W, 112 min.

CONTENT: Focuses on a crooked man who uses and abuses everyone   ★★★★
INTENDED AUDIENCE: Adults
STARRING: Paul Newman, Melvyn Douglas, Patricia Neal, Brandon de Wilde
DIRECTOR: Martin Ritt

This film tells the story of a man, Hud, played by Newman, who is so greedy that he is willing to spread hoof-and-mouth disease among cattle just to make money without concern for the damage it will cause the other ranchers. As the movie develops, Hud slides deeper and deeper into moral degradation, totally violating the western ideal of fair play and Christian community. Hud is a model of the corrupt sinner, who seems so striking and charming on the surface, and yet is underneath full of mean-spirited greed. In stark contrast to Hud, is Melvyn Douglas's portrayal of the man who believes in and upholds traditional, biblical values. He almost seems like an anachronism in today's world. Definitely a Western worth watching.

HYPERSAPIENS (1968)

RATING: PG ★★
CONTENT: Minor swearing, but no nudity or violence
INTENDED AUDIENCE: Adolescents, adults
STARRING: Ricky Paul Golden, Sydney Penny, Keenan Wynn
DIRECTOR: Peter Hunt

Ricky Golden stars as Dirt, a human being enamored with the beauty and mystical powers of an alien named Robin, who has stowed away with her sister, Tavy, on a spaceship that has landed on Wyoming's grassy plains. It's a beautiful spot, but nothing like the moon. The film also follows the exploits of Kirby, a whimsical, three-eyed, three-armed alien animal who allies himself with Grandpa, played by Keenan Wynn.

Dirt takes the two alien girls and Kirby to Grandpa's home, thinking they will be safe there. While at Grandpa's, Kirby develops a taste for gasoline. Even though Dirt attempts to promote a peaceful alliance between the aliens and the residents of Wyoming, conflict ensues. A barbecue for a senator proves disastrous as Kirby's desire for gasoline leaves all the motorists stranded.

The film is a lighthearted, comical adventure story, slightly marred by a preoccupation with the supernatural powers of the aliens, but reveals no ungodly (or godly) intent. Neutral enough for most audiences **C.U.**

IMAGEMAKER (1986)

RATING: R
CONTENT: Profanity and nudity
INTENDED AUDIENCE: Adults
STARRING: Michael Nouri, Anne Twomey, Jerry Orbach
DIRECTOR: Hal Weiner

Imagemaker is another *Power*—the story of the manipulation of the media by politicians. In this film, a Washington reporter exposes media manipulation and almost gets killed by the mean power brokers. Profanity and nudity make it unacceptable for Christians, even though it is a clever, slick production. Furthermore, the plot gets too contrived, and the ending is very weak.

IMPURE THOUGHTS (1986)

CONTENT: Very mild bad language and brief shadow nudity
INTENDED AUDIENCE: Adults
STARRING: Brad Dourif, John Putch, Lane Davies, Terry Beaver
DIRECTOR: Michael A. Simpson

This low-budget comedy was made in Atlanta entirely by Atlantans. From a technical point of view, it is a good movie, but from a theological point of view, it misses the mark by a mile. The story is not interesting enough to recommend watching a movie whose theological underpinning is so confused. There is no doubt that it was produced with the best of intentions, but it fails for lack of careful realization.

A soldier and a businessman meet in purgatory and are soon joined by two more of their classmates from St. Jude's parochial school. Each classmate reviews his life to see why he is in purgatory, and one by one they discover the impure thoughts that led them to this holding station on their way to heaven. They disappear and head to the next level of purgatory.

It is clear that no one intended for this to be as anti-Christian as it is. Sad to say, but the characters are looking for something they can do to save themselves. There is nothing that we have to do, or can do, to save ourselves, however. The film also suggests that we are saved or condemned by our works, not by Jesus Christ.

Impure Thoughts is a slow, surrealistic movie. There is some nudity seen through a shower door, and there are a few profanities. However, the worst aspect is its theological weaknesses. For that reason, it should be avoided.

INCENDIARY BLONDE (1945), 113 min.

CONTENT: Nothing overtly objectionable   ★★
INTENDED AUDIENCE: Adults
STARRING: Betty Hutton, Arturo de Cordova, Charlie Ruggles, Barry Fitzgerald
DIRECTOR: George Marshall

Incendiary Blonde is a fanciful takeoff on the legendary life of the prohibition sensation, Texas Guinan. The movie starts with a scene of a 1909 wild west show and rodeo. Texas Guinan (Hutton), watching the parade pass by, leaves the sidelines and sings and dances along the parade route until stopped by her father. She next enters the bronco-riding contest and loses, but demands to ride again, saying the saddle cinch was deliberately loosened. She wins the fifty dollar prize. When she goes for the money, the show's owner, Bill Kilgannon (de Cordova), asks her to join the show. She starts in as a trick rider and is so good that she is made the star of the Wild West Show. From there it's onward and upward as she ends up on Broadway!

Texas Guinan was a legend in her time—a loud, bawdy, flamboyant character, famous on the New York scene during the gangster era of Prohibition. The film skips over the sleaziness and corruption of the era and is presented with taste and compassion for her life-long love for the man in her life (who happens to be married).

The problem with the movie is that adulterous affair. Although the affair is never consummated, the very suggestion of the depth of Bill and Texas's love, when he is married and has children, is an affront. God hates adultery and divorce and Christians should too. **R.A.**

THE INQUIRY (1987), 110 min.

CONTENT: Nothing objectionable   ★★★
INTENDED AUDIENCE: Families
STARRING: Keith Carradine, Harvey Keitel, Phyllis Logan
DIRECTOR: Damiano Damini

The Inquiry tells the story of a Roman official, Taurus, who is sent to Palestine by Emperor Tiberius to find the missing body of the rebel Jesus of Nazareth, who was crucified three years earlier. Taurus is a very careful inquisitor, and Pontius Pilate, the Roman governor, is worried that Taurus's inquisition might reflect badly on him.

In the process of searching for Jesus' body, Taurus becomes confused. His original theory that the body was stolen is disproved, as is each one of his succeeding theories until he comes to the moment of realization that the resurrection did occur. This Italian film leads us inexorably to the conclusion, that either the resurrection is real or nothing is real.

Beautifully photgraphed, this film has some elements of a costume drama. However, it is a powerful apologetic for the resurrection. Highly recommended.

INVADERS FROM MARS (1986)
RATING: PG
CONTENT: Mild language
INTENDED AUDIENCE: Teenagers and adults
STARRING: Karen Black, Hunter Carson, Timothy Bottoms, Laraine Newman, James Karen, Bud Cort, Louise Fletcher
DIRECTOR: Tobe Hopper

A rip-off of a classic science-fiction movie, this film is simply an excuse for expensive special effects. When a young boy sees a UFO land and tells his parents about it, they do not believe him. Soon his father and other people are possessed by Martians. The marines save the day by wiping out the aliens. The boy wakes up, and his parents tell him it was just a dream. As he is going back to bed, he sees a spacecraft landing and knows that it was not a dream.

The story is not bad, but the realization is very weak. The boy flip-flops from fear to heroics for no reason. There are many gaps in the plot. You will probably want to avoid *Invaders from Mars* unless you are a science-fiction buff. **K.K.**

INVASION OF THE BODY SNATCHERS (1953) B&W, 80 min.
CONTENT: Nothing objectionable   ★★★★
INTENDED AUDIENCE: Families
STARRING: Kevin McCarthy, Dana Wynter, Larry Gates, King Donovan, Carolyn Jones
DIRECTOR: Don Siegel

Invasion of the Body Snatchers remains one of the most suspenseful, exciting science-fiction films of all time. It tells the story of a small town in California that is slowly being taken over by alien pods. Within each pod, there is a person who replaces a person in the town. Finally, it is only the doctor who has come in to examine the situation who escapes. In the last scene, he runs toward the big city trying to warn traffic on the highway of what is happening. As he does so, a truck load of pods passes him heading for the big city.

This is a suspenseful, exciting movie. Recommended for those who like science-fiction films.

INVASION USA (1986)
RATING: R
CONTENT: Profanity and violence
INTENDED AUDIENCE: Adults

STARRING: Chuck Norris
DIRECTOR: Joseph Zito

Invasion USA tells the story of a superman, played by Chuck Norris, who fights off invading Russians. Our hero, however, has feet of clay—he swears and steals. This poorly directed film is fatally flawed. Don't see it.

THE IPCRESS FILE (1965), 108 min.

CONTENT: Minor swearing and some violence   ★★★
INTENDED AUDIENCE: Adults
STARRING: Michael Caine, Nigel Green, Guy Doleman, Sue Lloyd, Gordon Jackson
DIRECTOR: Sidney J. Furie

Two rival sections in the British Secret Service are involved, and it is the discrepancies in the actions of the two section chiefs (Guy Doleman and Nigel Green) that leads Palmer into suspecting a double agent. The Russians are also suspected. Palmer discovers information that threatens his life, and is unsure who is working for whom, so he goes underground to uncover the mystery.

The Ipcress File is a tense, relentlessly absorbing espionage thriller, with such perfect casting that you almost think the actors are born for their parts. The story revolves around Palmer, who is placed in a new division of the Secret Service in the hope of tracking down the abductors of a top-level scientist. It seems that a "brain drain" is taking place, and Palmer is to investigate. This film so overshadows such movies as *The Spy Who Came in from the Cold*, *Torn Curtain* and *Topaz* that it could very well be the finest spy thriller of the sixties. There is some minor swearing in the movie. **B.G.**

IRON EAGLE (1986)

RATING: PG–13
CONTENT: Profanity
INTENDED AUDIENCE: Adults and teenagers
STARRING: Louis Gossett, Jr., Jason Gedrick
DIRECTOR: Sidney Furie

Good action and fancy dogfights in supersonic fighters cannot save the second-rate script of this film. It is the unbelievable tale of a teenager who steals an air force jet fighter to rescue his father from an Arab country, which resembles Libya. It's pure teen fantasy.

The only redeeming point is the positive father-son relationship. The music is often out of place. In parts, the movie is painfully slow. There is almost no real conflict or drama, and the plot is illogical. Bad dialogue, profanity, and embarrassing overacting make this a bomb.

ISLANDS IN THE STREAM (1977), 105 min.

RATING: PG   ★★★
CONTENT: Strong language, obscenities
INTENDED AUDIENCE: Adults
STARRING: George C. Scott, David Hemmings, Claire Bloom, Julius Harris,
   Susan Tyrrell
DIRECTOR: Franklin J. Schaffner

Tom Hudson (Scott) feels himself to be a failed husband, a man who has buried himself away from the world and then suddenly finds the world at his doorstep. His three sons by a former marriage arrive to spend the summer with their "old man." He wants to show his sons that he is still capable, and teaches one of them how to fish for Marlin. Yet the world creeps ever closer as he learns that his oldest son had been killed in battle.

Distressed at his existence on the island, Tom decides to leave for Key West. He becomes involved with a group of refugees, picking them up from their sinking boat. His own craft is attacked by Cuban coast guard boats, and a gun battle ensues. Tom's best friend is killed; he finally resorts to violence to save himself and others.

Other than for some mild off-color language, this is a strong, sensitive film that portrays the importance of being involved with others. **B.G.**

IT'S A MAD, MAD, MAD, MAD WORLD (1963), 192 min.

CONTENT: Nothing objectionable   ★★★
INTENDED AUDIENCE: All ages
STARRING: Spencer Tracy, Milton Berle, Sid Caesar, Buddy Hackett, Ethel Merman, Mickey Rooney, Dick Shawn, Phil Silvers, Terry Thomas, Jonathan Winters, Edie Adams, Dorothy Provine, Jimmy Durante, Eddie "Rochester" Anderson, Jim Backus, Ben Blue, Art Carney, William Demarest, Peter Falk, Paul Ford, Buster Keaton, Don Knotts, Carl Reiner, the Three Stooges, Joe E. Brown, Andy Devine, Sterling Holloway, Jesse White, Arnold Stang, Jerry Lewis
DIRECTOR: Stanley Kramer

The story begins when Milton Berle, henpecked by his wife and his mother-in-law (Ethel Merman), comes across a dying motorist in the California desert. The dying man (Jimmy Durante) tells Berle about a treasure of $350,000, which is stashed away somewhere. Several other motorists have arrived and hear Durante whisper the clue again, only to die. By now, characters played by Winters, Hackett, Rooney, and others know something big is happening and rush to their cars to pursue the cash. What ensues is an insane, snowballing comedy as the secret spreads to dozens of people. Everyone gets caught up in the attempt to find the money, using every conceivable means of transportation from stolen airplanes to a mule.

There are wild and hilarious scenes throughout the movie, such as Mickey Rooney and Buddy Hackett on board a twin engine plane with a passed out pilot. They don't know how to fly. Or when Sid Caesar, who is trapped in the basement of a hardware store, gives up trying to get out with tools when he finds dynamite!

It's a Mad, Mad, Mad, Mad World! is slapstick comedy and a most enjoyable film. **B.G.**

IT'S A WONDERFUL LIFE (1946), 129 min.

CONTENT: Nothing objectionable   ★★★★
INTENDED AUDIENCE: All ages
STARRING: Jimmy Stewart, Donna Reed, Thomas Mitchell, Lionel Barrymore, Ward Bond
DIRECTOR: Frank Capra

It's snowing on Christmas Eve, and the camera pans across the town's houses, circa 1946. The voices of the individual people are heard as they pray to God, petitioning the Lord for help in their lives. It seems that many of them are asking for help for a man named George Bailey.

The story focuses on George, a respectable, earnest, and concerned businessman and citizen. However, George feels that life is passing him by. His kid brother is a decorated war hero, but George has had to be content running the family business, a building and loan association.

Things take a turn for the worse one day, and George says he wishes he was never born. However, his guardian angel convinces him otherwise, and George returns home to a joyous Christmas Eve in Bedford Falls, with family and friends who know him, and he has an entirely new outlook on life. *It's a Wonderful Life* is one of the greatest movie of all times—and it is a testimony to the good news! **B.G.**

JAGGED EDGE (1986)

RATING: R
CONTENT: Profanity, nudity, and violence
INTENDED AUDIENCE: Adults
STARRING: Jeff Bridges, Glenn Close
DIRECTOR: Richard Marquand

Jagged Edge could have been a good suspense drama, but it is ruined by profanity, nudity, and violence. Again Hollywood has taken a good story and destroyed it. When a wealthy heiress is brutally murdered, all signs suggest that her husband is the killer. He hires a female attorney who gets him off, but the trick ending makes you think that he might be the murderer.

I won't reveal the murderer, but the movie is not worth seeing anyway. The direction is weak. Glenn Close is unprofessional as the lawyer. The courtroom scene is absurd. Definitely not recommended.

JAKE SPEED (1986)

RATING: PG ★★★
CONTENT: Mild language and violence
INTENDED AUDIENCE: Adults
STARRING: Wayne Crawford, John Hurt, Dennis Christopher
DIRECTOR: Andrew Lane

This film is a comic book come to life in the tradition of Indiana Jones. Here, a teenage girl is kidnapped to be sold into white slavery in the Middle East. In a movie first, her family prays for forgiveness for the kidnappers. The grandfather pulls out a copy of a paperback about the exploits of Jake Speed. The sister tracks down the real Speed who rescues people so that he can write best-selling paperbacks about his adventures. Indeed, Speed rescues the kidnapped sister.

This cute, lightweight movie does not take Jesus' name in vain, and it has no nudity and little violence. The problem is that the script is not as tight as it should be, so the movie misses the mark. However, it is fun for action-adventure fans and won't harm anyone. Furthermore, it features the fine acting talents of John Hurt. **K.K.**

JEWEL OF THE NILE (1985), 146 min.

RATING: PG
CONTENT: Profanity and sexual looseness

INTENDED AUDIENCE: All ages
STARRING: Michael Douglas, Kathleen Turner
DIRECTOR: Lewis Teague

In this sequel to *Romancing the Stone,* don't expect the humor and action of the first film. *Jewel of the Nile* is a dud. Besides falling flat, it is full of profanities and sexual looseness. I review it only to tell you to keep away and try to keep your friends away from this anti-Christian movie, which extols the virtues of the Sufis who are a confused, ragged sect of Islam. Don't waste your time.

JONI (1980)

RATING: G   ★★★★
CONTENT: Nothing objectionable
INTENDED AUDIENCE: All ages
STARRING: Joni Eareckson, Bert Remsen
DIRECTOR: James Collier

Joni is the heartwarming story of how a young girl's tragedy became a triumphant witness for God. Joni Eareckson is a young, spirited girl growing up in a Christian home. While playing in shallow water during a vacation, Joni dives in and breaks her neck. She is found by one of her sisters and rushed to the hospital. Despite surgery and medical help, the doctors conclude that Joni will never walk again. The family is torn in a battle of egos, emotion, attitude changes, and rationalization. Joni displays a deep bitterness and resentment toward God for allowing the accident to happen. She cries out to God in anger, and despairs when there is no immediate response to her prayers.

Joni steadily progresses in her physical therapy, and becomes better adjusted, accepting her condition. Slowly she regains the use of her arms, and learns to write and draw with her teeth. As Joni blooms into a talented artist and a more confident woman, she realizes that it has been God who has carried her the entire way. At the end of the film, Joni makes an appeal for each viewer to evaluate his or her relationship with God and to truly seek Him if they do not know Him. **B.G.**

JOSHUA THEN AND NOW (1986)

RATING: R
CONTENT: Immorality, profanity, and ill-advised actions
INTENDED AUDIENCE: Adults
STARRING: James Woods, Alan Arkin
DIRECTOR: Ted Kotcheff

Another movie that has a good story undermined by immorality, profanity, and foolishness, *Joshua Then and Now* is in bad taste. It does have a profound story of the evils of social climbing and envy embedded in it that needs to be told. But there are not enough good elements to save it.

THE JOURNEY OF NATTY GANN (1985)

RATING: PG   ★★
CONTENT: Profanity

INTENDED AUDIENCE: Families
STARRING: Meredith Salenger, Ray Wise
DIRECTOR: Jeremy Paul Kagan

The story of a young girl who faces incredible hardships to find her father is excellent, but it has been sabotaged by the Hollywood obsession with profanity. The premise is very positive: "Love triumphs over fear and alienation." The scenes with the wolf, who becomes Natty's protector, are excellent.

It is the Great Depression. At the beginning of the movie, Natty's father leaves her to look for work in the logging camps of Oregon. The woman who looks after her is a mean, selfish, profane creature who lies to Natty and pushes her around. Natty runs away to find her father, and she gets into one exciting adventure after another. Finally, in a touching sequence, she finds her father. It's unfortunate that this beautiful, tender family movie has been destroyed by profanity.

JUDGMENT AT NUREMBERG (1961), 189 min.

CONTENT: Nothing objectionable   ★★★★
INTENDED AUDIENCE: Mature audiences
STARRING: Spencer Tracy, Maximilian Schell, Burt Lancaster,
   Richard Widmark, Judy Garland, Montgomery Cliff
DIRECTOR: Stanley Kramer

This film is a gripping saga that serves as a reminder of the sinful nature of man. *Judgment at Nuremberg* portrays the famous war crimes trials held in 1948 in Nuremberg, Germany, where leading Nazis, accused by the Allies of brutal crimes, were tried. The story confronts that common rationalization for inhumane behavior, epitomized by Maximilian Schell's statement, "We were only following orders!"

Produced in a semidocumentary format in black and white, the film is perhaps Kramer's best, with many international stars performing in this movie. Highly recommended. **B.G.**

KANGAROO (1987)

RATING: R   ★★
CONTENT: A small amount of violence, sexual situations,
   and off-color language
INTENDED AUDIENCE: Adults
STARRING: Judy Davis, Colin Friels
DIRECTOR: Tim Burstall

There is trouble in paradise in this treatment of D. H. Lawrence's story of love, violence, and intrigue set in Australia. The famous writer Richard Somers (Colin Friels) and his wife Harriet (Judy Davis) flee post-World War I Europe in search of a freer, more tolerant world in which to rebuild their marriage. In a cottage looking out over the vast Pacific Ocean, they believe they have found their dream. However, Kangaroo (Hugh Keays-Byrne), who is the charismatic leader of "the diggers," a secret fascist army, attempts to seduce Somers into embracing his ideas. When Somers refuses, he and Harriet are threatened by the same crude, political thuggery they tried to leave behind in Europe.

Kangaroo was one of the finest films presented at the American Film Market in 1987.

However, caution is recommended because of the small amount of psychological violence and the few earthy, passionate scenes in the movie. **B.G.**

KAOS (1986)

(Subtitles)
CONTENT: Very brief nudity ★★★
INTENDED AUDIENCE: Adults
STARRING: Enrica Maria Modugno, Claudio Bagagli, Ciccio Ingrassia, Franco Franchi, Pasquale Spadola, Margarita Lozano, Omero Antonutti
DIRECTORS: Paolo and Vittorio Taviani

Kaos is five stories freely adapted for film by Paolo and Vittorio Taviani from a collection by the famous Italian author, Luigi Pirandello. This film is magnificent and emotive. The flawless cinematography is beautiful. The acting is superb. This three-hour movie is subtitled, but that in no way detracts from the complete understanding and immersion of the audience into each story.

Kaos is set in late nineteenth-century Sicily. The first story, entitled "The Other Son," tells of a slightly mad widow with three sons. The next story is "Moon Sickness." A bride of twenty days, seemingly content with her marriage and her lot in life, is confronted with a husband who becomes strangely violent at the appearance of the full moon. The third story, "The Jar," is a funny episode about a very wealthy, very proud olive grove owner. The fourth story is called "Requiem." A wealthy baron is asked by a group of gypsies squatting on his land for a free plot to be deeded to them as a burial ground. The fifth story is "A Talk With Mother." After the death of his mother, a man returns to his childhood home, which is filled with memories, and he has an imaginary talk with his mother.

This beautiful movie uses a few literary devices that are not totally biblical, but it is not intentionally antibiblical. There are some positive references to faith and prayer. It would be totally suitable for Christian adults were it not for the very brief nudity in the second story. **D.R.**

KARATE KID II (1986)

RATING: PG ★★★
CONTENT: Very little off-color language
INTENDED AUDIENCE: All ages
STARRING: Ralph Macchio, Noriyuki "Pat" Morita
DIRECTOR: John G. Avildsen

This delightful, mellow, enjoyable movie is not marred by nudity, sex, or cruel violence, and there is very little off-color language. The movie starts by showing the end of *Karate Kid*. Karate Kid's instructor goes back to Okinawa, which he left forty years earlier to avoid fighting with his best friend over the woman they both loved. His friend thinks that he is scared, but the instructor reasons that it is better to avoid a fight than to provoke one. His friend has now become very commercial and has left the way of life essential to karate.

The Karate Kid ends up in a match with this man's student, and the Kid wins. Good triumphs over evil. In other words, have values and stick with them, and don't give in to evil. This positive movie with a positive message is okay. **K.K.**

KING KONG (1933) B&W, 100 min.

CONTENT: Nothing objectionable   ★ ★ ★ ★
INTENDED AUDIENCE: Adults
STARRING: Robert Armstrong, Fay Wray, Bruce Cabot, Frank Reicher
DIRECTOR: Merian C. Cooper, Ernest Schoedsack

The original *King Kong* is a masterpiece of adventure. The story is about a film producer who hears tales of prehistoric animals living on an island in the South Pacific. He
goes there and finds a fifty-foot ape who promptly carries off his leading lady. She is
rescued, and the ape is returned to New York and put on display. The ape, King Kong,
breaks loose and wreaks havoc on the city.

This was one of the first films to use stop-action, frame-by-frame photography successfully. Dino De Laurintiis's 1976 remake is a poor substitute. His forty-foot robot
failed to work and was replaced by an actor in an animal skin. If you want excitement,
action, and adventure, see the original film, not the remakes.

KISS OF THE SPIDER WOMAN (1985)

RATING: R
CONTENT: Sodomy, homosexuality, and godlessness
INTENDED AUDIENCE: Adults
STARRING: William Hurt, Raul Julia, Sonia Braga
DIRECTOR: Hector Babenco

This boring, embarrassing movie vividly portrays the lust of a male homosexual who
seduces his cell mate. There is no splendid tale here. In fact, this film is not appropriate
viewing for any person.

KNIGHTS AND EMERALDS (1987)

CONTENT: Some off-color innuendo and bad language   ★ ★ ★
INTENDED AUDIENCE: Adults
STARRING: Warren Mitchell, Rachel Davies, Christopher Wild,
    Beverley Hills, Bill Leadbitter
DIRECTOR: Ian Emes

Set in an industrial town in England, *Knights and Emeralds* tells the story of two
bands: one of them white, one of them black. The white band used to be the perpet-
ual winner of national band contests, but has seen better days. They are opposed by a
black marching band that is walking away with all the honors. The white band doesn't
make it into the championships, but the black band does. However, the first routine
they do is a traditional routine, and they don't win enough points; so it looks as though
they are going to lose. They decide that they have nothing to gain by playing white
music, so they go out and play black music and finish with an incredible number that
wins the championship.

This is a classic story of the underdog coming from behind and winning. An enjoyable film, there is some risqué language.

LABYRINTH (1986)

RATING: PG

CONTENT: Grotesque goblins
INTENDED AUDIENCE: Adolescents
STARRING: David Bowie
DIRECTOR: Jim Henson

In this film, evil creatures are really good guys in disguise or misunderstood or figments of the imagination that have no power over anyone or anything. Therefore, ferocious goblins, fairies, and demons are named (nominalism), toyed with, and dismissed with the understanding that things are not real, "not always what they seem," and evil has no power over the heroine. This view of reality is pernicious because it undermines the reality of sin and the necessity of salvation through faith in Jesus.

A young teenage girl, Sarah, who is infatuated with fairy tales, thinks that her stepmother is a wicked witch, that no one understands her, and that her baby brother Toby receives all the attention she deserves. One night she calls to the goblins to take Toby away, and they do. She recants, but it is too late. The goblin king tells her that she has thirteen hours to solve the riddle of the Labyrinth maze and rescue Toby, or Toby will be turned into a goblin.

Sarah fulfills the quest with unusual ease with the help of monsters, goblins, and dwarfs, much to the goblin king's chagrin. In the process, she learns to love her brother and others.

Although there is no reality to the evil in this film, the ugly grotesqueness of the creatures can frighten children. All in all, it is acceptable only for adolescents and dedicated movie buffs, as long as the fallacy of discounting evil and the heresy of nominalism is made clear to the viewer from the first.

LADY AND THE TRAMP (1955), 75 min.

RATING: G ★★★★
CONTENT: Nothing objectionable
INTENDED AUDIENCE: Families
STARRING (voices): Peggy Lee, Stan Freberg
DIRECTOR: Hamilton Luske

Love triumphs over every obstacle in this dog-from-the-wrong-side-of-the-tracks story. The movie opens with a husband giving his wife a cute little puppy for Christmas, whom they name Lady. Meanwhile, on the wrong side of the tracks, Tramp is growing up as a wild dog. One day after both Lady and Tramp have grown up, Tramp sees Lady and falls in love.

Tramp talks Lady into going out for an adventurous prowl but the dogcatcher catches Lady after Tramp talks her into disturbing some chickens. She is humiliated by being in the dog pound and is angry at Tramp for getting her in trouble. When she is released to go home, she is put in the doghouse. Lady sees a rat coming into the house to bite her owner's little baby and breaks loose to go to the rescue. Tramp happens by at the same time and goes in through the window to kill the rat. And everyone lives happily ever after. See it if you can. **L.**, **P.** and **J.B.**

LADY JANE (1986)

RATING: PG–13 ★★★★
CONTENT: A very biblical message; however, very brief shadow
nudity restricts the audience

INTENDED AUDIENCE: Adults
STARRING: Helena Bonham Carter, Cary Elwes
DIRECTOR: Trevor Nunn

Lady Jane is a beautiful historical movie that mature Christians should support. It is directed in the manner of *A Man for All Seasons* and clearly sets forth the key issues of the Reformation and biblical theology.

Lady Jane Grey was the cousin of King Edward VI, Henry VIII's sickly son, who died in his youth. Lady Jane was crowned by the Reformed Christians to try to stop Mary I from becoming queen and reintroducing Roman Catholicism into England. John Dudley (the Duke of Northumberland) engineered the crowning to keep the church property, which had been misappropriated by the English nobility, from being restored to the church. Lady Jane ruled for nine days and was beheaded at the age of seventeen with her father and her husband.

In Lady Jane's disputes with the Roman inquisitor, she demonstrates that faith in Jesus is the only means of salvation (as opposed to salvation being found in the church), and she states the right of every person to read the Bible because that is the way to learn about the Lord and His kingdom. Even the Roman inquisitor is moved by her piety, and as she is being beheaded, he proclaims that she will be in heaven that day.

This film is an excellent presentation of true faith. There is no profanity or violence. However, there is brief nudity in an innocent love scene between Jane and her new husband. Therefore, it is not for teenagers or children, but only for mature Christians who are willing to look beyond the conventions of the film industry and see an outstanding Christian movie.

THE LAST VOYAGE (1960), 91 min.

CONTENT: Mild obscenities   ★★★
INTENDED AUDIENCE: All ages
STARRING: Robert Stack, Dorothy Malone, George Sanders, Edmund O'Brien, Woody Strode
DIRECTOR: Andrew Stone

This relatively unknown film is one of those truly exciting cliffhangers that will rivet you to your seat as an overage ocean liner goes slowly but spectacularly to a watery grave. Using a condemned ocean liner as his set, the director was able to capture an extraordinary sense of a ship actually going down. Fine actors and a taut, action-oriented script that places well-defined characters in a life-threatening circumstance make this an engrossing disaster film.

It is recommended family viewing if you like suspense and heroics. There is nothing objectionable in it. **B.G.**

LAWRENCE OF ARABIA (1962), 221 min.

CONTENT: Violence, although it is not gory or graphic;
homosexual innuendos and mild off-color language   ★★★★
INTENDED AUDIENCE: Adults
STARRING: Peter O'Toole, Omar Sharif, Arthur Kennedy, Anthony Quinn, Jose Ferrer, Anthony Quayle, Jack Hawkins, Alec Guinness
DIRECTOR: David Lean

David Lean's epic adventure about the exploits of T. E. Lawrence is a film a viewer should see on a big screen. The story is about Lawrence, a British army officer who is stationed in the Middle East during World War I. Lawrence begins his mission from Cairo, when he is assigned to investigate the progress of the Arab revolt against the Turks.

Lawrence befriends King Feisal (Alec Guinness), and they march across the treacherous Nafud Desert in northern Arabia, for a surprise attack on the Turkish stronghold at Aqaba. Yet even when victory comes, the various Arab tribes cannot continue their unity, and Lawrence, now a Colonel, bids farewell to those who will be ruling.

Filmed on location in Jordan, Morocco, and Spain, this movie was awarded an Oscar for Best Picture. Recommended despite some off-color innuendos. **B.G.**

LEGAL EAGLES (1986)
RATING: PG   ★ ★ ★
CONTENT: Off-color language
INTENDED AUDIENCE: Adults
STARRING: Robert Redford, Debra Winger, Daryl Hannah
DIRECTOR: Ivan Reitman

This thrilling romantic comedy set in the legal and art worlds of New York is an A picture, which is rare these days. The production value is head and shoulders above most films. The acting is superb, with Redford giving the best courtroom argument ever heard in a movie to date.

The story revolves around a hot-shot New York district attorney who gets involved with a loony defense attorney in solving an art swindle. The problem with the movie is a loose script that doesn't quite explain all the plot twists. However, the suspense is very good, and the movie is very funny. There is a brief affair, but it is seen as a sin that causes the young man to lose his job. He repents of his actions. No nudity, mild language, and almost no violence make this acceptable viewing. *Legal Eagles* is pure entertainment. It is not profound, but it is well done.

LEGEND (1986), 130 min.
RATING: PG
CONTENT: Anti-Christian views and pagan superstition
INTENDED AUDIENCE: Children and families
STARRING: Tom Cruise, Mia Sara
DIRECTOR: Ridley Scott

This boring ode to pagan superstition portrays a dualistic, nontheistic universe in which light and darkness are locked in a power struggle. The unicorns are the guardians of the light. The demons, goblins, and fairies working for the devil are attacking and killing off the unicorns, plunging the universe into darkness. The hero combats the evil Lord of Darkness to rescue the princess and free the universe from its curse of icy winter night.

Legend depicts a mythic realm that denies the reality of God. It has no profanity and no nudity, but don't let the PG rating fool you. It is a totally anti-Christian movie. **J.G.**

LETHAL (1986)

RATING: PG–13
CONTENT: Sex and profanity
INTENDED AUDIENCE: Adults
STARRING: Michael Billington, Denise DuBarry, Michael Ansara
DIRECTOR: Dwight Little

This run-of-the-mill CIA-KGB spy drama never works and never has you on the edge. A KGB double agent wants to defect to America, but his son is still on the side of the Soviets. In the end, the son comes to him, and all works out for him to defect. Aside from sex and profanity, a poor screenplay is enough to make you avoid this movie. **E.R.**

LETTER TO BREZHNEV (1986)

RATING: R
CONTENT: Sex, profanity, theft, and mean spirit
INTENDED AUDIENCE: Adults
STARRING: Peter Firth, Alfred Molina, Alexandra Pigg
DIRECTOR: Chris Bernard

Set in Liverpool, the story revolves around Elaine, a young working-class girl, who falls in love with a Russian sailor, Peter, on shore leave. When he goes back to Russia, she tries to get him back so that they can get married, but the USSR will not let him out. Finally, she writes to Brezhnev, and he sends her a ticket to come to Russia. The British Foreign Office tries to restrain her and even lies to keep her in England. In the end, she takes off for Russia, but we never find out what happens to her.

The film's upside-down world view is demonstrated by the contradictory facts of the story. Although it is clear that Russia will not let Peter out of the USSR and Great Britain will let Elaine leave, the movie tries to convince us that England is worse than Russia. Aside from this, sex, profanity, theft, and mean spirit make this movie unacceptable.

LIGHT OF DAY (1987)

RATING: PG–13   ★★★
CONTENT: Some off-color language and unsavory locations
INTENDED AUDIENCE: Teenagers and adults
STARRING: Michael J. Fox, Joan Jett, Gena Rowlands
DIRECTOR: Paul Schrader

Light of Day tells the story of a lower-middle-class, rust-belt family: Patti, an angry, rebellious, would-be rock star who has a baby, Benji, out of wedlock to punish her "born again" mother; Joey, Patti's brother who wants to do good, but has been led astray by his older sister; their Dad, who lives in the limbo of retirement; and, Mom, a strong believer who loves her family. Patti hates her mother, refuses to visit her mother on Christmas and has to be dragged by Joey to her mother's birthday dinner, which Patti leaves in anger when her mother starts to pray. Joey tells her that her mother didn't mean any harm and that Mom has the right to her beliefs. But Patti won't listen.

Mom comes down with incurable cancer, and, begrudgingly, Patti comes to see her. Mom asks Patti if she has ever done anything to Patti that Patti can't forgive. Patti breaks down and forgives her mother and begins to cry. Patti also forgives the local pastor who fathered Benji out of wedlock. Then Mom asks Patti if Patti will agree to join her in heaven. Having lived with Mom's strong evangelistic Christianity all her life, Patti knows what this means and says, "Yes."

This film exposes the weakness of rebellion and nihilism and lifts up forgiveness and God's love. Christians should exercise caution, however, because there is some tough material in this excellent movie.

LIGHTNING: THE WHITE STALLION (1986)

RATING: PG   ★★
CONTENT: Mild off-color language
INTENDED AUDIENCE: Children and teenagers
STARRING: Mickey Rooney, Susan George, Isabel Lorca
DIRECTOR: William A. Levey

Barney Ingram (played by Mickey Rooney) is a millionaire who has gambled away his white stallion that is worth millions. Unfortunately, the horse is stolen, and it looks as if Barney's creditors are going to get the opportunity to break every bone in his body. Fortunately for Barney, the horse is safe, being kept by a girl named Stephanie, who does not know the horse is stolen but who is riding him in contests to win money for an eye operation.

Barney's creditors find the horse and try to steal it. They chase Stephanie but she rides to Barney. They pull a gun on Barney. The bad guys lose the gun, and Barney picks it up, scares them off, and gives the horse to Stephanie. Stephanie goes to the national horse show and wins. She gets the eye operation.

Good triumphs over evil in a nice family picture that is not too well produced. **P.B.** and **J.B.**

THE LIGHTSHIP (1986)

RATING: PG–13   ★★★
CONTENT: Some obscene language and some violence
INTENDED AUDIENCE: Mature adults
STARRING: Robert Duvall, Klaus Maria Brandauer
DIRECTOR: Jerzy Skolimowski

This movie tells the tale of three men, a dandy and two uncouth thugs, who board a U.S. Coast Guard lightship (a small ship anchored as a floating lighthouse) after their boat breaks down nearby. The three men turn out to be felons who have robbed a bank and escaped by boat. The six crewmen on the lightship, including Captain Heller (played by Klaus Maria Brandauer) and his wayward adolescent son, are held at bay by the hoodlums.

Throughout the story, the Captain maintains his loyalty to his crew and preserves the honor of his command, as demonstrated when he puts his life on the line when the felons want to break anchor. The Captain knows that other ships in the dense fog depend on the lightship for guidance, and they would be in grave danger if the lightship were not visible in its anchored position.

The Lightship is recommended as a tale of integrity and loyalty, values in short supply in our day. **B.G.**

LILIES OF THE FIELD (1963) B&W, 94 min.

CONTENT: Nothing objectionable   ★★★★
INTENDED AUDIENCE: All ages
STARRING: Sidney Poitier, Lilia Skala, Francesca Jarvis, Stanley Adams
DIRECTOR: Ralph Nelson

This wonderful little film was the vehicle that launched Sidney Poitier's career and made him the first black star to win an Oscar. Poitier plays ex-GI Homer Smith, a happy-go-lucky drifter who comes across a group of five nuns, Iron Curtain refugees, maintaining a rundown convent on the edge of the desert in Arizona. The nuns badly need aid and talk Homer into staying and helping them build a new chapel. The story explores the relationships between Homer and the nuns, and how they continually charm him into completing the chapel. Best of all, they draw him close to faith in Jesus Christ.

Lilies of the Field is recommended viewing for all ages, a great movie that will bring you closer to God. **B.G.**

THE LION IN WINTER (1968), 135 min.

RATING: PG   ★★
CONTENT: Swearing, violence, adult situations, and adult themes
INTENDED AUDIENCE: Adults
STARRING: Peter O'Toole, Katharine Hepburn, Jane Morrow, Anthony Hopkins,
   Nigel Stock, Nigel Terry
DIRECTOR: Anthony Harvey

The question of who will be the heir to the throne of King Henry II is the theme of this film, with Henry as a growling, robust man in a contest of wills with Queen Eleanor of Aquitaine. The three sons, John, Richard the Lionhearted, and Geoffrey, bicker among themselves and plot individually as they vie for father Henry's throne. The plot is an intricate, interwoven tangle of human relationships, deals, and all sorts of intrigue.

Here is a family that hates with such villainy that if ever the concept of love existed for them, it has become only a distant memory. They have no love for one another; no love of God; and no caring for anyone, except for a love of self. Each family member is filled with hatred and only interested in gaining power at the expense of the others. This tough movie is very well done, but caution is recommended. It is not a godly movie, but it is a good portrait of the politics of sinful humans. If you are firmly rooted in a biblical world view, the film provides an instructive look at the government of man apart from God. **B.G.**

LONG DAY'S JOURNEY INTO NIGHT (1962), 136 min.

CONTENT: Adult situations, profanities, and minor vulgarities   ★★
INTENDED AUDIENCE: Adults
STARRING: Katharine Hepburn, Sir Ralph Richardson, Jason Robards, Jr.,
   Dean Stockwell
DIRECTOR: Sidney Lumet

This film chronicles the unraveling of the Tyrone family: a mother who is a drug addict; an alcoholic son; another son dying from tuberculosis; and a father who is an

aging matinee idol with intolerable pride and insecurity. The family has no values—
only morals that are relative. One minute the father loves his son, the next he hates him;
one minute the brother loves his younger brother, the next he is about to rip his throat
out.

Throughout the night, the inner feelings, or horrors, of each Tyrone family member
surface. By morning, they sit exhausted, hung over, and destroyed. This world, fashioned by Eugene O'Neill after his own family, is one of suffering, pain, remorse, loneliness, and emptiness. It is devoid of those qualities provided to us and for us by God:
love, hope, forgiveness, and understanding. These wretched souls know no solace,
only bitterness and frustration. There is little soul-searching here. Rather, they try to
drown their individual souls with alcohol, narcotics, and lies. This is a portrait of a
family without God. **B.G.**

THE LONGEST DAY (1962) B&W, 169 min.

CONTENT: War violence (but not graphic) and minor swearing   ★★★★
INTENDED AUDIENCE: Adults
STARRING: John Wayne, Robert Mitchum, Richard Todd, Henry Fonda,
   Robert Wagner, Eddie Albert, Sean Connery, Curt Jurgens, and Robert Ryan,
   among others
DIRECTORS: Ken Annakin, Andrew Marton, and Bernhard Wicki

Based on Cornelius Ryan's book of the same name, *The Longest Day* is a three-hour
action picture chronicling the Allied invasion of Normandy beach in France on June 6,
1944. Historically accurate and vivid in its portrayal of the many heroes of that day
(and there were many), the film shows the events leading up to the actual invasion and
gives us both the German and the Allied perspectives. From Eisenhower's decision to
go, even under marginal weather conditions, to the waves of supply ships on the
beach to support the forward-moving Allied troops, the film captures all the details of
this milestone event of the Second World War.

Filmed in black and white, the picture has the look of newsreel footage, with an
authenticity in the battle scenes that is most convincing. The staging is on a massive
scale. It gives us glimpses of war as hell and of how men and women at times ask for
heaven's intervention in such barbarity. It is well worth seeing in its entirety. **B.G.**

LOST HORIZON (1937) B&W, 118 min.

CONTENT: Some interesting reflections on paradise and free will   ★★★★
INTENDED AUDIENCE: Adults
STARRING: Ronald Colman, Jane Wyatt, H. B. Warner, Sam Jaffe
DIRECTOR: Frank Capra

Lost Horizon tells the story of a small group who find themselves in the lost valley of
Shangri-La. Life seems almost too perfect, and they want to get back to the real world
of life and death. Against the advice of the spiritual leader of this so-called paradise on
earth, the High Lama, they leave with one of the women of Shangri-La who has fallen in
love with the hero, Robert Conway (Ronald Colman). As soon as they are out of the
valley, she ages and dies in front of their eyes.

The film is an interesting reflection on Eastern mystical visions of paradise, and how
those ultimate, illusory realities are really a prison that denies man his God-given indi-

viduality and freedom. Shangri-La is not so much a paradise as it is a half-state of existence that prohibits the freedom to grow and change.

Lost Horizon is an immortal classic that should turn us away from counterfeit visions of paradise. Recommended.

THE LOVE BUG (1969), 107 min.

RATING: G   ★★★
CONTENT: Nothing objectionable
INTENDED AUDIENCE: Families
STARRING: Dean Jones, Michele Lee, Buddy Hackett
DIRECTOR: Robert Stevenson

Herbie, a Volkswagen Beetle with its own unique personality and ideas as to where it wants to go, involves itself in the romance of stars Dean Jones and Michele Lee. The film offers plenty of slapstick and laughs, aimed at the younger crowd, though adults will enjoy the antics, too. If you can suspend reality about cars being only sheet metal and glass, Herbie the Volkswagen is for you. This film is silly and fun for children. **B.G.**

LUCAS (1986)

RATING: PG–13   ★★
CONTENT: Profanity and obscenity
INTENDED AUDIENCE: Teenagers
STARRING: Corey Haim, Kerri Green, Charlie Sheen
DIRECTOR: David Seltzer

A film one would like to like, *Lucas* has everything going for it, but it is fatally flawed by profanity and obscenity. Lucas is a young genius who falls in love with the new girl in town, Maggie, who is older than he is. She likes Lucas and enjoys being with him, but she does not love him.

Lucas is devastated by this rejection. He tries out for the football team to win her love. During a game, Lucas goes in to play, but he is beaten to a pulp by the bigger players. However, everyone at the school is moved by Lucas's courage, and he ends up being the school hero after he gets out of the hospital. This positive, loving, important story has been rendered unacceptable because of bad language.

MAD MAX BEYOND THUNDERDOME (1985), 93 min.

RATING: PG–13   ★★
CONTENT: Harsh, cruel violence and profanity
INTENDED AUDIENCE: Young adults
STARRING: Mel Gibson, Tina Turner
DIRECTORS: George Miller, George Ogilvie

Mad Max movies have become cult favorites among people of very different philosophical and theological perspectives. The first two were simple stories of a hero who saves the besieged nice people from the horrible mutants some time in the future after the third world war. The only trouble with the third movie, *Mad Max Beyond Thunderdome,* is that the moviemakers have forgotten that the good guy has to stay in character to be a hero of any value.

The movie has several false starts, finally deciding to start the cohesive story of Mad Max rescuing the weak in the middle of the movie after the incidents in the Thunderdome. The movie also has several false conclusions, finally ending up with Mad Max becoming the focus of a new religious cult that worships him as a savior. This elevated status of Mad Max sets the movie firmly against a biblical world view.

This movie is exciting, but the flaws make one wonder whether all the violence and grotesque characters are worthwhile wading through to get to the time-honored "good triumphs over evil" premise. It should be avoided by biblical Christians who are interested in looking on what's good and pure.

THE MALTESE FALCON (1941) B&W, 101 min.

CONTENT: Nothing objectionable ★★★★
INTENDED AUDIENCE: Adults
STARRING: Humphrey Bogart, Mary Astor, Sydney Greenstreet, Peter Lorre, Gladys George, Jerome Cowan, Lee Patrick, Elisha Cook Jr, Barton MacLane, Ward Bond
DIRECTOR: John Huston

The Maltese Falcon tells the story of Sam Spade, detective. When his partner is killed, Spade finds himself involved with a group of villains who are trying to locate the famous Maltese Falcon, a gem encrusted statue worth thousands of dollars.

The acting by Humphrey Bogart, Sidney Greenstreet, and Peter Lorre is excellent. The dialogue is clean, clear, and crisp. Director John Huston took the movie almost word for word from the novel by Dashiel Hammett. The film is a work of art.

THE MAN WHO CAME TO DINNER (1941) B&W, 112 min.

CONTENT: Nothing objectionable ★★★★
INTENDED AUDIENCE: Adults
STARRING: Bette Davis, Ann Sheridan, Monty Woolley, Richard Travis, Jimmy Durante
DIRECTOR: William Keighley

The Man Who Came to Dinner is a funny, insightful movie based on the famous Broadway play by George S. Kaufman and Moss Hart. The play concerns Sheridan Whiteside, who slips and falls on the ice in front of a well-to-do home in the Midwest and is taken in by the friendly and courteous good Samaritans living therein. Once ensconced in the bosom of the family, he proceeds to repay their kind hospitality by intimidating one and all with his barbed invectives and egotistical boorishness. Fun and highly recommended. **R.A.**

THE MANCHURIAN CANDIDATE (1962) B&W, 126 min.

CONTENT: Excellent insight into brainwashing ★★★★
INTENDED AUDIENCE: Adults
STARRING: Frank Sinatra, Laurence Harvey, Janet Leigh, Angela Lansbury
DIRECTOR: John Frankenheimer

During the Korean War, the Chinese communists capture an American army patrol, which they take to Manchuria where the soldiers are brainwashed into believing that one of them is a hero. This "hero" has really been transformed into a communist operative, whose American agent is his mother, who is the wife of a conservative senator running for vice president of the United States. The communist plans call for the senator to win the election, and then for the "hero" to assassinate the president elect at a rally.

A classic thriller, *The Manchurian Candidate* contains one of the screen's best karate matches between Sinatra and Henry Silva, who plays a communist agent posing as a houseboy. The acting is superb, as is the screenplay and expert direction. See it.

THE MANHATTAN PROJECT (1986)

RATING: PG–13   ★★
CONTENT: Mild profanity
INTENDED AUDIENCE: Adults
STARRING: John Lithgow, Christopher Collet, Cynthia Nixon
DIRECTOR: Marshall Brickman

The Manhattan Project is a pretty good suspense film with a message that backfires. The message is "stop building bombs," but the movie proves that mutually assured deterrence works to keep the hero alive. Although the plot is highly improbable, the film works because of good pacing and a clear sense of jeopardy.

Paul Stephens, a teenager with an aptitude for science, discovers that the government has built a top secret plutonium plant near his home town. Paul and his girlfriend decide to expose the plant by stealing some plutonium and building a bomb to show the world how dangerous the stuff is. But there is no real motivation for Paul to go to such trouble to make the bomb. There are gaps in the logic of the script, which never proves the point it leads up to proving. Furthermore, Paul is not an attractive hero, that is, he does some morally suspect things. Still, the movie is good entertainment, though marred by mild profanity. Caution is recommended.

MANHUNTER (1986)

RATING: R
CONTENT: Profanity and violence
INTENDED AUDIENCE: Adults
STARRING: William Peterson, Kim Kreist, Richard Roth, Joan Allen, Bryan Cox
DIRECTOR: Michael Mann

Director Michael Mann does for FBI agents in this film what he has already done for "Miami Vice" cops, but *Manhunter* has twice the action and the plot of a "Miami Vice" episode on television. This is a well-shot, well-acted movie with a well-written screenplay that is not predictable. However, this slick high-tech detective thriller starts to unwind as it progresses.

During an intense psychic game, an FBI agent conditions himself to think like the depraved killer he is stalking. The killer is a demented psychotic who plays God, thinking that thereby he will become a god (shades of Nero). You won't be able to figure out this plot in five minutes. However, the profanity and violence makes it unacceptable. **K.K.**

MARCH OF THE WOODEN SOLDIERS (1934) B&W, 73 min.

CONTENT: A fun filled movie for the family   ★★★★
INTENDED AUDIENCE: Children and the young at heart

STARRING: Stan Laurel, Oliver Hardy, Charlotte Henry, Felix Knight
DIRECTOR: Gus Meins, Charles Rogers

Two of the screen's most beloved comedians join with Victor Herbert's music (*Babes in Toyland*) to portray the eternal struggle of good versus evil. Laurel and Hardy play the toymaker's assistants, who misinterpret an order from Santa Claus and create a set of giant soldiers. However, these soldiers proved to be a great blessing when bogeymen invade toyland.

The acting in this film is excellent: the villain is lecherous Barnaby, played by Harry Kleinbach, and our heroes are Laurel and Hardy, daffy, creative and hilarious. Just remember that this 1934 version is a great screen classic, not the later versions. See it. **B.G.**

MARIE (1985)

RATING: PG–13   ★★★
CONTENT: Mild obscenity
INTENDED AUDIENCE: Adults
STARRING: Sissy Spacek
DIRECTOR: Roger Donaldson

There used to be a rule of thumb in Hollywood that true stories make bad films. *Marie* almost succeeds in bringing a true story to the screen, but in the end, we are left with the feeling that something is missing, that some parts of the story do not make dramatic sense, and that Marie has more to her than the script or sweet Sissy Spacek will let us know.

This true story of a woman who stands up to corruption in the governor's office and triumphs over the political hacks trying to bury her is the classic example of good triumphing over evil. There are certain positive Christian elements: Prayer works, Jesus is confessed, and God is revered. At the same time, the bad guys swear, and evil is shown to be evil. The trouble is that it is too long, and there are too many loose ends. The film is okay, but not great.

MARTY (1955) B&W, 91 min.

CONTENT: Nothing objectionable   ★★★★
INTENDED AUDIENCE: Adults
STARRING: Ernest Borgnine, Betsy Blair
DIRECTOR: Delbert Mann

Marty is the touching story of an average Joe, a thirtyish, unmarried Bronx butcher living at home with his aging, sometimes nagging, Italian mother. Marty lives a lonely life, spending much of his time with his pals, usually a dateless Saturday night. His search for love culminates in his meeting a plain-Jane schoolteacher at a local dance.

A compassionate story about ordinary people everywhere, the film was so overwhelmingly received that it collected Best Actor Award for Borgnine, Best Picture, Best Director, Best Screenplay, with nominations for Best Supporting Actor and Actress, and Best Cinematography. It was also given Best Picture of the Year by the New York Film Critics and the National Board of Review. One of the finest dramas to come out of the fifties. **B.G.**

MARY POPPINS (1964), 140 min.

CONTENT: Magical thinking ★★
INTENDED AUDIENCE: Families
STARRING: Julie Andrews, Dick Van Dyke, David Tomlinson, Glynis Johns,
    Ed Wynn, Arthur Treacher, Reginald Owen, Elsa Lancaster
DIRECTOR: Robert Stevenson

This film tells the story of a British family, the Banks, who want to hire a Nanny to take care of the two children so that the mother can be involved in social issues and the father can devote more time to his work. It seems as if the parents don't have time for their children, but keep them only as ornaments, something everyone is supposed to have.

Mary Poppins, who rides an umbrella through the air almost like a witch riding a broomstick, comes to take care of the children and teach them the questionable lesson that love and joy are more important than responsibility. As the story unfolds, there are great songs and superb dance routines. Even the parents come to see the error of their ways.

All in all, a fun film, but with some not so subtle digs at otherwise worthy institutions and at biblical morality and responsiblity. View it with discernment.

MASS APPEAL (1985), 99 min.

RATING: PG ★★★★
CONTENT: Nothing objectionable
INTENDED AUDIENCE: All ages
STARRING: Jack Lemmon, Charles Durning
DIRECTOR: Glen Jordan

Mass Appeal shows the confrontation between a young seminarian, who is committed to God's truth, and an elderly alcoholic priest, who has comfortably feathered his nest by avoiding conflict and pandering to his parishioners. The seminarian forces the priest to see that he has sold God short and to take a stand for God's kingdom. At the same time, the priest helps the seminarian see how he really despises the people he must love if he is going to minister to them.

Naturally, there are flaws. The final sermon is weak and avoids being centered on Jesus; the young seminarian specializes in proof-texting his own opinions with suitable Scripture; and the power of repentance is ignored. However, the movie presents Jesus as Lord and Savior, condemns ministers in His church who compromise with the world system for their own comfort, and shows how denominations can insulate themselves from His Word by following the false traditions of men. In other words, it treats Christianity from a Christian perspective. These are lessons all of us need to learn, and for that reason, Christians should see it.

MAXIE (1985)

RATING: PG
CONTENT: Demonic possession, spiritism, and psychic sex
INTENDED AUDIENCE: Adults
STARRING: Glenn Close, Mandy Patinkin
DIRECTOR: Paul Aaron

In this half-baked story, a dead flapper from the 1920s possesses a modern woman so that she (the flapper) can break into movies. If this sounds like a dumb plot, you are right. It's an advertisement for demonic possession, spiritism, and psychic sex. And it also pokes fun at the church and portrays a priest in an unfavorable light. Avoid this obnoxious film.

MIDNIGHT COWBOY (1969), 113 min.

RATING: R
CONTENT: Very strong language, vulgarities, obscenities, nudity, adult
    situations presented graphically, and some violence
INTENDED AUDIENCE: Adults
STARRING: Jon Voight, Dustin Hoffman
DIRECTOR: John Schlesinger

Although the movie features outstanding performances by Hoffman and Voight, the story of a young Texan who comes to New York City to make it as a gigolo is rotten to the core. It is clear that this young man has no moral perspective, and it is this antibiblical, amoral perspective the movie is foisting on the audience. The young man ends up being hustled and finding much pain and loneliness.

When first distributed in 1969, this film was rated X and was not carried by some theaters. However, it is a sad commentary on the state of the motion picture industry that this gritty portrayal of lives wrecked by their own sinfulness won Academy Awards for Best Picture, Best Director, and Best Screenplay. This film is offensive in almost every area (language, sexual, thematic, etc.) and is definitely not for Christians.

MILDRED PIERCE (1945) B&W, 113 min.

CONTENT: Serious drama dealing with some tough subjects   ★★★★
INTENDED AUDIENCE: Adults
STARRING: Joan Crawford, Ann Blyth, Zachary Scott, Eve Arden
DIRECTOR: Michael Curtiz

Mildred is a hard working, divorced housewife, who opens a restaurant chain and devotes her life to satisfying every selfish whim of her daughter. Mildred marries the socially prominent but penniless Zachary Scott so that her daughter can have a home life, too; but to spite her, her daughter and stepfather have an affair that ends in murder. A beautifully photographed, suspenseful film, *Mildred Pierce* teaches a lesson about indulging in wickedness and selfishness that everyone needs to see.

MINI: THE ADVENTURES OF JENNY

RATING: G
CONTENT: Magic
INTENDED AUDIENCE: Families
STARRING: Beverly Ann Bailey, Rebecca Trued
DIRECTOR: Peter Nason

Mini bills itself as the first family feature motion picture made exclusively for video-store sale. It is a very low-budget film produced on videotape by Jackson Bailey, who painted the world's largest mural on the life of Christ. The film looks professional and would have succeeded if it were not for the script that had no hint of jeopardy, which is necessary to hold an audience's attention.

Jenny is physically handicapped, and her parents try to prepare her for life by making sure she knows how hopeless her situation is. While Jenny is feeling sorry for herself one day in her room, Mini, the magic clown, appears and takes Jenny on fantasy journeys where she can walk, run, dance, and do everything she has always wanted to do. Eventually, through her fantasies, Jenny learns to have confidence in herself, and in the last scene she miraculously walks.

It would be nice to be able to praise this film, but it cannot be recommended because it falls into the magic thinking trap. It tries to avoid debate by dealing with faith as positive mental attitude, wish fulfillment, and magical thinking. It has an illusory perspective toward the world rather than a realistic perspective that is at the heart of the Christian faith. Furthermore, it is a slow, flawed movie.

MIRACLE ON 34TH STREET (1947), 97 min.

CONTENT: Nothing objectionable except that children should be   ★★★★
     told the difference between the myth of Santa Claus and the
     reality of Jesus the Christ
INTENDED AUDIENCE: All ages
STARRING: Maureen O'Hara, John Payne, Natale Wood, Edmund Gwenn, Gene
     Lockhart, William Frawley
DIRECTOR: George Seaton

Set in New York City, this poignant comedy revolves around the great Macy's department store and its Christmas parade. Doris (Maureen O'Hara), who is the director of the parade, is divorced and raising her eight-year-old daughter. The girl has been sheltered by her mother, and has not been allowed to mature as normal children do, with fantasies, fables, and fun. The day of the parade, the hired "Santa Claus" for the Christmas float gets drunk. Just in the "Nick" of time, along comes an elderly gentleman with a real white beard, whom Doris hires on the spot to play Santa.

Within days, Chris Kringle, as he calls himself, has the store in a turmoil as he tells shoppers to go elsewhere for items Macy's doesn't have and causes an uproar with the in-store psychiatrist. It seems that Mr. Kringle claims to be the real Santa Claus, and his persistence in this claim opens a pandora's box for Macy's, the Supreme Court of New York State, and even the Post Office.

Miracle on 34th Street is a clever blend of humor and pathos with an uplifting message of forgiveness, understanding, and faith that continues to charm audiences of all ages. **B.G.**

THE MIRACLE WORKER (1962) B&W, 107 min.

CONTENT: Nothing objectionable   ★★★★
INTENDED AUDIENCE: Adolescents and adults
STARRING: Ann Bancroft, Patty Duke, Victor Jory, Andrew Prine
DIRECTOR: Arthur Penn

This film version of the brilliant Broadway play by William Gibson tells the story of Helen Keller, a blind, deaf girl who receives help from teacher Anne Sullivan. Sullivan, a patient woman, who comprehends the darkness and silence that Helen has lived with all her life, struggles, often violently, with her student. The two have knock-down, drag-out fights as Helen bucks the very hands that try to help her. The dramatic import of these early scenes leave one drained, realizing the uphill battle that both of them face before any achievements will be realized.

Expertly directed by Arthur Penn, the film won both Ann Bancroft and Patty Duke Oscars for best actress and supporting actress. Duke was the youngest actress up to that time to ever be awarded an Oscar. *The Miracle Worker* is a testimony to love and compassion. An emotional blockbuster for young and old to see. **B.G.**

MISHIMA (1985)

(Subtitles)
RATING: R
CONTENT: Homosexuality, nudity, and sadism
INTENDED AUDIENCE: Adults
STARRING: Ken Ogata
DIRECTOR: Paul Schrader

This film is an ode to a self-centered homosexual who commits suicide to get out of the world he hates. It attempts to be an arty testimony to the superiority of Japanese culture, but it comes off as a story about a demented sodomite who is preoccupied with sex and death. This movie is full of violence, cruelty, and explicit pornography. Avoid it.

THE MISSION (1986), 107 min.

RATING: PG   ★★★
CONTENT: Brief Amazon native nudity, violence, and minor sexual laxity
INTENDED AUDIENCE: Adults
STARRING: Robert De Niro, Jeffrey Irons
DIRECTOR: Roland Joffe

The Mission is an epic movie that skirts the border between the heresy of liberation theology and the orthodoxy of biblical Christianity. The story focuses in on the Jesuit, Father Gabriel, played by Jeffrey Irons, who has evangelized the Indians and is the guiding spiritual light of the mission, and Mendoza, played by Robert De Niro, who is a slave trader who comes to Christ and becomes a Jesuit as a result of a disastrous feud with his brother, the witness of Father Gabriel, and his reading of the Bible. However, when the Portuguese send in troops to forcefully take the mission away from the Jesuits and the Indians, Mendoza forsakes his vows and reverts to armed violence in a futile attempt to fight off the Portuguese. By encouraging and helping the Indians to fight, he releases a bloodbath wherein most of the Indians and all the Jesuits die, ill equipped to fight the Portuguese. The ending is ambiguous and lacks a clear affirmation of the fact of resurrected, eternal life in Christ.

For Christians who want a beautifully acted movie and who can put up with brief native nudity and pagan immorality (which is shown to be bad), *The Mission* is worthwhile film fare that will entertain and instruct the viewer about the problems that have always confronted the institutional church. Some of the photography in *The Mission* is truly extraordinary.

MISTER ROBERTS (1955), 123 min.

CONTENT: Some moral laxity   ★★★

INTENDED AUDIENCE: Adults
STARRING: Henry Fonda, James Cagney, William Powell, Jack Lemmon
DIRECTOR: John Ford and Mervyn LeRoy

Mister Roberts is an officer aboard the USS Reluctant, a Navy cargo ship in the Pacific during World War II. The ship is sailing from tedium to apathy as Roberts struggles to be transferred to a place where he can join the actual fighting. He is beloved by the crew and other officers because he champions their cause to the insane captain of the ship. Roberts rooms with Ensign Pulver, a loony misfit who is always in trouble. Everyone on the ship hates the captain and his beloved palm tree. The laundry room explosion, the Captain's palm thrown overboard, and the creation of scotch from chemicals are memorable moments in the film. A worthwhile movie masterpiece, marred only by an antiauthority attitude.

MR. SMITH GOES TO WASHINGTON (1939), 130 min.

CONTENT: Nothing objectionable   ★★★★
INTENDED AUDIENCE: Adults
STARRING: Jimmy Stewart, Claude Rains, Jean Arthur, Harry Carey,
   Thomas Mitchell, Beulah Bond
DIRECTOR: Frank Capra

Jefferson Smith (Stewart) is chosen by the political machine to fill the shoes of an outgoing Senator, but only as a rubber stamp for the bigwigs. Smith, a young man of principle and dignity, refuses to compromise his position and tries to expose corrupt political practices. In one of the more memorable scenes ever filmed, Smith, a hesitant, stammering figure collapses during a filibuster. With Claude Rains eloquent magnetism and speaking powers confronting Smith, the scene suggests Smith's innocence and frailty as he is assaulted by power brokers. Jimmy Stewart received his first Oscar nomination for this performance. **B.G.**

MODERN TIMES (1936) B&W, 87 min.

CONTENT: Nothing objectionable   ★★★
INTENDED AUDIENCE: All ages
STARRING: Charles Chaplin, Paulette Goddard, Chester Conklin, Henry Bergman
DIRECTOR: Charles Chaplin

In *Modern Times,* Chaplin's little Tramp is a victim of an assembly line; he has a nervous breakdown in the face of the pressure to become a human machine. When the factories close, the Tramp is tossed from one temporary job to another. This film, is really a collection of comic vignettes underscoring the effect of the Depression on the workers of the world. Funny and poignant, it is a classic. Chaplin's last silent film and the last appearance of the little Tramp.

MONA LISA (1986)

RATING: R
CONTENT: Nudity, sex, perversity, bad language, and profanity
INTENDED AUDIENCE: Adults
STARRING: Bob Hoskins, Cathy Tyson, Michael Caine
DIRECTOR: Neil Jordan

144

This film is raw pornography that has been exhibited as a work of art. In addition, the hero is a crook, and the lead character is a prostitute with a female lover. Don't even consider seeing it. **G.O.**

MOSES, THE LAWGIVER (1975), 141 min.

RATING: PG ★★★
CONTENT: Some violence
INTENDED AUDIENCE: Adolescents, adults
STARRING: Burt Lancaster, Anthony Quayle, Ingrid Thulin, Irene Pappas, Mariangela Melato
DIRECTOR: Gianfranco DeBosio

With a good script from Anthony Burgess, who later wrote the screen play for *Jesus of Nazareth,* this well crafted blend of epic spectacle and intimate narrative provides the viewer with an excellent portrait of Moses and his people. Lancaster is impressive as the Hebrew Patriarch who leads the Israelites from their bondage in Egypt to the Promised Land. The film follows Moses from his birth to the people's eventual settling in the Jordan Valley. It is a literal interpretation of the events described in the Bible, from the famous ten plagues brought down upon the Egyptian Pharaoh and his people, to the crossing of the Red Sea.

Although not as spectacular as *The Ten Commandments,* this film was two years in the making and is a very worthy rendition of the biblical message. The realistic presentation of various punishments may be too strong, and not suitable for young children, however. **B.G.**

MOTHER TERESA, 80 min.

CONTENT: Nothing objectionable ★★★★
STARRING: Mother Teresa
PRODUCER: Ann and Jeannette Petrie

This documentary on the life and work of Mother Teresa of Calcutta is as straightforward as the subject herself. Virtually unknown before receiving the Nobel Peace Prize in 1979, Mother Teresa now travels the world, delivering speeches, meeting heads of state, and receiving various accolades. These travels form the basis for the film, as the camera crew energetically follows the small woman through over half a dozen cities on as many continents.

Overall, the film seems as spare as the lifestyle of its subject. The expected deification of Mother Teresa is noticeably absent. Her message, however, is simply and boldy stated: to know and serve Jesus Christ and thus serve His creation. In Mother Teresa's world, those much abused words love, justice and holiness burn with the intensity of their true meaning. Highly recommended. **B.S.**

MOVERS AND SHAKERS (1985), 80 min.

RATING: PG ★★
CONTENT: Some off-color language
INTENDED AUDIENCE: Adults
STARRING: Walter Matthau, Charles Grodin
DIRECTOR: William Asher

Movers and Shakers provides a clear insight into the crassness of Hollywood. A studio executive tries to keep his word to a former executive by producing a movie on a topic that begs to be treated sexually, but he refuses to treat it that way. He brings in a writer and a director, but they get nowhere trying to develop the theme. Finally, the failure of the project becomes clear to everyone, and they move on to more absurd Hollywood projects.

Unfortunately, this movie is too slow; however, it is a realistic look at the most powerful industry in the world today. Surprisingly, there is very little off-color language.

MRS. MINIVER (1942) B&W, 134 min.

CONTENT: Nothing objectionable   ★★★★
INTENDED AUDIENCE: Adults
STARRING: Greer Garson, Walter Pidgeon, Teresa Wright, Dame May Whitty,
   Henry Travers, Richard Ney
DIRECTOR: William Wyler

A beautiful, emotive movie, *Mrs. Miniver* tells how hard it was on the British home front during the early days of World War II. The film opens in a quiet village on the eve of war where Kay and Clem Miniver live. The stationmaster grows roses and enters one, named for Mrs. Miniver, in the annual flower show (a competition perpetually won by the snobbish Lady Beldon). While her husband is involved in the drama of Dunkirk, Mrs. Miniver single-handedly captures a downed Nazi pilot. Returning home, Mr. Miniver notes, "Oh, darling, I'm almost sorry for you, having such a nice, quiet, peaceful time when things were really happening, but that's what men are for, isn't it—to go out and do things while you women folk look after the house?" Highly recommended.

MURPHY'S LAW (1986), 141 min.

RATING: R
CONTENT: Foul language, excessive violence, and nudity
INTENDED AUDIENCE: Adults
STARRING: Charles Bronson, Carrie Snodgrass, Robert Lyons
DIRECTOR: J. Lee Thompson

Action fans should mourn the fact that tight plots and solid action have given way in Hollywood to foul language, excessive violence, and nudity. The story line of this film is good, but the realization stoops to conquer.

Charles Bronson plays a Los Angeles cop faced with all kinds of problems, including tracking down a killer. Bronson's character is the only one with a modicum of integrity in an insane world. The most interesting aspect of the film is the fact that the female killer had been conditioned by her parole officer to think that she could do anything she wanted to do. Overall, there are too many negative elements to make this a recommended film. **J.C.J.**

MURPHEY'S ROMANCE (1986)

RATING: PG–13
CONTENT: Adultery, profanity, and ungodly viewpoints
INTENDED AUDIENCE: Adults
STARRING: Sally Field, James Garner

DIRECTOR: Martin Ritt

Sally Field plays a lonely single parent who moves to a small town to start a horse farm. She meets James Garner. They fall in love. They end up together—not married—but together.

The mediocre, immoral plot is topped by foul language, and Christianity is mocked. Avoid this film. **J.G.**

THE MUSIC MAN (1962), 151 min.

RATING: G ★★★★
CONTENT: Nothing offensive
INTENDED AUDIENCE: All ages
STARRING: Robert Preston, Shirley Jones, Paul Ford, Buddy Hackett,
  Hermione Gingold
DIRECTOR: Morton DaCosta

This dancing, singing, all-American musical classic is a thoroughly enjoyable two and a half hours of pure entertainment. Robert Preston stars as Professor Harold Hill, a city-slicker, flim-flam man who cons the citizens of the small Iowa town of River City into organizing a high school band so he can sell them musical instruments. However, he doesn't know how to read a note of music, and the instruments don't exist! He is selling them fraudulent contracts, with a sizable portion as down payment. Hill tries to skip town, but is unmasked by Marian (Shirley Jones), the town librarian.

The Music Man is chock full of memorable hit songs, such classics as, "Ya Got Trouble (right here in River City!)," " 'Till There Was You," "Marian the Librarian," and the unforgettable "Seventy-Six Trombones." This is a four-star film, and classic family entertainment. If you haven't seen it, you are missing a winner. **B.G.**

MUTINY ON THE BOUNTY (1935) B&W, 132 min.

CONTENT: Great action and scenery ★★★★
INTENDED AUDIENCE: All ages
STARRING: Charles Laughton, Clark Gable, Franchot Tone, Dudley Digges
DIRECTOR: Frank Lloyd

This film tells the powerful true story of the eighteenth century mutiny aboard the British naval vessel *Bounty*. The mutineers, who were led by Fletcher Christian, set their sadistic master, Captain Bligh, adrift, after which they settled in the Pitcairn Islands. Their descendants populate the islands today. The despicable Bligh and some of the remainder of the crew also made it to safety in a lifeboat with very little provision, definitely one of the most remarkable feats of seamanship ever.

Mutiny on the Bounty won the Academy Award for best picture. Charles Laughton was excellent as the heinous Bligh. Definitely a movie worth seeing.

MY AMERICAN COUSIN (1986)

RATING: PG ★★★
CONTENT: Nothing objectionable
INTENDED AUDIENCE: All ages
STARRING: Margaret Langrick, John Wildman
DIRECTOR: Sandy Wilson

Twelve-year-old Sandra Wilcox's voice is heard through the darkness, "Dear Diary: Nothing ever happens." Aided by a flashlight she continues to read her diary underneath the bed covers, "I first met my American Cousin in the golden summer of 1959." Thus begins a summer full of adventure as the Wilcox family is aroused from sleep only to find the unexpected arrival of California teenage relative, Butch, at their front door.

Sandra's father, John, owner of a cherry orchard ranch in British Columbia enquires if Butch has gotten into trouble with the police, or worse, gotten some girl in trouble. Butch replies, "No," while Uncle John explains to Aunt Kitty that Butch does come from a very decent family—American, but decent nevertheless.

Put to work in the cherry orchards, Butch is less interested in production quotas than the more industrious Canadian teenagers. He soon skips the work scene, driving his fish tail, firehouse red Cadillac convertible over gravel top dirt roads on the make for chicks. Cousin Sandy agonizes with growing pains, constantly quarrels with her mother, and chuckles at her father's attempt at explaining the phenomena of male and female attraction.

There is no nudity, or profanity, or violence in this film, which mirrors the growth within families and stresses true value instead of material gain. Recommended. **G.O.**

MY CHAUFFEUR (1986)

RATING: R
CONTENT: Profanity and nudity
INTENDED AUDIENCE: Teenagers
STARRING: Deborah Foreman, E. G. Marshall, Sam Jones
DIRECTOR: Daniel Beaird

Very little plot holds together this story of sexual escapades. The lead character is a young woman who becomes a very popular chauffeur. The film has no redeeming values. Don't let teens see it. **J.C.J.**

MY FAIR LADY (1964), 170 min.

CONTENT: Great songs and great story ★★★★
INTENDED AUDIENCE: All ages
STARRING: Rex Harrison, Audrey Hepburn, Stanley Holloway, Wilfrid Hyde-White, Gladys Cooper, Theodore Bikel
DIRECTOR: George Cukor

My Fair Lady tells the well-known story of how Professor Henry Higgins, bets with Colonel Pickering that he can turn a cockney guttersnipe, Eliza Doolittle, into a lady. He does, and in the process he falls head over heels in love with her. This is perfect movie entertainment. The acting, the direction, the music, the photography, the costuming, the set design—in fact, every aspect of the film is perfect. Songs such as "Why Can't the English," "Wouldn't It Be Loverly," "I'm an Ordinary Man," "With a Little Bit of Luck," "The Rain in Spain," "I Could Have Danced All Night," "Show Me," and many others are unforgettable. A movie of hope, love, and joy, *My Fair Lady* is a must.

MY LITTLE PONY (1986)

RATING: G ★★
CONTENT: Animated cartoon
INTENDED AUDIENCE: Children

STARRING (Voices): Danny DeVito, Tony Randall, Madeline Kahn, Cloris Leachman
DIRECTOR: Michael Joens

My Little Pony is a cartoon feature based on a toy. The ponies, who live in an idyllic country, are confronted by three witches trying to show how mean they are. The mother witch wants her daughters to shape up and be as bad as she is. The witches create smooze, a blob that covers everything. Some of the ponies escape and find the flutter ponies who drive back the smooze. All ends well, and good triumphs over evil.

This innocuous movie shows evil as evil and good as good. Young children will love it, but adults will be bored.

MY NAME IS NOBODY (1974), 115 min.

RATING: PG ★★★
CONTENT: Minor swearing and cowboy violence, but not gory
INTENDED AUDIENCE: Adults
STARRING: Henry Fonda, Terence Hill, R. G. Armstrong, Geoffrey Lewis
DIRECTOR: Tonino Valerii

This Italian production was the logical extension of the "spaghetti westerns," such as Clint Eastwood's Italian pictures. This tongue-in-cheek, spaghetti western spoof mixes real and mythical characters together in an unusual blend, with the audience almost believing that the central character, played by Henry Fonda, was indeed the legendary sheriff, Jack Beauregard. Actually, Beauregard never existed, but in this film he is forced to take on the Wild Bunch, another mythical creation of Western lore.

This is a fun movie, laughing at itself as it parodies the genre of moviemaking it is copying. A character named Nobody succeeds in making Sheriff Jack the legendary hero, as Jack is forced to take on the entire Wild Bunch. If Westerns are your type of entertainment, then this film is a light, almost fanciful movie you will enjoy. However, caution is recommended because of some swearing. **B.G.**

MY SIDE OF THE MOUNTAIN (1969)

RATING: G ★★★
CONTENT: Nothing objectionable
INTENDED AUDIENCE: Families
STARRING: Theodore Bikel, Ted Eccles
DIRECTOR: James Clark

With elements much like the story of Heidi, this film has a young Canadian boy leaving his parents to live alone in the mountains. The boy meets a retired folk singer who helps him adjust to the Canadian winter and reconcile with his parents.

Excellent nature photography added to the Canadian mountain background makes this fine family fare. It's a moving story of separation and reconciliation of a boy and his parents. **B.G.**

MY SWEET LITTLE VILLAGE (1986)
(Czech)

CONTENT: Mild off-color language and implied sexual situations ★★★
INTENDED AUDIENCE: Adults

STARRING: Unavailable
DIRECTOR: Jiri Menzel

My Sweet Little Village is a pleasant movie about many, many characters in a small village and their attitudes and temptations, loyalties, practicalities, and tendernesses. The "center of the wheel" is the character of a retarded adult who lives in a house that his parents willed to him upon their deaths. The atmosphere, acting and directing are superb, though the humor and drama are somewhat predictable. **S.S.**

MYSTERIOUS ISLAND (1960), 100 min.

CONTENT: Nothing objectionable   ★★★
INTENDED AUDIENCE: All ages
STARRING: Gary Merrill, Michael Callan, Herbert Lom
DIRECTOR: Cy Endfield

Escaping from a Southern prison camp during the Civil War, a group of men flees to safety aboard a hot-air balloon. Taking off in a storm, the balloon carries them away across the sea, and they crash land on to a tropical island somewhere in the ocean. The crew discovers two other stranded castaways (Beth Rogan and Joan Greenwood). Soon, all the castaways realize that the island is inhabited by oversized animals. They battle with giant birds, bees, and crabs!
Mysterious Island is a fun movie, with excellent special effects. **B.G.**

THE NAME OF THE ROSE (1986)

RATING: R   ★★
CONTENT: An earthy sexual encounter
INTENDED AUDIENCE: Adults
STARRING: Sean Connery, F. Murray Abraham
DIRECTOR: Jean-Jacques Annaud

This film is adapted from Umberto Eco's international best selling medieval detective story, which tells the story of a fourteenth century Franciscan abbey in Italy where the best minds in Christendom come to investigate charges of heresy. In the process of investigating the heresy, William of Baskerville (who resembles a combination of Sir Francis Bacon and Sherlock Holmes) is confronted by a series of murders. William's deductive and investigative abilities are extraordinary, but the murderer cleverly avoids detection until the end. There is an unnecessary, extended, raw sexual encounter in the movie. For that reason, this movie is not for most Christians. **L.B.**

NATIONAL VELVET (1945), 125 min.

CONTENT: Nothing objectionable   ★★★★
INTENDED AUDIENCE: All ages
STARRING: Elizabeth Taylor, Mickey Rooney, Reginald Owen,
    Donald Crisp, Angela Lansbury
DIRECTOR: Clarence Brown

This captivating, heartwarming, family drama tells the story of plucky twelve-year-old Velvet Brown, the butcher's child who disguises herself as a boy and rides her horse in England's Grand National Steeplechase. Set in the twenties in the English countryside, the story follows Velvet as she trains with "The Pi," as her horse is called. The bum kid (Rooney) works with her and the horse, making ready for the day of the climactic race.

The film pulls at the heartstrings, but doesn't yank at them. A well-paced, thoroughly enjoyable movie, which ends on the high note of an excitingly staged Grand National competition. **B.G.**

A NIGHT AT THE OPERA (1935) B&W, 96 min.

CONTENT: Nothing objectionable ★★★★
INTENDED AUDIENCE: All ages, but humor that only adults
  will understand
STARRING: The Marx Brothers, Margaret Dumont, Kitty Carlisle, Allan Jones,
  Sig Rumann
DIRECTOR: Sam Wood

Otis B. Driftwood (Groucho) has been hired to introduce Mrs. Claypool (Margaret Dumont) to society, but as of yet, he hasn't even shown for dinner. The bellboy pages him, "Paging Mr. Driftwood, Mr. Driftwood. . . ." Driftwood is having dinner directly behind Mrs. Claypool. He joins her, and tells her of his plan to have her underwrite an opera and get her into society.

The film moves at a brisk pace as Groucho introduces Mrs. Claypool to Herman Gottlieb, director of the New York Opera Company. After formal introductions, they part, and Groucho meets with Chico (who plays Forelo, manager of the world's greatest tenor). What ensues is one of the funniest scenes in movie history, as they negotiate a contract.

Other classic scenes include the famous stateroom scene aboard a steamship. Before the scene is over, dozens upon dozens of people are filling the room almost to its ceiling. The opera is finally performed, but not without Groucho selling peanuts in the aisles and Harpo and Chico playing baseball in the orchestra pit. Sheer zaniness and side-splitting fun. **B.G.**

'NIGHT MOTHER (1986)

RATING: PG–13
CONTENT: Suicide and humanism
INTENDED AUDIENCE: Adults
STARRING: Sissy Spacek, Anne Bancroft
DIRECTOR: Tom Moore

'Night Mother is about a woman's last two hours with her mother. The daughter, Jesse, tells her mother, Thelma, of her intentions to commit suicide. Although the pensive and meticulous Jesse and the loquacious Thelma contrast in terms of their personalities, spiritually they are alike: separated from God. All of the real action in 'Night Mother centers in the emotional tug of war within and between Thelma and Jesse. Their confrontation opens up old wounds and inflicts new ones. Wonderful performances by Sissy Spacek and Anne Bancroft make these women very poignant.

Although this film is devoid of nudity and profanity, teenagers should not see it. As reported in the September 11, 1986 issue of the New England Journal of Medicine, researchers have found that teenage suicide goes up by 5 percent to 7 percent after watching a dramatic program on suicide or a news report on suicide. Although a well-

made film, 'Night Mother has an anti-Christian world view. Our suggestion: Avoid it.
E.S.

9½ WEEKS (1986)

RATING: R
CONTENT: Sadomasochistic pornography
INTENDED AUDIENCE: Adults
STARRING: Mickey Rourke, Kim Basinger
DIRECTOR: Adrian Lyne

This film is billed as a love story, but don't believe it. This movie is pure sadomasochistic pornography. Avoid it.

1984 (1984), 123 min.

RATING: R ★★★
CONTENT: The stark cruelty of inhuman statism and some inconsequential
nudity that is definitely not erotic
INTENDED AUDIENCE: Adults
STARRING: John Hurt, Richard Burton, Suzanna Hamilton, Gregor Fisher
DIRECTOR: Michael Radford

This film tells the story of Winston, who lives in Oceana, which is one of three totalitarian states that have divided up the world. Winston is one of a number of people who program the news/encyclopedia, which changes the past to suit the Party and Big Brother. Winston deletes words, people, and events and changes meanings to suit Big Brother. Winston is guilty of thought crime. He hates Big Brother and wants to break out of the monotony of the state. His problem is that he remembers the past and therefore knows that Big Brother manipulates the people.

1984 should be required viewing for anyone who thinks socialist statism is the answer to the world's problems. This film vividly portrays the evil of totalitarian communism, showing that humanity is the depraved product of original sin, and statism is a hothouse breeding ground for the worst in mankind. Although there is some nudity, this film is recommended for its message.

NO DEPOSIT, NO RETURN (1976), 111 min.

RATING: G ★★
CONTENT: Nothing objectionable
INTENDED AUDIENCE: All ages
STARRING: David Niven, Darren McGavin, Don Knotts, Herschel Bernardi,
Barbara Feldon
DIRECTOR: Norman Tokar

No Deposit, No Return follows a pair of moppets who engineer their own kidnapping via a pair of bungling crooks (McGavin and Knotts) to get plane fare to surprise their mother (Feldon) with a visit. The story reveals that mother has been selfishly neglecting them for her magazine career. A pair of tough gangsters move into the kidnapping for real, and a pair of detectives fail to crack the case, until Uncle David Niven carefully provides a happy ending.

The film does end on an unusual note, as each of the characters does a moral swerve for the better. Children should enjoy the film and overlook its technical difficulties, mismatched special effects shots, and sloppy set construction. Harmless adventure, but not one of the better films to come from the Disney studios. **B.G.**

NO RETREAT, NO SURRENDER (1986)

RATING: PG   ★ ★
CONTENT: Spiritism
INTENDED AUDIENCE: Young adults
STARRING: Kurt McKinney, J. W. Fail
DIRECTOR: Corey Yuen

At first glance, the film seems to offer pure entertainment—no sex, no nudity, and no foul language, just action where the good guy wins. However, there are some disturbing aspects since it conjures up, perhaps unwittingly, the evil of spiritism.

The story involves Jason Stillwell, whose father runs a karate center in Los Angeles. The Mob tries to extort protection money from the father, and their evil Russian karate expert breaks Dad's leg. Jason and his father move to Seattle where Jason prays at the grave of the famous karate expert Bruce Lee. Bruce appears as Jason's spirit guide and teaches him karate in a house Jason has converted into a Shinto temple. The Mob backs a national karate match in Seattle, and the Russian challenges all comers only to be defeated by Jason.

Because calling up the spirit of the dead is condemned in the Bible, Jason's prayer to Bruce Lee, perhaps only a plot device in the movie, is sinful, and his studying at the hands of the departed is an abomination. Therefore, this film is unacceptable. **J.S.** and **K.D.**

NO SURRENDER (1986)

CONTENT: Mild off-color language and profanity   ★ ★
INTENDED AUDIENCE: Adults
STARRING: Bernard Hill, Mark Mulholland, Joanne Whalley
DIRECTOR: Peter Smith

This intriguing British movie just falls short of worthwhile viewing. A newly employed nightclub manager finds himself set up by the disgruntled former manager. For New Year's Eve, several strange groups are booked into the club, and all kinds of complications arise. But the new manager successfully solves the problems.

Some very positive facets of this film are marred by the new manager's going off with the barmaid, who talks him out of going home to his wife. This moment of moral failure cuts against the grain of the rest of the movie. This ending demonstrates that the writer did not have a biblical world view, but put his faith in heroes. However, the film has many good points to recommend it, except for some mild off-color language and profanity.

NORTH BY NORTHWEST (1959), 136 min.

CONTENT: Nothing objectionable   ★ ★ ★ ★
INTENDED AUDIENCE: All ages
STARRING: Cary Grant, Eva Marie Saint, James Mason, Jesse Royce Landis, Leo G. Carroll
DIRECTOR: Alfred Hitchcock

This film tells the story of Roger Thornhill, a business executive who is mistaken for a secret agent who doesn't even exist. Thornhill is kidnapped and is unable to prove his innocence to the head of a spy ring, Philip Vandamm. For the rest of the film, Roger tries to escape Vandamm's clutches. He ends up at Mount Rushmore in a frightening chase over the steep face of the monument.

This film is one of Hitchcock's best, a thrilling, suspenseful masterpiece that will keep you on the edge of your seat. See it. **B.G.**

NOT QUITE PARADISE (1986)

RATING: R(?)
CONTENT: Brief nudity, promiscuity, and obscenity
INTENDED AUDIENCE: Adult
STARRING: JoAnn Pakula, Sam Robards, Todd Graff, Kevin McNally
DIRECTOR: Lewis Gilbert

This story of five people who volunteer to go to Israel to harvest melons on a kibbutz makes a moderately interesting slice-of-life film and part of the new crop of small group portraits that has become popular. Most of the film is character development of a blond American, a soldier from Northern Ireland, a young American Jew, an Englishwoman who claims she is a nurse, and an Australian chicken farmer. Toward the end, a group of Muslim terrorists take the kibbutz hostage, but they are saved by an Israeli military raid. Don't waste your time on this dull film. **K.K.**

NOTHING IN COMMON (1986)

RATING: PG ★★
CONTENT: Frequent profanity and promiscuity
INTENDED AUDIENCE: Adults
STARRING: Jackie Gleason, Tom Hanks
DIRECTOR: Garry Marshall

Nothing in Common begins in poor taste but ends up being a loving, moving film. The filmmaker's heart is in the right place, but the loose sexual mores and the foul language make this movie off-limits for Christians.

An obnoxious, self-centered, up-and-coming creative director at an advertising agency is taking the world by storm only to be pulled up short by the problems confronting his has-been father. The ultimate premise ("love triumphs over selfishness") and the moral ("love is a decision you have to make") are biblical, but the journey that the young man has to follow to get to the realization of the truth is very rough. It is true to life for him to emerge from selfishness to caring and love for his father. Unfortunately, this transformation is not tied to Jesus Christ. Also, the life he leads before his transformation is too licentious. All in all, the film is not for Christians.

THE NUN'S STORY (1959), 151 min.

CONTENT: Nothing objectionable ★★★★
INTENDED AUDIENCE: Adults
STARRING: Audrey Hepburn, Peter Finch, Dame Edith Evans, Peggy Ashcroft,
    Dean Jagger, Beatrice Straight, Colleen Dewhurst
DIRECTOR: Fred Zinnemann

This is an exceptionally appealing story about how a young woman becomes a nun. The story follows Sister Luke as she serves in the Belgian Congo during the forties. Stationed with Dr. Fortunati (Finch) under harsh living conditions, she is disturbed by his agnostic criticisms of her life and fights obedience and pride within herself.

She returns to Belgium and learns of her father's death at the hands of the National Socialists (Nazis). Her Order will not allow her to serve in the Belgian underground, but because of her insistence the Order releases her from her vows. Audrey Hepburn and the fine cast surrounding her are exceptional. The character of Sister Luke has many layers of personality, each giving us a glimpse of her inner and outer turmoil. Highly recommended. **B.G.**

THE NUTTY PROFESSOR (1963), 107 min.

RATING: G   ★★★
CONTENT: Nothing objectionable
INTENDED AUDIENCE: All ages
STARRING: Jerry Lewis, Del Moore, Stella Stevens, Kathleen Freeman
DIRECTOR: Jerry Lewis

Professor Julius Kelp, a nerdy, bespeckled, chemistry teacher, devises a formula to change into another person, much like Dr. Jekyll and Mr. Hyde. Kelp's secret formula transforms him into his alter-ego, Buddy Love, a loud, brash character, who is also suave and definitely a ladies man. This is perfect for Kelp, who wants to impress a cute coed (Stevens). Kelp doesn't realize that he cannot control Buddy, and soon, Buddy becomes even more egotistical as he realizes his powers over both men and women.

The two personalities intermingle within Kelp. During the senior prom, he transforms in front of everyone from Buddy back to Kelp, but not before confessing his deceptive ways and realizing the value of truth. Taken by his confession, the coed feels empathy for Kelp and the romance continues.

Like all of Lewis's films, *The Nutty Professor* contains clever sight gags and great comic support, especially from Freeman, Moore, and Howard Morris. The film also moralizes about truth and falsehood and is instructive therefore. **B.G.**

OFF BEAT (1986), 133 min.

RATING: PG   ★★★
CONTENT: Off-color language
INTENDED AUDIENCE: Young adults
STARRING: Judge Reinhold
DIRECTOR: Michael Dinner

Off Beat is a cheerful, funny, and kindhearted police comedy. Everything about it is upbeat, except for some off-color language that is totally unnecessary.

The story is far-fetched, but not outlandish. A librarian agrees to do a favor for a policeman friend, Abe, by impersonating Abe in the police benefit play tryouts. To his amazement, the librarian lands the part and falls head over heels in love with a pretty policewoman in the play. He even unintentionally solves several crimes while wearing Abe's uniform. This is pretty good entertainment, except for the mild bad language, and good triumphs over evil. It is almost, but not quite, on target. **J.C.J.**

THE OFFICIAL STORY (1986)
(Subtitles)

CONTENT: Nothing objectionable   ★★★
INTENDED AUDIENCE: Adults
STARRING: Norma Aleandro, Hector Alterio
DIRECTOR: Luiz Puenzo

This well-made Argentine film tells of a woman who begins to fear that her five-year-old adopted daughter was stolen from one of the people who disappeared during the military government of the late 1970s. Unfortunately, the film depicts all anarchists and Communists as good and all conservatives as bad. *The Official Story* is a great movie flawed by a totally wrong-headed premise.

OKLAHOMA! (1955), 143 min.

CONTENT: Nothing objectionable   ★★★★
INTENDED AUDIENCE: Adult
STARRING: Gordon MacRae, Shirley Jones, Rod Steiger, Eddie Albert
DIRECTOR: Fred Zinnemann

With a superb cast headed by Gordon MacRae and Shirley Jones, this film version of the famous Broadway play is an exciting, moving production. MacRae plays Curly, a cowboy who loves Laurey (Jones), but their happiness is threatened by Jud Fry, a local farmhand (Rod Steiger). The plot is merely a vehicle to allow for some of the best choreography and music ever to be filmed. The great score includes "Kansas City," "The Surrey with the Fringe on Top," "People Will Say We're in Love," "Oh, What a Beautiful Mornin'," and the rousing title song, "Oklahoma!". The entire family will be singing along with the cast in this energetic and enthusiastic production. **B.G.**

THE OLD MAN AND THE SEA (1958), 89 min.

CONTENT: Nothing objectionable   ★★★★
INTENDED AUDIENCE: All ages
STARRING: Spencer Tracy
DIRECTOR: John Sturges

Spencer Tracy plays an old man who, for eighty-four days at sea, has caught nothing. Each day he goes out in his boat, but returns with not a single fish. Everyone has lost faith in him, except a little boy who makes coffee for him and reads him the newspaper. Finally, the old man catches a giant fish the size of his little boat. However, sharks devour it, as he helplessly tries to defend his catch. He returns with nothing.

The Old Man and the Sea deals with heroism and man's conflict with nature, as many Hemingway stories do. Tracy, who is alone on the screen for sixty of the eighty-six minutes, is a virtual one-man show. His towering ability as a leading actor is clearly seen in his performance. Highly recommended. **B.G.**

THE OMEN (1976), 110 min.

RATING: R   ★★★
CONTENT: Violence
INTENDED AUDIENCE: Adults

STARRING: Gregory Peck, Lee Remick, David Warner, Billy Whitelaw
DIRECTOR: Richard Donner

Spurned by the critics when first released, *The Omen* seems to improve with age. Loosely based on the book of Revelation, the story follows Robert Thorn, ambassador to Great Britain, who adopts a son the same night his wife loses their natural son in childbirth. Five years later, the Thorn family is overwhelmed by bizarre circumstances involving the adopted son, Damien. A priest warns that the child is not human, but the son of Satan.

A photographer teams up with Thorn to try to uncover the mystery of Damien. They read from Revelation about the Antichrist and realize that Damien is fulfilling the prophecy. They learn that the only way the Antichrist-Damien can be killed is to sacrifice the child with a set of knives on holy ground. Reluctant at first, Thorn eventually attempts to sacrifice the Antichrist, but he is killed before he can do it. As Thorn is eulogized, young Damien intently watches the proceedings on the lawn in front of the White House. He smiles as his godfather, the president of the United States, holds his hand.

The film ventures into new ground by depicting the Antichrist and is very slick in a melodramatic way. Even though it is a commercial product from a Hollywood studio, it invokes the name of Jesus Christ as the Savior and the only way to triumph over Satan. Though there will be countless critics of the film's interpretation of the Antichrist, the film is guided by a measure of Christian theology. It is entertaining and recommended with the caution that it is violent and theologically askew in parts of the story line. It is not a great movie, but it makes several solid biblical points about salvation. **B.G.**

ON THE BEACH (1959), 134 min.

CONTENT: Grim portrayal of the lethal poisoning of all mankind from nuclear fallout; adult situations; no swearing, no violence, no nudity   ★★★
INTENDED AUDIENCE: Adults
STARRING: Gregory Peck, Fred Astaire, Ava Gardner, Anthony Perkins
DIRECTOR: Stanley Kramer

This film, set in Australia after World War III, is one of the most provocative of this genre ever produced. It faithfully follows the novel by Nevil Shute, with the entire earth eventually poisoned by nuclear fallout and the last remaining survivors helplessly awaiting the onset of the lethal clouds.

The strong cast gives brilliant, understated performances of people faced with their own impending and inevitable deaths. The character studies provide us with a strong juxtaposition between life and death. The film reiterates over and over again that life is sacred, although man's sinfulness has brought him to the brink of destruction. We get quick glimpses of Christianity at work, as a preacher speaks to his outdoor audience, telling them the message of Christ.

On the Beach is not pleasant because of the message it delivers. Its tone is very somber, yet the film is brilliant and provides much food for thought even today, many years since its release. As Christians, we know that the end will not come through nuclear poisoning or annihilation. We know that the end will be just a beginning for us, and we will live forever with the King of kings. Therefore, the despair of the film turns Christians away from the true focus, which is to witness to Him. A good film, it must be viewed with caution. **B.G.**

ON THE WATERFRONT (1954), 108 min.

CONTENT: Some violence, but not graphic   ★★★★
INTENDED AUDIENCE: Adults
STARRING: Marlon Brando, Lee J. Cobb, Eva Marie Saint, Rod Steiger, Karl Malden
DIRECTOR: Elia Kazan

This stark, powerful drama is about corruption among New York City longshoremen, and how muscle and money can do or take care of almost anything. Brando portrays Terry Malloy, a stevedore who dreams of becoming a boxing champion. Terry finds out how things get done on the waterfront and proceeds to expose the criminals who control the union. This is the classic story of David versus Goliath, where Terry is David and the union is Goliath.

The movie marked the debut of Leonard Bernstein's career as a cinematic composer, and Saint's first film as an actress. They both received Oscars. *On the Waterfront* is a masterpiece that exposes the underside of life. Recommended. **B.G.**

ON VALENTINE'S DAY (1986)

RATING: PG   ★★★
CONTENT: Nothing objectionable
INTENDED AUDIENCE: Adults
STARRING: Hallie Foote, William Converse-Roberts, Michael Higgins,
    Steven Hill, Rochelle Oliver, Matthew Broderick
DIRECTOR: Ken Harrison

Well-to-do Elizabeth Vaughn shocks her town by running away from home on Valentine's Day of 1917 to marry Horace Robedaux, a decent young man who only has humble prospects. Although her wealthy parents cross their daughter out of their lives, their pain is as genuine as that of the young couple.

Elizabeth and Horace make do in a rented room, and their love draws people into their lives, such as: their impoverished, alcoholic landlord, Bobby Pate; the spinster, Miss Ruth, who pines for Pate; a simple-minded young girl from down the street; and the eccentric, wealthy George Tyler, who is related to just about everyone in town.

Come Christmas, Elizabeth's family agrees to visit because they know that Elizabeth is about to have a baby. During the reconciliation that follows, many truths come to light. The brilliant ensemble acting keeps the story in balance. We care about all the characters in this small Texas town. Scriptwriter Horton Foote has given us a true valentine of a movie. See it. **L.B.**

ON THE EDGE (1986), 126 min.

RATING: PG
CONTENT: Nudity and profanity
INTENDED AUDIENCE: Young adults
STARRING: Bruce Dern, Bill Bailey, Jim Haynie
DIRECTOR: Rob Nilsson

On the Edge is *Chariots of Fire* without the gospel. In fact, it substitutes mysticism for redemption. A 1964 Olympic runner, who was disqualified, makes a comeback twenty years later in the Californian Mountain Race. At the very end of the race, the runner has a mystical experience and waits for all the other runners to cross the finish line at the same time.

Nudity and profanity add to the unsavory aspects of this utopian, anti-Christian movie. The acting is good, and there is some redemption of relationships. But overall, the film is not for Christians. **R.W.**

ONCE BITTEN (1985), 133 min.

RATING: PG–13
CONTENT: Homosexuality, transvestism, and premarital sex
INTENDED AUDIENCE: Young adults
STARRING: Lauren Hutton, Jim Carrey, Karen Kopins
DIRECTOR: Howard Storm

This loser promotes homosexuality, transvestism, and premarital sex. The vampire countess tells her victim that the cross doesn't work any more to ward off vampires, but sex will. This film mocks the church and every biblical value. Avoid it.

ONCE UPON A TIME IN THE WEST (1969), 165 min.

RATING: PG   ★★★
CONTENT: Some violence, with Fonda and his gang gunning down a
    father and his sons (not explicit); shootings and hangings, all Italian
    Western style; and mild swearing
INTENDED AUDIENCE: Adults
STARRING: Henry Fonda, Charles Bronson, Jason Robards, Jr., Claudia Cardinale,
    Jack Elam, Keenan Wynn, Gabriele Ferzetti
DIRECTOR: Sergio Leone

In what could be described as the grandest Italian Western ever produced depicting the settling of the American West, *Once Upon a Time in the West* is a large budget picture (by Italian standards) that earned the phrase: "It took the Italians to finally show American film producers how to make a real Western." The film spans many years and many characters, and it runs over two hours in length. Good triumphs over evil as Charles Bronson slays the killer of his brother and father in a gun duel near the end of the film. **B.G.**

ONE CRAZY SUMMER (1986)

RATING: PG   ★★
CONTENT: Mild swearing
INTENDED AUDIENCE: Teenagers
STARRING: John Cusak, Demi Moore
DIRECTOR: Savage Steve Holland

Unfortunately, this film fails for want of a good script. It is a friendly, loving comedy with no profanity, no nudity, and no promiscuity. However, as it stands, it is painfully dull and has absolutely no continuity.

A young man who has no athletic ability wants to study art rather than follow in the footsteps of his famous basketball-playing forebears. Caught between his desires and the demands of his family, he takes the summer off and goes to Nantucket Island, where he falls in love with a girl who has been cheated out of her inheritance by an unscrupulous land baron and his preppie son. After a series of light engagements and dull jokes, our hero and his girl defeat the opposition, and all ends well. Too bad something so positive could not have been more entertaining.

ONE DAY IN THE LIFE OF IVAN DENISOVICH (1971), 100 min.
RATING: G ★★★★
CONTENT: Adult themes involving a Soviet prison labor camp
INTENDED AUDIENCE: Adults
STARRING: Tom Courtney, James Maxwell, Alfred Burke
DIRECTOR: Casper Wrede

Set in 1950, this heart-breaking account of Soviet slave labor camps in Siberia is a grim reminder of the warnings issued by Alexander Solzhenitsyn whose novel is the basis for this film. *One Day* details the horrors of just one day in the life of Ivan Denisovich, who is sentenced to ten years hard labor in Siberia for the "crime" of trying to escape from a German prisoner-of-war camp. The film follows his daily routine, from rising early in the morning in the bitter, sub-zero cold, to working all day at hard labor and then bedding down in a freezing bunk after a meal of thin fish broth and frozen porridge. A true portrayal of the corrupt Soviet system. **B.G.**

ONE MAGIC CHRISTMAS (1985)
RATING: G ★★
CONTENT: Faith in Santa Claus
INTENDED AUDIENCE: Families
STARRING: Mary Steenburgen, Gary Basaraba, Michelle Meyrink
DIRECTOR: Phillip Borsos

A powerful, heart-rending movie that equates Santa Claus with the Deity, *One Magic Christmas* is an excellent apologetic for having faith. But faith in what? Santa Claus? The Christmas spirit? Unfortunately, the writers never tell us that the only secure faith is in Jesus Christ.

A mother has lost the Christmas spirit because her husband is out of work. Her daughter asks Santa in a letter to give her mother the Christmas spirit, and an angel from Santa mails the letter for her. The husband is shot in a bank holdup, the two children are kidnapped, and the mother finally calls out to Santa, at which point the husband comes back to life and the children are found safe.

This is a movie with some promise that lets down God and Christians. If you take your children to see it, tell them that Jesus is the answer, not Santa Claus.

OPERATION DAYBREAK (1975)
RATING: PG ★★★
CONTENT: Minor swearing and some violence
INTENDED AUDIENCE: Adults
STARRING: Timothy Bottoms, Joss Ackland, Anthony Andrews, Anton Diffring, Martin Shaw
DIRECTOR: Lewis Gilbert

This film is a true, realistic war story set in Czechoslovakia in 1942 at a time when the country was occupied by the Nazis. The Allies are looking for a way to change their dismal fortunes. The Czechs are looking for relief from their dreaded "protector," Reinhard Heydrich's SS Grupenfuhrer, second in command only to Hitler in the Third Reich. Heydrich ruthless methods and numerous executions earned him the name "the Hangman of Europe."

Heydrich's schedule is watched, and the underground provides information on his movements. He is finally assassinated when a grenade thrown into his open touring car explodes and wounds him. The assassin rushes to the car, sees Heydrich alive and shoots him until his gun is empty. Heydrich dies a few days later, but not before the entire male population of the village of Lidice is murdered in retaliation.

If you like war movies, or you are interested in recent history, you will like *Operation Daybreak*. **B.G.**

OTELLO (1986)

RATING: PG   ★★★
CONTENT: Nothing objectionable
INTENDED AUDIENCE: Adults
STARRING: Placido Domingo, Katia Ricciarelli, Justino Diaz, Petra Malakova,
    Urbano Barberini
DIRECTOR: Franco Zeffirelli

Otello tells the story of a proud Moor who is destroyed by his jealousy when his ensign, Iago (whom Otello slighted), takes revenge on him by treacherously leading Otello to suspect his wife's fidelity. Consumed with rage, Otello kills his bride and brings death and destruction on himself.

Many opera purists have criticized the movie because director Zeffirelli cut out over half an hour of the opera's score. However, Zeffirelli rightly contends that film is its own art form, and he is not doing any more to Verdi's opera than Verdi did to Shakespeare's tragedy. There is no doubt that *Otello* has its flaws, but nonetheless it is a beautiful adaptation of a great opera. **L.B.**

THE OTHER SIDE OF THE MOUNTAIN (1975), 103 min.

RATING: PG   ★★★
CONTENT: Nothing objectionable
INTENDED AUDIENCE: Adolescents, adults
STARRING: Beau Bridges, Marilyn Hassett
DIRECTOR: Larry Peerce

As a best bet to make the U.S. Olympic team for 1956, Jill Kinmont is determined to beat her only close rival in the Snow Cap Race, but she loses control coming downhill and plunges over a precipice, breaking her neck and severing her spinal cord. Based on a true story, the film recreates Jill's story of tragedy and triumph.

Jill's boyfriend, Dick "Mad Dog" Beuk (Beau Bridges), suggests to Jill that they should get married. Dick makes promises of a "dream house with ramp ways" for her wheelchair. Although his plans are never realized, the story reveals how those close to Jill must also adjust to her handicap. A good film. **B.G.**

OUT OF AFRICA (1985)

RATING: PG   ★★
CONTENT: Adultery and promiscuity

INTENDED AUDIENCE: Adults
STARRING: Robert Redford, Meryl Streep
DIRECTOR: Sydney Pollack

This beautifully filmed movie shows that immorality leads to loneliness and death. Unfortunately, the writer does not seem to understand the story, so we are left with a muddled plot. The heroine doesn't seem to realize that her problems stem from her poor choice in men; she chooses men with no scruples.

Robert Redford seduces Meryl Streep while she is the wife of a total cad who has given her a venereal disease. The movie then shows us that adultery leads to death, although the sin is not explicitly condemned. In spite of the stars and the excellent direction, the film is unfit for Christians.

OVER THE TOP (1987)

RATING: PG   ★★★
CONTENT: Some crude language and rough locations
INTENDED AUDIENCE: Adults
STARRING: Sylvester Stallone, David Mendenhall, Robert Loggia, Susan Blakely
DIRECTOR: Menahem Golem

Over the Top tells the story of an independent truck driver, Lincoln Hawks, who is barely making it, who shows up at an expensive military academy to pick up his twelve-year-old son, Mike, whom he hasn't seen for ten years. Mike's mother is dying and wants Mike to get to know his father whom her father, Jason Cutler, chased off ten years earlier because he felt "Linc" was not worthy of his debutante daughter. For years, the father-in-law has been keeping Linc from his son.

At first, Mike wants no part of the father who deserted him and his mother. Linc is honest about the fact that he made a dreadful mistake and has enough character not to rationalize it. Mike and Linc grow to love one another, with Linc showing Mike something about character and love that Mike had not known under his grandfather's influence.

This movie is recommended for fathers and their teenage sons. There are some rough spots in the film, but it does take a moral approach.

PALE RIDER (1985), 113 min.

RATING: R   ★★
CONTENT: Violence and obscenity
INTENDED AUDIENCE: Adults
STARRING: Clint Eastwood, Michael Moriarty, Carrie Snodgrass
DIRECTOR: Clint Eastwood

This good but flawed Western almost attains a Christian perspective on good and evil. Clint Eastwood plays a gunfighter turned preacher who goes back to gunfighting to save the weak from a ruthless robber baron. The trouble is that it touches on Christianity without developing the logical ramifications of a Christian world view on the actions of the hero. Clint, as the preacher, doesn't seem to wrestle with his decision to resort to gunfighting. Furthermore, his character is flawed by his falling into an adulterous relationship without giving it a second thought (there is no on-camera sexual encounter).

The violence is very rough, and the language is strong. The preacher does cause the mining camp to consider love, justice, community, and the fight against evil. The film is to be avoided by anyone with a weak stomach, but anyone who wants to see a film-maker striving to understand the good might want to see it.

PAPA WAS A PREACHER (1986)

RATING: G   ★★★★
CONTENT: Nothing objectionable
INTENDED AUDIENCE: All ages
STARRING: Robert Pine, Georgia Engel, Dean Stockwell, Imogene Coca
DIRECTOR: Steve Feke

Papa Was a Preacher tells the story of a Methodist preacher, Paul Candler, who has a loving wife and seven children, and who is called to revive a Texas church that has fallen on hard times. Through the grace of God acting in the father's life, the church is saved from the bank, and we are treated to the beautiful story of how a Christian family works together under the headship of Jesus Christ to overcome adversity.

The script, direction, and acting in this movie are commendable. There are some minor flaws, and it is apparent that the budget was tight, but, in all, this is a beautiful movie, funded and produced by a *church* in Dallas, Tex. We need to support movies such as this.

THE PAWNBROKER (1965), 116 min.

CONTENT: Brief nudity and masochism
INTENDED AUDIENCE: Adults
STARRING: Rod Steiger
DIRECTOR: Sidney Lumet

The Pawnbroker is the movie that knocked the legs out from under morality in motion pictures because the National Council of Churches honored it with an award in spite of the fact that it featured nudity. Incidentally, the film made Rod Steiger a star.

This depressing movie deals with one man's inability to face reality. Sol Nazerman, a Nazi prison camp survivor, lives in self-imposed isolation. He operates a pawnshop in Harlem, which he owns, but it is used by a crime kingpin to launder illegal profits. He finally breaks out of his stupor when his assistant gets shot and killed as he foils a robbery and saves Nazerman's life.

This sad, pathetic story focuses on the hopelessness most people feel in life. Although it does show some spark of love when the assistant sacrifices himself to save Nazerman, the film is not for Christians. **K.G.**

THE PEANUT BUTTER SOLUTION (1986)
(Subtitles)

CONTENT: Nothing objectionable   ★★
INTENDED AUDIENCE: All ages

The Peanut Butter Solution is a modern fairy tale about a compassionate little boy who learns to deal with the real world by facing his fears. The boy feels sorry for some beggars, so he gives them some change. Later, he goes with a friend to visit the house

163

where they live. He climbs in through a window, is scared, screams, and climbs out, but he can't remember what he saw. Since the fright causes him to lose all his hair, he finds a home remedy for baldness. But he uses too much peanut butter in the concoction, and his hair starts to grow out of control. An unemployed art teacher kidnaps the boy and some other children, and he starts to produce paintbrushes with the boy's hair. Eventually, all the children are rescued, and the little boy's hair starts to grow normally after he climbs into a realistic picture of the old house that the magical art teacher painted.

The message of this French comedy—that facing the truth helps to overcome fear—is positive. The movie is delightfully produced. Some brief magical moments are not objectionable because this is traditional fairy tale material brought into movie format. It is fun, fanciful, family viewing. **D.R.**

PINOCCHIO (1940), 88 min.

CONTENT: Nothing objectionable ★★★★
INTENDED AUDIENCE: Families
STARRING (Voices): Dickie Jones, Cliff Edwards
DIRECTOR: Ben Sharpsteen, Hamilton Luske

Pinocchio is a Walt Disney masterpiece, telling the story of the friendly woodcarver, Gepetto, who makes a wonderful puppet, Pinocchio, and wishes that the puppet would come to life. His wish is granted, but Pinocchio still has to prove himself worthy to become a real boy. A small cricket, Jiminy, promises to help him by being his conscience. Pinocchio proves to be all too human in many ways, going through many troubles of his own making, but he finally realizes that love is more important than selfishness and is turned into a real boy. A beautiful movie with many biblical undertones, this film shows that Pinocchio is only a creature until he turns from his rebellion and accepts his father's love. Highly recommended in spite of some references to magic. **P.B.** and **J.B.**

PLACES IN THE HEART (1984), 110 min.

RATING: PG ★★★★
CONTENT: Mild swearing and some risqué scenes
INTENDED AUDIENCE: All ages
STARRING: Sally Field
DIRECTOR: Robert Benton

The movie opens with the great hymn "Blessed Assurance." A small-town Texas family is praying before dinner. The husband, who is the sheriff, is called away to deal with a drunk black teenager who is raising a ruckus at the railroad yard. As the sheriff speaks to the boy, the boy accidentally shoots him. The boy is lynched by the angry citizens. After that, the widow's stark courage enables her to face the unscrupulous bank manager, the depression, the weak cotton market, and tornadoes. Her determination triumphs over incredible adversity.

Places in the Heart is an endearing, poetic vision of the recent past in small-town America. God is accorded a place in its heart. This film is a witness to the resurrection of the saints. In the last scene, all the townspeople, even those who have died during the movie, come together to share communion in church. Highly recommended viewing.

PLANET OF THE APES (1968), 120 min.
RATING: G   ★★★
CONTENT: Some off-color language
INTENDED AUDIENCE: Families
STARRING: Charlton Heston, Roddy McDowell, Kim Hunter
DIRECTOR: Franklin Schaffner

Astronauts from current times land on a planet inhabited by intelligent apes, where humans are wild, live in trees and behave like animals. Is everything topsy-turvey? Yes. *Planet of the Apes* takes a look at a lot of our social, religious, political, and artistic values through the eyes of an ape!

The major drawback to this movie, other than some off-color language, is an allusion to evolution. In this case, apes got more intelligent and humans much less. Easily-offended viewers may wish to avoid the film. **L.R.**

PLATOON (1986)
RATING: R
CONTENT: Excessive profanity, obscenity, and violence
INTENDED AUDIENCE: Adults
STARRING: Tom Berenger, William DeFoe, Charlie Sheen
DIRECTOR: Oliver Stone

Platoon is an overrated, dishonest movie that pushes anti-Americanism and communism. It is a dull, spotty, mediocre movie that has been commended by some because of its leftist perspective, not because it is a well-made film (which it is not).

Platoon tells the story of a college dropout, Chris Taylor, who volunteers for the Army because he is convinced that his fellow soldiers will teach him about life, and the war will be his passage to manhood. Chris joins his unit in the jungle and is soon wounded when they are ambushed by the Vietcong they are tracking.

The soldiers in the platoon are divided between two sergeants, Elias and Barnes, who symbolize good and evil, respectively. At one point in the movie, outraged by the death of his friends, Chris begins to take part in a mission of revenge on a Vietnamese village, but then is repelled by the brutality of his comrades. In the end, Chris is wounded again and airlifted out of a battle saying: "Those of us who did make it have an obligation to build again, to teach others what we know and to try with what's left of our lives to find a goodness and a meaning to this life."

Most of the critics who have reviewed this movie were not in Vietnam and have no idea what the war was like in 1967. However, many do share Director Oliver Stone's leftward leanings and like *Platoon* because it confirms their worst suspicions about the nature of the Vietnamese War. A better movie about the war in Vietnam is *Go Tell the Spartans*. Christians should avoid *Platoon* because of excessive profanity, obscenity, violence, and a dishonest portrait of history.

PLENTY (1985)
RATING: R
CONTENT: Drug use, profanity, promiscuity, and perverted values
INTENDED AUDIENCE: Adults

STARRING: Meryl Streep, Charles Dance, John Gielgud
DIRECTOR: Fred Schepisi

Plenty promises more than it delivers. It is a profane, boring portrait of progressive insanity. A British World War II heroine has a one-night stand during the war and is haunted by the memory of her elusive lover. After selfishly destroying her husband's career and then finding her wartime lover, she collapses into a dope-smoking haze. Her lover abandons her to the dope, and she drifts into dreams of lost innocence.

This film is a portrait of deceit, selfishness, cruelty, and madness. Full of profanity and perverted values, it is spiritually empty. Don't see it.

POLTERGEIST II: THE OTHER SIDE (1986), 127 min.
RATING: PG–13
CONTENT: Witchcraft, demonic elements, and spiritism
INTENDED AUDIENCE: Children and families
STARRING: JoBeth Williams, Craig Nelson
DIRECTOR: Brian Gibson

This film attacks Christianity and lifts up witchcraft and spiritism. It suggests there is something stronger than invoking the name of Jesus Christ to defeat demons, and that "something" is a family's love for one another.

A family beleaguered by demons, a little girl with psychic powers, and evil spirits led by a man dressed like a preacher are some major elements of this film that present a completely upside-down world view. Christians should not support this film.

POWER (1986)
RATING: R   ★★
CONTENT: Swearing and some promiscuity
INTENDED AUDIENCE: Adults
STARRING: Richard Gere, Julie Christie, Gene Hackman
DIRECTOR: Sidney Lumet

Power tells the straightforward story of a public relations man, a political power broker, and a reporter who are caught in the gruesome game of politics. A well-produced movie with competent actors, it contains some swearing and a brief sex scene. It is not for Christians. **B.A.**

PRETTY IN PINK (1986)
RATING: PG–13   ★★★
CONTENT: Mild off-color language
INTENDED AUDIENCE: Teenagers
STARRING: Molly Ringwald
DIRECTOR: Howard Deutch

A lighthearted 1980s Cinderella story about a girl from the wrong side of the tracks who finds Prince Charming, *Pretty in Pink* is well directed and cast, but some mild off-color language detracts from the film. However, it is acceptable viewing for teenagers and others who might be interested in this story.

PSYCHO III (1986)

RATING: R
CONTENT: Nudity, cruel violence, and evil doings
INTENDED AUDIENCE: Adults
STARRING: Anthony Perkins
DIRECTOR: Anthony Perkins

Norm is out of jail. He is shown in flashbacks stuffing birds and his mother. He dresses up like Mom and kills beautiful women to take revenge on himself and his mother. A beautiful girl falls for him and is killed by accident. He gets caught by the police and goes off to jail with his mother's arm concealed under his coat.

Anthony Perkins directed this sequel to the famous *Psycho,* but he is no Hitchcock. Nudity, cruel violence, and evil doings are its hallmarks. This movie is definitely *not* recommended. **J.C.J.**

THE PURPLE ROSE OF CAIRO (1985), 84 min.

RATING: PG   ★ ★ ★ ★
CONTENT: Mild swearing and risqué situations
INTENDED AUDIENCE: Adults
STARRING: Mia Farrow, Jeff Daniels
DIRECTOR: Woody Allen

The Purple Rose of Cairo is one of the most accurate and poignant theological statements ever made, although Woody Allen probably did not intend it as such. The process of producing a film is a great, if not perfect, illustration of the Trinity. If we imagine reality as a movie, God the Father can be seen as the writer-creator who directs the movie production as the Holy Spirit and then steps into the film to resolve the conflict as an actor in the person of Jesus Christ. God is one and the same God, fulfilling three different roles. The characters within the film are unconscious of the reality outside the movie and know that reality only through the lead, Jesus, coming into their reality. This is an imperfect analogy, but it is extremely helpful. Woody Allen comes close to capturing this analogy here.

The movie is set during the depression. Cecilia's husband is unemployed, and when she loses her job, she escapes to the theater where a B movie is playing. After she has watched the movie several times, the leading man, Tom, steps out of the picture, out of the screen, and into her life. The other characters are in chaos, unable to continue the story of the movie, and they argue with the audience about what they should be doing.

The focal point of the movie occurs when Cecilia leads Tom into a church where he asks who Jesus is. She tells him that Jesus is God who created the heaven and the earth. Tom says that he does not have the concept of God written into his character. She says that God is similar to the writers who created him, in that God created everything that exists. At this point the actor Gil, who played Tom in the production of the movie, comes on the scene and wrestles with Tom underneath the cross. The two natures—the good Tom and the evil Gil—are wrestling for the love of the heroine. The person he was created to be fights with the fallen self underneath the symbol of creation and redemption.

Finally, Gil tricks Tom into going back into the picture by winning Cecilia's affections with false promises. Then, as soon as Tom is back on screen, Gil heads back to Hollywood, leaving Cecilia with her memories and her dreams.

There are many more levels of theological meaning in this film. Clearly, it should be seen for its gospel associations. It is truly wonderful that God can call unbelievers to communicate His story.

THE QUEST (1986)

RATING: PG   ★★★
CONTENT: Nothing objectionable
INTENDED AUDIENCE: Families
STARRING: Henry Thomas, Tony Barry
DIRECTOR: Brian Trenchard-Smith

The Quest is an exciting, fun film from Australia which adults and children can enjoy. The only problem is the brief, almost innocuous references to magic, which is shown really to be previously unexplained physical phenomena. This is not a Christian film, but it will not offend Christians.

The Quest opens with a man sitting in a boat in a muddy pond. Suddenly, there is a chug, chug, chugging sound and this "thing" comes out of the water and pulls the boat under the water! Is it some hoax or a stone-eating monster named Dunkagin? The suspense builds. Everyone is spooked and the dialogue is quite funny. A character named Cody decides to find out about the monster of the pond. He decides to go on a quest to meet the "monster" face to face. In the end courage triumphs over fear.

This is a good movie, although there are some references to magic you might want to discuss with your children. **L.B., P.B.** and **J.B.**

QUICKSILVER (1986)

RATING: PG   ★★
CONTENT: Some profanity
INTENDED AUDIENCE: Teenagers and adults
STARRING: Kevin Bacon, Jami Gertz, Paul Rodriquez
DIRECTOR: Tom Donnelly

Although this movie has potential, it does not deliver. The problem is that the plot does not hold together. It begins as the interesting story of a young stockbroker who goes bust and finds himself a new life as a bicycle messenger, but it ends up being a stale chase through the streets of San Francisco, pursuing an evil drug pusher.

The acting is excellent. The actors are relatively unknown, but they show real talent. The direction is good. However, the morals are suspect, and the plot is weak. *Quicksilver* is not worth your time.

THE QUIET EARTH (1986)

RATING: R
CONTENT: Frontal nudity
INTENDED AUDIENCE: Adults
STARRING: Bruno Lawrence, Alison Routledge, Peter Smith
DIRECTOR: Geoff Murphy

The Quiet Earth is a New Zealand remake of *The Night of the Comet* and *The World, the Flesh and the Devil*, only now the cause of the destruction of mankind is the United States. One man who survives the cataclysm spends most of the movie being petty. He finds two other survivors. The world is on the brink of a new age of weirdness.

Good production values cannot help this film become more than mediocre. Brief frontal nudity takes it out of the boundaries of acceptable viewing. **B.G.**

THE QUIET MAN (1952), 129 min.

CONTENT: Nothing objectionable   ★★★★
INTENDED AUDIENCE: Adults
STARRING: John Wayne, Maureen O'Hara, Victor McLaglen, Ward Bond, Barry Fitzgerald
DIRECTOR: John Ford

The Quiet Man takes place in Ireland, where ex-boxer Wayne has come to leave behind his troubles in America. He wants to be a "quiet man," and find peace in the Irish countryside. It takes some time, especially after he falls in love with fiery Maureen O'Hara and has to settle the score between himself and new brother-in-law Victor McLaglen. In one of the grandest donnybrooks ever staged, Wayne and McLaglen fight it out, becoming the best of friends afterwards.

The film develops a very strong sense of family and tradition, with sentiment and love-for-the-land subtleties that John Ford weaves through the story. Filmed in the lovely Irish countryside, the scenery is breathtaking. Highly recommended. **B.G.**

RADIO DAYS (1987)

RATING: PG   ★★
CONTENT: Limited profanity, occasional irreverence, and some crude humor
INTENDED AUDIENCE: Adults
STARRING: Mia Farrow, Diane Keaton, Julie Kavner, Michael Tucker, Diane Wiest, Seth Green, Jeff Daniels, Tony Roberts
DIRECTOR: Woody Allen

Radio Days is Woody Allen's semi-autobiographical, boyhood recollection of the big-band melodies and radio fantasies of the forties when, as one reviewer has noted, "viewers were listeners and little bald men with big voices could be superheroes." The movie is a collage of vignettes presented in chronological order and keyed to popular songs and radio programs of the era. Although this is a well-made movie, it falls short of the vision of the previous fourteen films Allen has made.

Set in the New York City beach community of Rockaway, the story features an extended Jewish family: mother, father, son (Woody's alter ego), and assorted aunts and uncles. In spite of the fact that the family members are very real, fat, somewhat unattractive, and bicker continually, it is clear that they love each other. Interwoven with the family story is the fantasy story of a cigarette girl at the famous Stork Club, Sally White, who makes it to the top to become a gossip columnist for the rich and famous.

It is Sally's story that most deeply mars the film. She sleeps her way to the top while still being portrayed as a sympathetic person. *Radio Days* cannot be recommended for Christians. **L.B.**

RAINBOW BRITE AND THE STAR STEALER (1985)

RATING: G ★★★
CONTENT: The mention of magic
INTENDED AUDIENCE: Children
STARRING: Animated characters
DIRECTORS: Bernard Deyries, Kimiel Yabuki

This is a surprisingly good movie that children thoroughly enjoy. The evil queen is realistically motivated by selfishness. The heroes, Rainbow Brite and Chris, are good, but not saccharine. In the end, courageous good triumphs over selfish evil. The only problem is the mention of magic, but it serves the purpose of stressing the need for goodness. If you see the film with your children, tell them the difference between magic and prayer.

A RAISIN IN THE SUN (1961) B&W, 128 min.

CONTENT: Nothing objectionable ★★★★
INTENDED AUDIENCE: Adolescents and adults
STARRING: Sidney Poitier, Diana Sands, Ivan Dixon, Lou Gossett, Ruby Dee, Claudia McNeil
DIRECTOR: Daniel Petrie

Sidney Poitier portrays Walter Lee Younger, a frustrated young man seeking dignity for himself and his family, as they struggle to live in a tiny house in a ghetto in Chicago. Lena Younger, Walter's mother, wants to use the dead father's insurance money to help her daughter through school and to buy a house. Walter sees the money as a way to break the chains of his poverty and economic enslavement. He wants to invest in a liquor store and remove himself from having to chauffeur a white man.

Though the story takes place primarily within the confines of their small home, it captures the essence of each of the actors and the dynamics of the Younger family. This is a worthy portrait of a family at odds, yet at peace with each other. Under many burdens, the Younger family still holds on to their dignity. Recommended. **B.G.**

RAN (1985)
(Subtitles)

CONTENT: Violence and cruelty ★★★
INTENDED AUDIENCE: Adults
STARRING: Tatsuya Nakadai, Akira Terao, Daisuke Ryu
DIRECTOR: Akira Kurosawa

The Japanese director Akira Kurosawa is a favorite with many critics, even though most of his films are clumsy, portentous, and poorly acted. *Ran* is a case in point. It is not bad, but it is a slow, stagy film that never quite captures the audience's attention.

Basically, it is a Japanese *King Lear*, even though it is based on the true story of a sixteenth-century Japanese warlord whose sons turn against him when he tries to give them their inheritance. Unlike *King Lear*, where the premise is "vanity leads to self-destruction," the premise here is muddled by the secondary plot of revenge. The premise turns out to be "revenge destroys a kingdom." The photography is excellent and makes the movie worth seeing in spite of its other defects. However, exercise caution; violence and cruelty fill this heroic epic.

RANGER COURAGE (1937) B&W

CONTENT: Good, clean, moral, old-fashioned Western　　　★★★
INTENDED AUDIENCE: Children of all ages
STARRING: Bob Allen, Martha Tibbetts, Walter Miller, Buzzy Henry, Bud Osborne, Bob Kortman, Harry Strang, Bill Gould, Horace Murphy, Jay Wilsey
DIRECTOR: Spencer Gordon Bennett

The wagon train is in the protective circle for the night. Soft music drifts across the scene. As the wagoneers prepare to bed down, a band of renegade Indians (really white men masquerading as Indians) attacks. The wagon train survives, but not without a fight in this Bob Allen, Ranger, film. A lot of action and adventure, as the good guys win out in the end. **R.A.**

THE RANGER STEPS IN (1936) B&W

CONTENT: Nothing objectionable　　　★★★
INTENDED AUDIENCE: Children and families
STARRING: Bob Allen, Eleanor Stewart, John Merton, Hal Taliaferro, Jack Ingram, Jack Rockwell, Jay Wilsey, Rafe McKee
DIRECTOR: Spencer Gordon Bennett

The Ranger Steps In opens with Martin (John Merton) telling his men that the Allens and the Warrens came West bringing their Kentucky feud with them. The Allens outnumber the Warrens two- or three-to-one, so he figures the Warrens will move on, then he can take over their property and sell it at a profit to the railroad men for a "right of way."

Martin watches the shooting feud between the two ranch groups. The Marshall (Jack Rockwell) tries to stop the gunfight by riding in under a flag of truce, but is shot at by Martin who wants the feud to continue. The Marshall (only wounded) says he'll call in the Rangers to stop the fighting, and that's when all the fun begins in this traditional, shoot-'em up Western. Good entertainment. **R.A.**

RATBOY (1986)

RATING: PG–13　　　★★★
CONTENT: Mild bad language
INTENDED AUDIENCE: Adults
STARRING: Sondra Locke
DIRECTOR: Sondra Locke

Ratboy tells the story of a mysterious boy who resembles a cross between a rat and a person. Ratboy is captured by some ex-convicts who want to sell him for a small fortune, but they themselves fall prey to an opportunistic woman who tries to turn Ratboy into a Hollywood star. Confused by the fact that everyone wants to use him, Ratboy prays to be free of the nightmare in which he is caught. He is a stranger in a strange land of greed and exploitation. Eventually, he escapes the clutches of all the "normal" people but leaves a gift for his female captor whom he loves.

Like *The Elephant Man*, *Ratboy* shows up the sinfulness of fallen man by the way people react to someone whose appearance is radically different from that of a normal human being.

This is an interesting movie, a worthwhile study of man's sinfulness, but its ambiguousness will make it too obtuse for most audiences.

RAW DEAL (1986)

RATING: R
CONTENT: Profanity and violence
INTENDED AUDIENCE: Adults
STARRING: Arnold Schwarzenegger, Kathryn Harrold, Darren McGavin, Sam Wanamaker
DIRECTOR: John Irvin

Raw Deal is a slick piece of action-violence. There are some human touches, in particular a touching scene of love and support at the end, but Arnold still has trouble convincing us that he is the person he is playing in this movie about a former FBI agent hired to destroy a Mafia family.

Suspense and conflict are sustained throughout this exciting movie. However, there are great gaps in logic. Furthermore, the language is vile, and the violence is gruesome. Although good triumphs over evil and the hero refuses to give in to the temptation of extramarital sex, this film is unsuitable for Christians.

REAL GENIUS (1985)

RATING: PG
CONTENT: Profanity and obscenity
INTENDED AUDIENCE: Teenagers
STARRING: Val Kilmer, Gabe Jarret, Michelle Meyrink
DIRECTOR: Martha Coolidge

This pretentious story of young geniuses defeating the greedy professor presents an anti-authority and antiwork viewpoint. Revenge is the only viable human motivation, according to this second-rate film. Excessive swearing and a sophomoric display of useless knowledge do nothing to help this weak story with weak characters. Not recommended.

RECKLESS RANGER (1936) B&W

CONTENT: Nothing objectionable   ★★★
INTENDED AUDIENCE: Children and their families
STARRING: Bob Allen, Louise Small, Mary MacLaren, Harry Woods, Jack Perrin, Jack Rockwell, Buddy Cox, Slim Whitaker
DIRECTOR: Spencer Gordon Bennett

Reckless Ranger is a fun, family film made when heroes wore white hats and the good guy was really good. Bob Allen plays twin brothers, Jim Allen and Bob Allen. The plot of the story develops around the heavies (the cattlemen) trying to drive the sheep-herders off the land by killing off the sheep. Bob, masquerading as his dead brother, Jim, lassos and captures two of the heavies involved in the hanging and brings them in. Good, clean entertainment. **B.A.**

RED RIVER (1948) B&W, 125 min.

CONTENT: Nothing objectionable   ★★★★

INTENDED AUDIENCE: All ages
STARRING: John Wayne, Montgomery Clift, Joanne Dru, Walter Brennan,
John Ireland
DIRECTOR: Howard Hawks

Red River is the classic Western, the story of the first cattle drive along the famed Chisholm Trail. The movie focuses on the relationship of a father, Tom Dunson, and his foster son, Matt Garth. Tom is a self-made cattle baron, who will not be stopped from doing what he wants by anyone. When a Mexican tries to stop Tom from building a ranch on land he has just claimed, Tom shoots and then buries him, reading from the Bible. Eventually, he finds himself in opposition to Matt as Matt takes his herd to Abilene. A real Western.

RED SONJA (1985), 88 min.

RATING: PG–13   ★★
CONTENT: Violence
INTENDED AUDIENCE: Young adults
STARRING: Arnold Schwarzenegger, Brigitte Nielsen, Sandahl Bergman
DIRECTOR: Richard Fliescher

This is the third *Conan* film starring the nice but musclebound Arnold Schwarzenegger. Here, Conan meets his match in the female warrior Red Sonja. Eventually, they team up to save the world from destruction by a talisman in the hands of a crazed queen. This is pure comic book fare—good action and adventure with lots of violence. It is acceptable to some, but not for the squeamish.

REMO WILLIAMS: THE ADVENTURE BEGINS (1985)

RATING: PG–13
CONTENT: Mysticism and anti-Christian world view
INTENDED AUDIENCE: Adults
STARRING: Fred Ward, Joel Grey, Charles Cioffi
DIRECTOR: Guy Hamilton

This is a perverse movie about a killer cop who is recruited by the president's supersecret SS to defend the state from unscrupulous free enterprise capitalists. The savior is an ancient Korean martial arts master who can walk on water. Unfortunately, he is dedicated to serving the state and death, and he teaches Remo all kinds of mystical things he can use to defeat his opponents. The values presented are inside out. Avoid it, unless you want to waste your time watching evil triumph over evil.

RETURN TO OZ (1985), 118 min.

RATING: PG   ★★★
CONTENT: Scary in parts
INTENDED AUDIENCE: Families
STARRING: Fairuza Balk, Nicol Williamson, Jean Marsh
DIRECTOR: Walter Murch

This is not a great picture on the order of *The Wizard of Oz* (1939); however, in terms of acceptable entertainment, it is far better than most films and should prove to be a children's favorite. What's missing in this film is the lighthearted joy of *The Wizard of Oz*. For some reason it captures the bleak fantasy of Frank Baum's books and avoids the enchantment.

The plot is simple. Good triumphs over evil as Dorothy's goodness, faithfulness, and love for her friends triumph over the evil Nome King and free the people of Oz who have been turned to stone. Some moments are too strong for young children. However, it shows the ugliness of evil and clearly identifies the good as the path to choose. The film is recommended, but don't compare it to the 1939 movie.

REVOLUTION (1985)

RATING: PG ★★★
CONTENT: Very mild language
INTENDED AUDIENCE: Adults
STARRING: Al Pacino, Donald Sutherland
DIRECTOR: Hugh Hudson

This story of a father and son who fight in the American Revolution seems to understand that the war was fought to protect the rights of each individual to be free, have a family, and own property without that property being stolen by the state through confiscation or excessive taxation. You may want to see it because it promotes these values.

There are a few minor flaws. The scope of the movie remains small, tightly focused on the lives of the father and son, and battle sequences leave much to be desired. Also, the dialogue drags in a few sections, and the internal logic of events does not always hold up or appear authentic. The casting is particularly uninspired, with the British portrayed in caricature rather than developed as real characters. Furthermore, the ending does not reach an emotional climax.

It is encouraging that the few sexual advances are quickly rebuked and shown to be wrong. It is particularly heartwarming to see a British officer pray the *Twenty-Third Psalm* and have his prayer answered. Overall, the film is pretty good entertainment.

RIO GRANDE RANGER (1936) B&W

CONTENT: Good, moral movie ★★★
INTENDED AUDIENCE: Children and their families
STARRING: Bob Allen, Iris Meredith, Paul Sutton, Hal Taliaferro, Robert Henry, John Elliot, Tom London, Slim Whitaker, Jack Rockwell
DIRECTOR: Spencer Gordon Bennett

Bob and Hal are called into the Texas Ranger office and told to do some undercover work in Shanto City, across the state line, where bad guy Jim Sayers gives sanctuary to marauding rustlers and bank robbers. Innumerable escapes follow till Bob finally rides off into the sunset with his gal. Another fine movie in this B Western series. **R.A.**

ROCKY IV (1985)

RATING: PG ★★★
CONTENT: Violence in the ring
INTENDED AUDIENCE: All ages
STARRING: Sylvester Stallone, Talia Shire, Burt Young
DIRECTOR: Sylvester Stallone

This has to be one of the most entertaining movies to come from Hollywood in a long time, and it has no profanity, nudity, or sex. Of course, it has its share of violence, but the violence is controlled in the boxing ring and is not malicious. It even has some clear references to prayer and the resurrection of Jesus.

Rocky comes out of retirement to fight a Russian challenger. Relying on good old American ingenuity and hard work, Rocky beats the doped-up, synthetic Russian. This is straight comic book material, but very enjoyable. It is a good, entertaining movie that is worth seeing.

A ROOM WITH A VIEW (1986)

CONTENT: Brief, distant nude swimming   ★★★★
INTENDED AUDIENCE: Adults
STARRING: Helena Bonham Carter, Denholm Elliott, Julian Sands, Maggie Smith
DIRECTOR: James Ivory

A Room with a View is an entertaining, enlightening, intelligent, beautiful, positive movie with no sex, no profanity, and no violence. This bright, cheery comedy of manners was adapted from E. M. Forster's novel by the same name. It provides a humorous look at the pretensions of the cultural gadflies of the Edwardian era. In our age of infatuation with culture, it is even more humorous to watch this film poke fun at the stuffy Edwardians who toured the Continent and became so adept at second-guessing art.

Aunt Charlotte and her charge, Lucy Honeychurch, leave their upper-middle-class world in England for a cultural tour of Florence. It is hard for these cultural aficionados to stay prim in the midst of the passionate Italians who created the beauty they are viewing, and Lucy falls for a young man she eventually marries. The only flaw is a brief, distant, male skinny-dipping scene that is so natural it will not offend most viewers, although it could have been omitted. On the other hand, the parson is a positive, sympathetic character. Highly recommended, with a caution as noted. **L.B.**

ROUND MIDNIGHT (1985)

RATING: PG(?)   ★★★
CONTENT: Very mild bad language
INTENDED AUDIENCE: Adults
STARRING: Dexter Gordan, Francois Cuzet
DIRECTOR: Bertrand Travanier

The movie chronicles the last years of Dale Turner, a famous blues saxophone player who died in the mid-1960s. If you love blues music, you'll love it. It is beautifully photographed. The moral—"the wages of sin is death"—is well worth remembering. However, the film also tells us that love can overcome sin, if the sinner sincerely repents.

The story begins with Dale clearly on his way out. He is an alcoholic and perhaps a drug addict. But some people help him dry out and get back on his feet. Dale begins to cut records again and regain his musical excellence. His recovery is short-lived, though, and he seems headed for self-destruction. Dale dies, never having repented. This is a good film with a poignant message. **E.R.**

RUMPELSTILTSKIN (1987)

RATING: G   ★★★

CONTENT: Magical thinking
INTENDED AUDIENCE: Families
STARRING: Amy Irving, Robert Symonds, Clive Revill, Priscilla Pointer,
John Moulder Brown, Billy Barty, Yael Uziely
DIRECTOR: David Irving

Rumpelstiltskin is set a long time ago in a small kingdom, where the beautiful Katie (Amy Irving) and her father Victor (Robert Symonds), a poor miller, live in a small cottage. Victor is a foolish braggart. One day, he boasts to another peasant that Katie can spin straw into gold. This information finds its way to the greedy King Mezzer (Clive Revill) and Queen Grizelda (Priscilla Pointer) who bring Katie to the palace and set her to work. But for the intervention of a scheming dwarf, Katie would be in big trouble! As it is, in the end she must outsmart even the dwarf. As is the case with all fairy tales, Christians must warn their children about the fact that these tales are pure fantasy and the magic in them is not real or commendable. Still, the movie is pretty good if handled with caution.

RUNAWAY TRAIN (1985)

RATING: R
CONTENT: Profanity, violence, and nudity
INTENDED AUDIENCE: Adults
STARRING: Jon Voight, Eric Roberts, Rebecca DeMornay
DIRECTOR: Andrei Konchalovsky

Jon Voight's powerful acting makes this sad tale work, but he can't move this *Runaway Train* off the wrong track, which is its existentialist world view. It has great action and great acting, but it is devoid of hope.

The opening prison scenes are some of the toughest, roughest, cruelest scenes ever filmed. This is a gruesome portrait of the worst in man—anti-authority, antihumanity. Furthermore, the script is second rate. Avoid this rough movie.

RUNNING MATES (1986)

RATING: PG(?)   ★★★
CONTENT: Mild swearing
INTENDED AUDIENCE: Adults
STARRING: Greg Webb, Barbara Howell
DIRECTOR: Michael Vanroff

This insightful, moral portrait of politics uses the romantic relationship between a young woman and a young man, children of opposing mayoral candidates, as a focal point. This film has no nudity or violence, and at one point, someone sings a song about Jesus. The innocence of the romance is in stark contrast to the rotten politics. Basically a wholesome movie, it is not great, but it is not bad entertainment. **J.C.J.**

RUNNING SCARED (1985)

RATING: R
CONTENT: Brief nudity, promiscuity, and offensive language
INTENDED AUDIENCE: Young adults

STARRING: Gregory Hines, Billy Crystal
DIRECTOR: Peter Hyams

Two Chicago cops are running scared, but they keep getting their man anyway. After many failures, they are pushed too hard by the leading drug dealer in Chicago and decide to stop running and get him. After a spectacular gunfight, they win the war, and justice triumphs.

Brief nudity, promiscuity, and offensive language undermine this positive story. Also, the dialogue is weak, and the first half of the movie is slow because there is no conflict. It is not worth your time.

RUTHLESS PEOPLE (1985)

RATING: R
CONTENT: Abundant profanity
INTENDED AUDIENCE: Adults
STARRING: Danny DeVito, Bette Midler, Judge Reinhold, Helen Slater
DIRECTORS: Jim Abrahams, David Zucker, Jerry Zucker

This is an antifamily, anti-Christian movie filled with sexual situations, nudity, and abundant profanity. The plot is rotten. A wealthy henpecked husband wants to kill his wife. But before he has a chance, she is kidnapped by two likable fortune hunters. The police suspect that he has actually killed his wife, so he reluctantly gives $2.2 million to the kidnappers to get the police off his back. The kidnappers get away with the money, and he ends up broke but happy with his wife.

This film features fraud, extortion, and coercion. It witnesses to the worst in man—his sin. Don't see it. **K.G.** and **D.G.**

THE SACRIFICE (1987)

RATING: PG ★★★
CONTENT: Shadow nudity, sexual situations, and supernaturalism, but
  also a strong witness to Jesus as Lord
INTENDED AUDIENCE: Adults
STARRING: Erland Josephson, Susan Fleetwood, Valerie Mairesse, Allan Edwall,
  Gudrun Gilsadottir
DIRECTOR: Andrei Tarkovskij

The Sacrifice is the story of Alexander, who is possessed by visions of the end of the world. His wife is cruel. His daughter doesn't care about him. The only real relationship he has is with his young son.

At one point, in the midst of a dream that the world is in the middle of a nuclear war, Alexander gets to his knees and prays the Lord's Prayer. Then he offers up his life and all he has to God. However, next he turns to superstition in his dream and goes to sleep with a witch to save the world. He awakes, but is still demented. He burns his house as a sacrifice, and ends up being carted away to the asylum. His son continues to water the dead tree they planted as some sort of memorial act of faith. In fact, this film is beautifully made, with no profanity and only a little shadow nudity. The trouble is, there is a mix of superstition and true faith. Recommended with caution.

SALVADOR (1986)

RATING: R
CONTENT: Excessive profanity, nudity, and violence
INTENDED AUDIENCE: Adults
STARRING: James Woods, Jim Belushi, Michael Murphy
DIRECTOR: Oliver Stone

This movie is an attempt to attack democracy and promote the goals of Communist revolutionaries. It is based on journalist Richard Boyle's trip to El Salvador in 1980. The Communist rebels are the heroes in Boyle's eyes, and all evil is laid at the feet of the legitimate government. The movie is constructed so that Boyle witnesses every questionable occurrence in Latin America, and the government of El Salvador and the right-wing paramilitary groups are portrayed as the guilty parties. Boyle reports all the evil perpetrated by the government, has sex, drinks, lies, curses, begs money, gets married (even though he is already married back in the States), and heads back to the USA, exhausted by his tour of the revolution. Boyle makes it clear that he hates all authority, especially American.

The problem is that the free world listens to reporters like Boyle and is seduced into believing the lies of a movie like this one until the revolution occurs and the truth is out in the open. Christians must counter with a biblical world view that condemns deceit and lifts up the truth. Avoid this film, and tell your friends to avoid it.

SANTA CLAUS (1985)

RATING: PG
CONTENT: Anti-Christian, sacrilegious, and boring
INTENDED AUDIENCE: Children
STARRING: Dudley Moore, John Lithgow, David Huddleston
DIRECTOR: Jeannot Szwarc

The first twenty minutes of this big-budget picture are an advertisement for consumerism run amuck—pure plastic pretending to be craftsmanship. The rest of the movie is a hackneyed replay of the big, bad businessman who tries to steal Christmas.

Too bad the producer's don't realize that they are the big, bad businessmen who are trying to steal Christmas by denying the Savior of the world. On the other hand, maybe they do realize what they are doing, since they keep alluding to Santa Claus as the chosen one and attach other messianic titles to him. Try not to let your children see it.

SEVEN BRIDES FOR SEVEN BROTHERS (1954), 102 min.

CONTENT: Nothing objectionable   ★★★
INTENDED AUDIENCE: All ages
STARRING: Jane Powell, Howard Keel, Jeff Richards, Russ Tamblyn
DIRECTOR: Stanley Donen

Set in 1850 in Oregon, this film tells the story of seven strapping, pioneer back-woodsmen, led by elder brother Howard Keel, who want wives. Keel goes into town and comes back with new bride Jane Powell, inspiring the other six brothers to do the same, simple as that. The brothers go into town and kidnap the girls they love and return to the ranch, but an avalanche keeps the angry townspeople out until spring arrives. When the snow melts and the townspeople confront the boys, the girls intervene because they love the brothers too much to have them shot.

With its toe-tapping musical numbers, written by Johnny Mercer and Gene de Paul, and choreography by Michael Kidd (who received a special citation from The National Film Board), it is easy to overlook the minor technical problems that trouble early color films. You'll love it. **B.G.**

SEVEN DAYS IN MAY (1964), 118 mins.

CONTENT: Minor swearing and adult situations ★★★
INTENDED AUDIENCE: Adults
STARRING: Burt Lancaster, Kirk Douglas, Fredric March, Ava Gardner, Edmund O'Brien, Martin Balsam
DIRECTOR: John Frankenheimer

A spylike thriller about a possible coup d'état in Washington, D.C., this film is a taut drama with a fine cast and a tight script. It is a well-crafted story that has us following the wrong trail—the trail of a threat from our own military rather than the real threat from the Communists.

The chairman of the Joint Chiefs of Staff heads a plot to overthrow the president of the United States and take control of the government on a Sunday in May. He is fearful of a nuclear disarmament treaty the president is negotiating with the Soviets, and he wants to take command before the USA is sold out to the Communists. But his allies in the attempted takeover desert him at the last moment, and the coup fails.

Seven Days in May presents a world view that undermines the defense of the free world and presents defense itself as the enemy of freedom rather than the God-given right to protect ourselves. In fact, it is a good presentation of the tack we have taken, which is to compromise in the misplaced hope that there is some goodness in the hearts of the Soviets. For biblical Christians, the film is an instructive study in how people can be stripped of the will to take a stand against the forces of evil. **B.G.**

SHANE (1953), 118 min.

CONTENT: Mild, fifties style violence ★★★★
INTENDED AUDIENCE: Adults
STARRING: Alan Ladd, Jean Arthur, Van Heflin, Jack Palance, Ben Johnson
DIRECTOR: George Stevens

Shane is a classic Western. Set in Wyoming's Grand Tetons in 1890, it is the tale of the cattlemen against the homesteading sod-buster. Shane, an ex-gunfighter, drifts into the area and becomes involved with one of the homesteaders (Van Heflin), his wife, and their young son.

The film is a brilliant work of genius, from its tight script, which realistically portrays life on the range, to the interplay between the characters: Heflin and his wife; Shane and their son; the cattlemen and the sod-busters. The story is the triumph of good over evil, which comes at a price: the homesteaders lose their farms, some even lose their lives. Yet, the film's tone is one of moral imperatives, tenacity, loyalty, and all the Christian virtues.

The acting is superb, with Ladd giving his finest performance. The director, George Stevens, handles the grimness of death, pathos and bittersweet rewards with equal effectiveness. A great movie. **B. G.**

SHANGHAI SURPRISE (1986)

RATING: R(?)
CONTENT: Profanity, vulgarity, and violence
INTENDED AUDIENCE: Teenagers and young adults
STARRING: Sean Penn, Madonna
DIRECTOR: Jim Goddard

The story takes place in 1937, the year of the Japanese occupation of Shanghai. The heroine and the hero—a poor little rich girl with a bleeding heart and a pseudoreligious cause and a handsome young man of the world—try to find five missing crates of opium so that wounded Chinese soldiers can be helped. Mix into the plot a silly missionary, a con man, a rickshaw chase, a cricket fight to the death, a night of amour, and Chinese torture. If it sounds like a grade-C soap opera, you are right.

The cinematography is excellent, but the story is implausible and the acting is weak. The movie is filled with profanity, vulgar jokes, and some violence. There is no nudity, but nothing else in the love scenes is left to the imagination. Sadly, the main attraction for teenagers and young adults will be Madonna and her husband, Sean Penn, who are certainly not good role models for young Christians. Christians should boycott this movie.

SHE DONE HIM WRONG (1933) B&W, 66 min.

CONTENT: Sexual innuendo   ★★
INTENDED AUDIENCE: Adults
STARRING: Mae West, Cary Grant, Noah Beery, Gilbert Roland, Rafaela Ottiano, David Landau
DIRECTOR: Lowell Sherman

This movie is of historical interest to Christians. *She Done Him Wrong* was one of the movies that galvanized churches into taking a stand against immorality in Hollywood in the early thirties. Looking at this movie from our vantage point today, it seems very mild. This change in our perspective speaks volumes about how the entertainment industry has decayed into a smut industry and how many of us have been corrupted by what we see.

The film is based on Mae West's stage play, *Diamond Lil*. Set in New York's Bowery in the 1890's, it tells of Gus Jordan, the boss of a nightclub, who is a counterfeiter and white-slaver and Miss West's beau. Cary Grant plays a notorious police agent, "The Hawk," masquerading as a missionary. In the conflict that ensues, the two men vie for Miss West. Not for Christians.

SHEER MADNESS (1985)

(Subtitles)
CONTENT: Feminism run amuck
INTENDED AUDIENCE: Adults
STARRING: Hanna Shygalla
DIRECTOR: Margarethe Von Trotta

Margarethe Von Trotta is a renowned German director and ardent feminist, and this film blames women's problems on men. Basically, men are boors who suppress women because they are afraid of women. This simplistic view illustrates a complete lack of biblical wisdom and Christian compassion.

The story involves Olga and her husband who meet neurotic painter Ruth and her husband Franz on a vacation. Most of the action focuses on problems between the latter two because he opposes an exhibition of her paintings. These characters are trivial and inane, and their primary problem is alienation from God. Not recommended. **K.K.**

SHIP OF FOOLS (1965), 149 min.

CONTENT: Nothing objectionable   ★ ★
INTENDED AUDIENCE: Adults
STARRING: Vivien Leigh, Jose Ferrer, Oskar Werner, Simone Signoret, Lee Marvin
DIRECTOR: Stanley Kramer

This film shows us everything from petty rivalries to racial prejudice, with a smattering of gratuitous sex, violence, and alcoholism. Set on a cargo/cruise ship making a voyage from Vera Cruz to Germany via Mexico in 1933, the film is a "human condition" movie of the sixties. Apparently *Ship of Fools* is trying to draw a parallel between the pre-war German race-hatred and anti-Semitism and to the social climate of early sixties America.

What does the film really say? That man is basically evil, and life is meaningless. There is no real happiness, no real security . . . it's all vanity. We're all selfish, blind people, clinging to what we perceive is ours as we stumble down the road of life. Not recommended unless one enjoys being depressed. **L.R.**

SHOAH (1986)
(Subtitles)
CONTENT: Nothing objectionable   ★ ★
INTENDED AUDIENCE: Adults
DIRECTOR: Claude Lanzmann

Shoah is the Hebrew word for "annihilation." In this nine-and-one-half-hour epic about the horror of the Holocaust, there is not one frame of newsreel footage. Instead, Claude Lanzmann asks blunt questions of survivors, guards, and anyone else who was associated with the extermination of millions of Jews.

This film is too long for most people, unless it is broken into parts and shown on television, but it is a moving Kaddish—a chant for the dead. Also, it underlines the sinfulness of man. **J.C.J.**

THE SHOOTING PARTY (1985), 108 min.

CONTENT: Very brief nudity   ★ ★ ★ ★
INTENDED AUDIENCE: Adults
STARRING: James Mason, Edward Fox, John Gielgud
DIRECTOR: Alan Bridges

This excellent film has strong Christian subplots. It speaks to us today by portraying life in 1913 through the focal point of a powerful premise, that is, "moral decadence leads to war." As we watch some of the English aristocracy who are assembled for a shoot of game birds, it becomes evident that they have lost their moral moorings. The one beacon of graciousness, the grandfather lord of the manor, has lost his drive to teach and disciple the younger generation who are seeking their own self-interests. At the end of the film, tending a common man who has been shot by one of the selfishly competitive aristocrats, the lord of the manor is barely able to say a prayer to commit the dying man to Jesus.

The acting is superb. The scene between the passionately wrong-headed, self-serving John Gielgud and the gentle lord of the manor, James Mason, is a classic. This confrontation alone makes it worth seeing. One brief nude scene underlines the theme of moral decadence. Unfortunately, this scene may keep some people from seeing this profoundly moral film, which ends with a prayer and the dedication of a man's life to our Lord and Savior. This film is a must for anyone who is interested in the roots of war and anarchy.

SHORT CIRCUIT (1986), 139 min.

RATING: PG   ★★★
CONTENT: Obscenity
INTENDED AUDIENCE: Adults
STARRING: Ally Sheedy, Steve Guttenberg
DIRECTOR: John Badham

Short Circuit opens with a spectacular war between dummy troops, conventional tanks, and five red-eyed robots, simulated by the military establishment and Nova Laboratories to obtain funding from visiting senators for a future robot army of America. All goes well until one senator asks to talk with the genius inventor, a young man ill at ease away from his computers and nauseated by society. Things get complicated when one robot escapes, and the military goes on a search-and-destroy mission to find it. We follow the robot through a roller-coaster adventure of dangerous attacks and escapes.

This movie has everything going for it that a good movie should have: adventure, humor, romance, imagination, freshness, and enjoyment. However, offensive dialogue kills the wonderful qualities that make the film worth seeing. **G.O.**

A SHOT IN THE DARK (1964), 101 min.

CONTENT: Some bawdy humor   ★★★
INTENDED AUDIENCE: All ages
STARRING: Peter Sellers, Elke Sommer, George Sanders, Herbert Lom,
    Tracy Reed, Burt Kwouk
DIRECTOR: Blake Edwards

Inspector Clouseau is looking for three killers who have committed murder under his very nose. He bumbles and stumbles into rivers, ornamental ponds and some risqué places trying to find out whodunit. *A Shot in the Dark* also plays upon the hilarious conflict between Clouseau and his long-suffering superior at the Surete, Inspector Dreyfus, as well as the competition between Clouseau and his karate-chopping valet, Kato.

This is a funny, but bawdy movie.

SILVER BULLET (1985), 135 min.

RATING: R
CONTENT: Foul-mouthed, occult attack on the church
INTENDED AUDIENCE: Adults
STARRING: Gary Busey, Everett McGill, Corey Haim
DIRECTOR: Daniel Attias

This film is another of writer Stephen King's occult attacks on the church. Here the foul-mouthed good guys finally kill the fundamentalist preacher who turns into a werewolf by night. Besides being an insult to God, it's a bad horror story. There is nothing to recommend it.

SILVERADO (1985), 213 min.

RATING: PG-13   ★★★
CONTENT: Mild obscenity
INTENDED AUDIENCE: All ages
STARRING: Kevin Kline, Scott Glenn, Rosanna Arquette
DIRECTOR: Lawrence Kasdan

This revival of the classical Western is good entertainment, but nothing special. The action is tight; the language is surprisingly mild; and the message of compassion, concern, and mercy is refreshing. However, the characters are weak and underdeveloped, and there are no real bonds of friendship. Furthermore, God has been left out of the town of *Silverado*, creating an unreal portrait of the Old West.

Four men team up to rid a town of a ruthless, cruel, and immoral sheriff. The sheriff has driven off or intimidated every honest person in the town until our four heroes stand up to him and his robber baron boss who hovers in the background. In the end, good triumphs over evil. In spite of its failings, it is worth seeing, and Hollywood should be financially encouraged to make more movies that are this upstanding.

16 DAYS OF GLORY (1986)

RATING: G   ★★★
CONTENT: Nothing objectionable
INTENDED AUDIENCE: All ages
STARRING: The athletes of the 1984 Olympics
DIRECTOR: Bud Greenspan

This well-made, entertaining documentary about the 1984 Olympics in Los Angeles is a movie the whole family can see and enjoy. There are a few flaws, however. It fails to focus on some of the more important sports and achievements. Also, there is no mention of the faith of some of the contestants. Furthermore, the film opens with an ode to Los Angeles instead of the United States of America. Human achievement and utopian brotherhood are the focal points rather than the spiritual character that gives so many athletes the winning edge. And the final hymn to the almighty Father is interpreted as a hymn to human achievement and the countries that participated. Yet the lack of a spiritual dimension does not detract from the fact that the film is exhilarating, triumphant, and worth seeing as an enjoyable insight into the drama of the Olympics.

SLEEPER (1973), 88 min.

RATING: PG   ★★
CONTENT: Mild off-color language and innuendo
INTENDED AUDIENCE: Adolescents and adults
STARRING: Woody Allen, Diane Keaton, John Beck
DIRECTOR: Woody Allen

Sleeper is Woody Allen's answer to *2001: A Space Odyssey*. Allen plays Miles Monroe, the timid owner of a Greenwich Village health food store, who goes into the hospital for a minor ulcer operation and gets cryogenically frozen. He is thawed two hundred years later. Miles awakes to find a world—totally different from 1973—where smoking and eating fatty foods are good for you, and prison inmates are forced to watch Howard Cosell as part of their incarceration.

The script presents twenty-first-century culture as a reflection of the worst elements within our present society. The problem with *Sleeper* is Allen's irreverence. There is off-color language and sexual innuendo. Viewer caution is recommended. **B.G.**

SMILE (1975), 113 min.

RATING: PG   ★★★
CONTENT: Some suggestive language and minor swearing
INTENDED AUDIENCE: Adults
STARRING: Bruce Dern, Barbara Feldon, Michael Kidd
DIRECTOR: Michael Ritchie

Smile takes a sacrosanct institution, the beauty pageant (in the film, "The Young American Miss Pageant") and presents it as a microcosm of the way many people picture the "ideal" American way of life: A house in the suburbs, two cars, club membership, success in a 9-to-5 job, and a happy marriage. The film follows several young girls who have entered the pageant in the hope of becoming a finalist, and, eventually, The Young American Miss. They are herded like cattle for processing, and admonished by a former beauty queen to "be yourself and keep smiling."

Smile points out that a life of things is a dead end. It is also a funny movie, but recommended with caution because of some indiscretion in the language. **B.G.**

SMOOTH TALK (1986)

RATING: PG–13
CONTENT: Vile language
INTENDED AUDIENCE: Adults
STARRING: Treat Williams, Laura Dern, Mary Kay Place
DIRECTOR: Joyce Chopra

Smooth Talk is an attempt at a serious coming-of-age film based on the story "Where Are You Going, Where Have You Been?" by Joyce Carol Oates. The character Arnold Friend is based on the so-called pied piper of Tucson who seduced and sometimes killed teenage girls in Arizona in the 1960s. A fifteen-year-old girl who has become obsessed with the opposite sex has her desires fulfilled, though not in the way she wanted, by Arnold Friend (A. Friend—get it?). This man in his thirties cajoles and browbeats her into driving off with him, and she comes back from the drive with a sober view of reality and sex.

The film illustrates that the wages of sin is death—in this case, the death of innocence. However, lapses in continuity and miserable direction turn what could have been a good morality tale into a confused nihilistic statement. The casting is awful, too. There is no overt sex, but the vile language removes any hope of recommending this movie for anyone.

SOLARBABIES (1986)

RATING: PG–13   ★★
CONTENT: No nudity, or obscene language. The rating is for violence.
INTENDED AUDIENCE: Teenagers, young adult
STARRING: Richard Jordan, Jami Gertz, Charles Durning
DIRECTOR: Alan Johnson

Solarbabies fits nicely into a "Mad-Max-with-an-extraterrestrial-angle-for-kids" genre. Set in the future some two thousand years, Earth has become a barren land, with its water depleted and people barely surviving on the desert plains. The story revolves around a group of four adolescents and their young six-year-old friend. All of them live in an "orphanage," which is actually a prison-of-sorts for youngsters run by the police. There, the children are indoctrinated into the mindset of the authorities, inculcating them with visions of violence and the use of police force to subdue all opposition. It is an Orwellian vision of controlling the masses.

If this all sounds somewhat farcical, it is. The movie, though well photographed and accompanied by a music score by Maurice Jarre *(Lawrence of Arabia, Dr. Zhivago, Grand Prix)*, has too many scenes that are unbelievable. The film doesn't have offensive language or nudity, but most adults will probably find the picture dull. Acceptable escapist fare for adolescents. **B.G.**

SONG OF THE SOUTH (1946)

RATING: G   ★★★★
CONTENT: Nothing objectionable
INTENDED AUDIENCE: All ages
STARRING: Lucille Watson, Ruth Warrick, Hattie McDaniel, James Baskett, Luana
    Patten, Bobby Driscoll
DIRECTOR: Harve Foster

This is one of Walt Disney's greatest movies about a young boy's friendship with a loving old black man on his grandmother's plantation.

Seven-year-old Johnny travels with his parents from Atlanta to his grandmother's plantation only to find out that his parents are separating. At the plantation, Johnny decides to run away to join his father in Atlanta, but is distracted by the voice of Uncle Remus who loves to tell delightful tales of Brer Rabbit and the Briar Patch to the children on the plantation. Upon meeting Uncle Remus, an immediate friendship is sparked.

Throughout the movie, Johnny runs into problems that Uncle Remus solves through his wonderful (beautifully animated by Disney) fables. Each of these stories revolves around an adventuresome rabbit, Brer Rabbit, who seems always to be easing in and out of trouble. Each fable is a parable which teaches a brief moral lesson. *Song of the South* is great entertainment and highly recommended for all ages. **L.N., P.B.** and **J.B.**

SPACE CAMP (1986)

RATING: PG
CONTENT: Excessively foul language
INTENDED AUDIENCE: Families
STARRING: Kate Capshaw, Lea Thompson, Kelly Preston
DIRECTOR: Harry Winer

When a group of young aspiring astronauts go to NASA's space camp for teenagers, the youngest becomes a good friend of a robot named Jinx. Jinx wants his friend to be happy by really blasting off into space. So Jinx arranges for the shuttle to fire when they are sitting in it, and the teenagers head off into orbit. Because the shuttle is not ready to go up, they have to work together under perilous circumstances to survive. Their team work allows them to triumph over adversity.

Space Camp could have been a good, acceptable movie if it were not for the excessively bad language. Also, the first half is very slow with no conflict, although the last half is exciting.

SPARTACUS (1960), 196 min.

CONTENT: Nothing objectionable   ★★★
INTENDED AUDIENCE: Families
STARRING: Kirk Douglas, Tony Curtis, Peter Ustinov, Jean Simmons,
Laurence Olivier, Charles Laughton
DIRECTOR: Stanley Kubrick

Spartacus is a big picture focusing on the revolt of the Roman slaves in 72 BC, also known as the Gladiator's War, which ended in six thousand slaves being crucified on the roads to Rome. (Spartacus broke out of the gladiator school at Capua, Italy, and fled to Mount Vesuvius where many fugitives joined him. After defeating several Roman forces, Crassus and Pompey put down the revolt.)

The movie is notable for its magnificent staging of gladiatorial combat, especially between Spartacus and Draba. Peter Ustinov is excellent as Batiatus, a snide, insinuating, witty former slave, and deserved the Academy Award he won for his performance. Worth seeing.

SPIES LIKE US (1985), 142 min.

RATING: PG
CONTENT: Obscenity and promiscuity
INTENDED AUDIENCE: Young adults
STARRING: Chevy Chase, Dan Aykroyd
DIRECTOR: John Landis

This dull, slow comedy is hardly worth your time. It is a sophomoric, anti-Christian story of two bozos who stop World War III. Not recommended.

SPRING SYMPHONY (1986)
(Subtitles)

CONTENT: Very brief nudity and promiscuity   ★★
INTENDED AUDIENCE: Adults

186

STARRING: Natassja Kinski, Herbert Gronemeyer, Rolfe Hoppe
DIRECTOR: Peter Schamoni

A biography of Clara Wieck, the wife of Robert Schumann, the great nineteenth-century romantic composer. Clara gave up her successful career as a pianist when she married. This film imparts a feminist consciousness to the well-known story of their long, difficult love affair. This modern view seems out of place in an otherwise accurate historical piece.

Spring Symphony is interesting, but the sexual situations and the strained world view make it suspect for most viewers. This romantic tragedy shows clearly how empty life is without God, but Robert and Clara never seem to realize that.

SQUARE DANCE (1987)

RATING: PG–13   ★★★
CONTENT: Strong Christian witness and some off-color language
INTENDED AUDIENCE: Adults
STARRING: Jason Robards, Jane Alexander, Winona Oyder, Rob Lowe
DIRECTOR: Daniel Petrie

Square Dance tells of a young girl's search for an answer to the fundamental question, "Who am I?" The spirited Gemma lives with her cranky grandfather, Pop (Jason Robards). On the verge of womanhood and pierced by the absence of a mother and father she has never even seen, Gemma finds solace and meaning in church work and good deeds. The tension in the film develops around the sudden arrival of her long lost mother and their struggle to re-establish a relationship. For a while, mother and daughter live together until both of them finally realize that Gemma really does belong to grandpa.

This film offers much food for thought. The main character is a Bible-believing Christian woman intent on living her life as such. She reads from the Bible and practices her Christian faith. At one point, Gemma asks one of the characters if he knows that Jesus Christ is his Lord and Savior. Highly recommended. **B.G.**

STAGECOACH (1939) B&W, 99 min.

CONTENT: Nothing objectionable   ★★★★
INTENDED AUDIENCE: All ages
STARRING: John Wayne, Claire Trevor, Thomas Mitchell, George Bancroft,
   Berton Churchill, Donald Meek, John Carradine, Lousie Platt, Andy Devine,
   Tom Tyler
DIRECTOR: John Ford

Stagecoach has often been billed the classic Western. The action is mainly in the last few minutes of the movie with an Indian attack on the stagecoach. Most of the movie is a character study that shows how the passengers interact with each other and change each other's lives. It is a character study unique among American Westerns. This is a film well-worth watching. It launched John Wayne's career.

STAND BY ME (1986)

RATING: R   ★★
CONTENT: Profanity

INTENDED AUDIENCE: Adults
STARRING: Will Wheaton, Richard Dreyfuss, River Phoenix, Corey Feldman,
   Jerry O'Connell
DIRECTOR: Rob Reiner

This artistic movie attempts to show a group of young boys coming of age, but it ignores God and shows the young men from a completely humanistic perspective. There is a lot of truth in the movie, because most people are cut off from their Creator, but the lack of a reference to God relegates this movie to mediocrity. And it fails in its attempt to provide insight into the true nature of people.

When one young boy says he knows where a dead body is, he and three friends make plans to find it. But their older brothers interfere and want to take the body. The animosity between the brothers suggests that there is no real brotherly relationship. Eventually, the younger boys take care of the situation by making an anonymous phone call informing the police of the body. Overall, there is nothing to commend this film. **J.C.J.**

STAR CRYSTAL (1986)

RATING: PG   ★★★
CONTENT: Very little bad language
INTENDED AUDIENCE: Adults
STARRING: Justin Campbell, Faye Bolt, John Smith
DIRECTOR: Lance Lindsay

Star Crystal is not a bad little science-fiction movie. A spaceship goes to Mars and picks up a rock, but the oxygen disappears and everyone aboard dies. A new ship goes out to find out what went wrong, and three more people die before a computer specialist figures out what happened. Though the plot is overshadowed by a lack of scope and quality and there is some bad language, it is acceptable entertainment. **L.B.**

STAR TREK IV: THE VOYAGE HOME (1986)

RATING: PG   ★★★
CONTENT: Minor profanity and obscenity that are put down as owing to
   a lack of education and intelligence
INTENDED AUDIENCE: All ages
STARRING: William Shatner, Leonard Nemoy
DIRECTOR: Leonard Nemoy

This film picks up where *Star Trek III* left off, with the crew of the Enterprise repairing a commandeered Klingon starship, while Dr. Spock is being retrained on Vulcan. The Federation is trying Admiral Kirk for destroying the Enterprise in his successful attempt to defeat the Klingons and save his crew. Kirk and company fix the spaceship and head for Earth only to find that an interstellar space probe is destroying the planet while looking for humpback whales that have been extinct for several centuries. Dr. Spock advises Kirk to try to take the Klingon ship back in time to the twentieth century to capture a humpback whale and bring it back to the twenty-third century to save the Earth.

After several humorous escapades in our century, Admiral Kirk and crew capture two humpback whales and get them back to Earth in the twenty-third century just in time to keep the planet from being destroyed. Courage triumphs over adversity in a magnificent way. An entertaining movie for the whole family.

STAR WARS (1977), 121 min.

RATING: PG   ★★★
CONTENT: Violence and some mysticism updated to a futuristic pantheism
INTENDED AUDIENCE: All ages
STARRING: Mark Hamill, Harrison Ford, Carrie Fisher, Alec Guinness, Peter Cushing
DIRECTOR: George Lukas

As pure entertainment, *Star Wars* is great science fiction, loaded with action, adventure, humor, love pathos, and, best of all, in the end good triumphs over evil. As a device to move the plot along, the idea of the Force (spirit over matter) works; as a theological statement it is a travesty. (When some eager young person asked Alec Guinness to explain about the Force, Mr. Guinness replied that he knew nothing about the Force, but he did know about Jesus Christ.)

George Lucas wrote and directed the *Star Wars* trilogy in the style of the serials of old. The Imperial Galactic Empire is ruled by the Grand Moff Tarkin and his evil aide, Lord Darth Vader. All that stands against these evil rulers, as they attempt to suppress the entire universe, are the rebel leader Princess Leia Organa, farmer Luke Skywalker, and starship pilot Hans Solo, who are aided by robots, anthropoids, rebels, Obi-Wan-Kenobe, and the light side of the Force. As with any good saga, in the end the good underdogs defeat the Evil Empire. A fun movie that is recommended with caution because of the mysticism that forms its world view.

A STREETCAR NAMED DESIRE (1951) B&W, 122 min.

CONTENT: A psychological look at the seamy, underside of life   ★★★
AUDIENCE: Adults
STARRING: Marlon Brando, Vivien Leigh, Karl Malden, Kim Hunter
DIRECTOR: Elia Kazan

A Streetcar Named Desire is a personal drama fashioned out of Tennessee Williams' life. The greatness of the story derives in part from the fact that it tells of an essential human conflict in visual terms. Blanche du Bois is valiantly trying to hold on to her faded gentility against the cruel badgering of her crude, brutal brother-in-law, Stanley Kowalski. Eventually, Stanley drives off Blanche's only beau and drives her into madness.

Vivien Leigh, Kim Hunter, and Karl Malden all won Oscars for their performances. The film was nominated for six additional Academy Awards including best actor for Brando. This film is strong stuff, showing the cruel face of the fallen human condition, but a great movie nonetheless.

SUBWAY (1985)
(Subtitles)

RATING: R   ★★
CONTENT: Profanity
INTENDED AUDIENCE: Adults
STARRING: Christopher Lambert, Isabelle Adjani
DIRECTOR: Luc Besson

This light French comedy is about a youth who is driven underground by society. The film is slightly rebellious in a youthful rite-of-passage way. Most of it is quite funny, but some of it is infantile. It is not Christian, but it won't hurt anyone. Love is the redemptive element that forces the trick ending. It would not be a bad film if it weren't for some profanity in the subtitles.

SUDDEN DEATH (1986)

RATING: R
CONTENT: Obscenity and nudity
INTENDED AUDIENCE: Adults

Sudden Death is a female *Death Wish*. It is pure exploitation of the vigilante theme. A woman who is raped becomes an avenger. In the end, she falls in love with the cop who is investigating her case. The worst part is not the language (mildly bad) or the very brief nudity, but the terrible script someone should have taken the time to re-write.

SULLIVAN'S TRAVELS (1941) B&W, 90 min.

CONTENT: Nothing objectionable   ★★★★
INTENDED AUDIENCE: Adults
STARRING: Joel McCrea, Veronica Lake, Robert Warwick, William Demarest,
   Porter Hall, Robert Greig, Eric Blore, Franklin Pangborn, Byron Foulger,
   Torben Meyer, Jimmy Conlin, Margaret Hayes
DIRECTOR: Preston Sturges

A filmmaker, John Sullivan, wants to research what poverty is like in America. Twice, he tries to escape the studio to go off by himself and find out what America is and what poverty is really like. His third attempt is a success when he gets clobbered by a bum, looses his clothes and his identification, and really gets amnesia. He wanders about the country, landing briefly in a Georgia chaingang, and eventually finds his way into a black church.

While watching a movie at the church, he comes back to his senses. Furthermore, he realizes that people want to see movies that make them laugh, not movies that emphasize the problems they face. Much food for thought here for Christians.

THE SUNSHINE BOYS (1975), 103 min.

RATING: G   ★★★
CONTENT: Nothing objectionable
INTENDED AUDIENCE: Adults
STARRING: Walter Matthau, George Burns, Richard Benjamin
DIRECTOR: Herbert Ross

Willy Clark (Matthau) and Al Lewis (Burns), a once-celebrated vaudeville comedy team, broke up years ago and have been feuding ever since. Clark refuses to be reconciled with Lewis, but the appeal of appearing on television, reunited and doing their routine, brings the two together. They sign up for the show, which turns out to be disastrous. The show bombs, and the results are both sad and funny.

Neil Simon's script (one of his best), gives us a fresh, stimulating look at older people, and the reality of losing our abilities as we age. Here, the two men have lost their ability to perform, but still have their professional spark and zeal. The script also tells us to listen for the clues of love even when the language may be cutting. Recommended. **B.G.**

SUPERMAN I, II, AND III (1978, 1981, 1983), 142 min., 127 min., 125 min.

RATING: PG   ★★
CONTENT: Fantasy. In *Superman II,* there is an off-camera affair between Superman and Lois.
INTENDED AUDIENCE: Families
STARRING: Christopher Reeve, Margot Kidder, Marlon Brando, Gene Hackman, Richard Pryor
DIRECTORS: Richard Donner (I), Richard Lester (II, III)

The *Superman* trilogy of movies is exactly what one would expect, a comic book series brought to the screen. All three are fun to watch, although the first is the best. *Superman II* is not for Christians, because Lois and the Man of Steel have an affair. This affair is probably an attempt to appeal to the mores of Hollywood and what Hollywood thinks that public wants. It is unfortunate because the plot of the second *Superman* is better than either of the other two with a clear battle waged between good and evil.

Christopher Reeve is excellent in all three movies, often running rings around the other actors. *Superman III* falls so short of the other two that it seems like a made-for-TV movie.

Much has been written in Christian circles about Superman as an humanistic, alternate Christ symbol. It is unnecessary to read this into the movie character. Taken as entertainment, *Superman I* is fun, *Superman II* should be avoided, and *Superman III* is so-so.

SUPPORT YOUR LOCAL SHERIFF (1969), 93 min.

RATING: G   ★★★
CONTENT: Nothing objectionable
INTENDED AUDIENCE: All ages
STARRING: James Garner, Joan Hackett, Walter Brennan, Harry Morgan, Bruce Dern, Jack Elam
DIRECTOR: Burt Kennedy

An amusing spoof on Western movies, this film provides many laughs as the adventurer-turned-sheriff Garner takes on the evil likes of Jack Elam and Walter Brennan. The most interesting aspect is Garner's portrayal of an honest man in the midst of no-good sinners. He refuses to step out of character and sink to the low level of his adversaries. Garner convinces the respectable people in the town to stand up for their rights and oppose the villains. They follow his good example and do so. Truly goodness wins over evil.

This is a positive movie your family will want to see if you haven't had the pleasure of seeing it already. The message of this movie says to support your local sheriff over the mean hombres of the world. **B.G.**

SWEET DREAMS (1985), 148 min.

RATING: PG–13
CONTENT: Profanity, obscenity, and promiscuity
INTENDED AUDIENCE: Adults
STARRING: Jessica Lange, Ed Harris
DIRECTOR: Karel Reisz

This foul-mouthed movie portrays country singing star Patsy Cline as an adulterous, selfish opportunist with a strange sexual craving for an overly sexed alcoholic. There is nothing to commend this film.

SWEET LIBERTY (1986), 147 min.

RATING: PG ★★
CONTENT: Profanity, promiscuity, and brief nudity
INTENDED AUDIENCE: Adults
STARRING: Alan Alda, Michael Caine, Michelle Pfeiffer
DIRECTOR: Alan Alda

This well-made movie is thoroughly entertaining but, unfortunately, full of subtle immorality. A history professor has written a book about a Revolutionary War battle, and a Hollywood film company buys the rights to the book, *Sweet Liberty*, and comes to town to film it on location. The professor clashes with the film company because the script distorts history. Yet for all his moral posturing, he is shown to be immoral.

The professor objects to the three audience-grabbing devices of defying authority, destroying property, and nudity, but in the process of mocking these film devices, they are used quite effectively in making this film. But we have to ask why they are used. Is the moviemaker making a statement that we must appeal to the spirit of the times to have a successful movie? The director of the movie within this movie says they are the three things people pay to see. Whatever the reason, be advised they are there. Overall, this is a good film, but beware its moral pitfalls.

SWISS FAMILY ROBINSON (1960), 126 min.

RATING: G ★★★★
CONTENT: Nothing objectionable
INTENDED AUDIENCE: All ages
STARRING: John Mills, Dorothy McGuire, James MacArthur, Tommy Kirk,
    Kevin Corcoran, Janet Munro, Sessue Hayakawa
DIRECTOR: Ken Annakin

Based on the classic story by Johann Wyss, the Disney movie version of *Swiss Family Robinson* is an escape into fantasy. En route to New Guinea in 1813, the Robinson family is shipwrecked during a storm and must start life anew on a deserted island. Salvaging all their worldly goods from the ship, they create their own paradise-on-earth as they fashion an entire homestead from the surrounding jungle.

However, just as the Garden of Eden came to an abrupt end with the introduction of evil, so too it is the case with the Robinson family as they learn of pirates in the vicinity. The family makes elaborate plans to repel their invaders and save their paradise from destruction.

There are a number of favorable references to God in the film. Also, the family is portrayed as possessing many Christian virtues. A film for the whole family! **B.G.**

THE SWORD AND THE STONE (1963)

CONTENT: Some antibiblical references to magic ★★
INTENDED AUDIENCE: Families
STARRING: Sebastian Cabet, Karl Swenson
DIRECTOR: Wolfgang Reitherman

Before the king, Uther Pendragon, dies at the beginning of this movie, he leaves his sword in a rock and tells his courtiers that whoever pulls the sword from the rock is the next king of Britain. Years pass and many try to pull the sword with no success. Merlin, the king's magician, has a vision of the boy who will be king falling through his roof. We cut to the orphan, Arthur, and his brother. Arthur is retrieving the arrows that his brother shoots and finds Merlin's house. He goes up to the roof to retrieve an arrow and falls through. He proceeds to have tea with Merlin. Through most of the movie, Merlin and Arthur get involved in many adventures as Merlin tutors Arthur.

The Sword and the Stone is the Disney movie version of the legend of King Arthur. It is a funny, entertaining, little movie that will delight your children, but you need to inform them about the evil of magic and taking that sort of thing seriously. Should be enjoyed only as light entertainment. **P.B.**

TAKE THE MONEY AND RUN (1969), 85 min.

RATING: PG ★★★
CONTENT: Nothing objectionable, but the humor is adult oriented
INTENDED AUDIENCE: Adults
STARRING: Woody Allen, Janet Margolin
DIRECTOR: Woody Allen

The first of many films directed by Woody Allen, this spoof of gangster films is full of sight gags and one-liners. It focuses on an inept thief who fumbles his way into jail when his schemes for pulling off heists fail.

This intellectual film has a nihilistic world view, typical of Woody Allen. It is not harmful entertainment and is quite humorous; however, caution is recommended for those who like straight-ahead story lines and clear-headed world views. It is not antibiblical, but neither is it biblical; rather, it is a series of insights into the mind of man that is profound but misses the point of man's sinfulness. If you like mental gymnastics, see it. **B.G.**

A TALE OF TWO CITIES (1935) B&W, 121 min.

CONTENT: A great movie ★★★★
INTENDED AUDIENCE: Adults
STARRING: Ronald Colman, Elizabeth Allan, Donald Woods, Basil Rathbone, Edna May Oliver
DIRECTOR: Jack Conway

This tale of the French Revolution shows the poverty and wealth of eighteenth-century France, the storming of the Bastille and the sensation-seekers at the guillotine, such as the infamous Madam Defarge, who knits as the heads roll into their bloody basket. All of Dickens' immortal characters, plots and subplots, are captured in the movie. It was a stroke of brilliance to use a few well placed subtitles that contribute to the viewer's sense of history.

After Carton's memorable speech as he goes to be beheaded, "It is a far, far better thing. . . . ," a biblical subtitle appears that was deleted from later remakes that moved in a more humanistic direction. Everyone should see this film.

THE TAMARIND SEED (1974), 123 min.

RATING: PG   ★★★
CONTENT: Nothing objectionable
INTENDED AUDIENCE: Adults
STARRING: Julie Andrews, Omar Sharif, Anthony Quayle, Dan O'Herlihy, Oscar Homolka
DIRECTOR: Blake Edwards

Avoiding the gimmickry and violence of most spy movies, writer/director Blake Edwards has fashioned a smooth, polished story about a woman (Julie Andrews) who is a British Foreign Service employee on vacation in Barbados. A Soviet diplomat (Omar Sharif) is attracted to her, but she is cautious because of a recent unhappy affair. Their relationship is under surveillance by intelligence officials on both sides, and they become increasingly involved in a series of diplomatic scandals. Subplots develop, and the story accelerates into a bloody climax, though it is not exploitive. The director chooses to reaffirm life rather than celebrate death.

The Tamarind Seed is a subtle blend of intricate relationships, motives, and moral imperatives, all of which are difficult to translate to film. However, director Edwards has done his work masterfully. **B.G.**

TARGET (1985)

RATING: R
CONTENT: Profanity and nudity
INTENDED AUDIENCE: Adults
STARRING: Gene Hackman
DIRECTOR: Arthur Penn

This is a so-so spy story about a father and son who can't get along until the wife-mother is abducted by spies and they learn to love each other as they rescue her from the East Germans. The family story of the father, son, and mother learning to love and appreciate each other is excellent, but the spy story is confused.

In the end, the movie tries to tell us that the East German spy is a family man, and the problem is with the opportunistic double agents who have no moral code. The movie is filled with profane language and has some nudity. It could have been a good film, but it doesn't quite make it.

THE TEN COMMANDMENTS (1956), 219 min.

CONTENT: Nothing objectionable   ★★★★
INTENDED AUDIENCE: All ages
STARRING: Charlton Heston, Yul Brynner, Edward G. Robinson, Yvonne DeCarlo, Debra Paget, Anne Baxter, Sir Cedric Hardwicke
DIRECTOR: Cecil B. DeMille

The film opens in Egypt, with the Israelites suffering under the bondage of their Egyptian masters. This story of Moses follows him from his birth to the time when he leads the Israelites to their home near the river Jordan. It brings this biblical hero to life—discovering his true identity as a Hebrew, being cast out in the desert, learning he is the one to free the Hebrews, encountering God in the burning bush, and eventually receiving the Ten Commandments on Mount Sinai.

The grandeur of this film is lost on a television screen because of its overwhelming sets, costuming, action sequences, and pageantry. It ranks with *Ben-Hur* and *The Greatest Story Ever Told* as the most impressive, if not the finest, film produced about the Bible. Skillful writing and fine acting, with Yul Brynner as Ramesses and Charlton Heston as a vibrant, energetic Moses, enhance the vividness of the events.

The Ten Commandments evokes many emotions, from excitement to tears. It is a moving portrayal of God's grand design for man and that design's origins with Moses and the Jewish people. There cannot be a more highly recommended film for everyone to see. This is moviemaking at its best. **B.G.**

TENDER MERCIES (1983), 93 min.

RATING: PG   ★★★★
CONTENT: Minor profanity
INTENDED AUDIENCE: Adults
STARRING: Robert Duvall, Tess Harper, Betty Buckley, William Brimley, Ellen Barkin
DIRECTOR: Bruce Beresford

Mac Sledge, after a drunken binge, wakes up at a motel penniless. He is a country and western singer whose career has been ruined by alcohol. He agrees to work for the owner, a widow named Rosa Lee, until the debt is paid. Rosa is a committed Christian, and as he stays to pay his debt, he gives up alcohol and comes to know Christ. In fact, in the movie he is baptized. Eventually, he grows to love Rosa Lee and her son and marries her.

Tender Mercies is a great, loving movie and a gift from God. Every Christian should see it, with the caution that there is minor profanity in the beginning of the movie in keeping with the message of change from sinner to saint.

THAT WAS THEN . . . THIS IS NOW (1985)

RATING: R
CONTENT: Obscenity, profanity, and sexual looseness
INTENDED AUDIENCE: Teenagers
STARRING: Emilio Estevez, Craig Sheffer, Kim Delaney
DIRECTOR: Christopher Cain

This movie starts with a car theft and goes on to tell the story of two losers who destroy everything they touch. And this silly, dull movie is not improved by the profanity and sexual looseness. Talk your teenagers out of going to it. There are much better films to see.

THAT'S ENTERTAINMENT (1974), 138 min.

RATING: G   ★★★★
CONTENT: Nothing objectionable
INTENDED AUDIENCE: All ages

STARRING: Gene Kelly, Fred Astaire, Bing Crosby, Debbie Reynolds,
Jimmy Stewart, and other MGM stars
DIRECTOR: Jack Haley, Jr.

This compendium of scenes from over one hundred of the best MGM musicals is a delight. Excerpts are from some of the finest scenes ever shot, with such notable inclusions as Gene Kelly and "Singin' in the Rain," Fred Astaire and Eleanor Powell dancing "Being the Beguine," Donald O'Connor doing his singing and dancing-of-sorts "Make 'Em Laugh," and the entire "American in Paris" ballet, to name but a few.

The film is narrated by many of the original performers and provides a sense of nostalgia as many of these fine actors and actresses relive their heydays as clips from their finest moments are displayed. This movie is a lasting reminder of the quality that infused films for decades. It stands out as a beacon, signaling how the movie industry used to pride itself on creativity and talent. **B.G.**

THERESE (1986)

CONTENT: Nothing objectionable ★★★
INTENDED AUDIENCE: Adults
STARRING: Cathleen Mouchet
DIRECTOR: Alain Cavalier

This film is a series of vignettes depicting the life of St. Therese, who, at the age of sixteen, entered a convent and died a few years later of tuberculosis due to the rigors of monastic life. (Twenty-eight years later she was canonized.) Therese had a genius for loving Jesus with all her heart, and this movie makes you want to love Him too. However, it should be noted that Therese's passionate spirituality is so unique that it is almost stilted. Therese's passionate love affair with Jesus stands in contrast with Mother Teresa's deep love for Jesus that empowers her to love others in word and deed.

The movie's strong point is an objective point of view toward the simple spirituality of Therese and the other nuns that allows full character development to reveal the motivations behind their behavior. As a result, the infighting and petty jealousies shown between Therese and her real-life sisters (all three sisters eventually joined the convent) are set beside scenes of genuine prayer and strong faith.

Therese depicts deep faith and commitment to Christ. On the other hand, Therese's faith is so emotional that it appears at times macabre, and, therefore, not nearly as poignant as the biblical faith of the average Christian. However, the film is well worth seeing, and is recommended. **B.S.** and **V.L.**

THE THIRD MAN (1949) B&W, 104 min.

CONTENT: Nothing objectionable ★★★★
INTENDED AUDIENCE: Adults
STARRING: Joseph Cotton, Alida Valli, Trevor Howard, Orson Welles
DIRECTOR: Carol Reed

Journalist Holly Martins travels from America to Vienna to work for a friend, Harry Lime. When he gets to Vienna, he finds out that Harry has been killed. Or has he? As Holly searches through Vienna to learn more of the death of his friend, he finds out more about the man than he ever cared to know. *The Third Man* is beautifully filmed and powerfully acted.

THE 39 STEPS (1935) B&W, 89 min.

CONTENT: Nothing objectionable   ★★★★
INTENDED AUDIENCE: Adults
STARRING: Robert Donat, Madeleine Carroll, Wylie Watson, Godfrey Tearle,
    Lucie Mannheim, John Laurie, Peggy Ashcroft, Helen Hayes, Frank Cellier
DIRECTOR: Alfred Hitchcock

The 39 Steps tells the story of a man who inadvertently gets involved with international intrigue. Richard Hannay is a colonial in England who attends a magic show featuring Mr. Memory. Mr. Memory's act starts a riot. A gun is fired, causing panic. A veiled, femme fatale grabs Hannay's arm and asks him to protect her. He takes her to his apartment. She tells him a story of a spy ring. In the middle of the night, she is knifed in the back and staggers into his room to croak a warning that "they" will get him next. One of Hitchcock's best films.

THIRTY SECONDS OVER TOKYO (1944), 138 min.

CONTENT: War film; no nudity, no bad language; minor violence   ★★★★
AUDIENCE: Adult
STARRING: Spencer Tracy, Van Johnson, Robert Walker, Robert Mitchum, Phyllis
    Thaxter.
DIRECTOR: Mervyn LeRoy

The forties inspired hundreds of films dealing with World War II. One of the greatest is *Thirty Seconds Over Tokyo*, based on the true story of the famous B-25 air raid against Japan.

Lt. Colonel Jimmy Doolittle, played very straight-faced by Spencer Tracy, conceives a plan to strike at the heart of Japan with a secret attack that is to be launched from the aircraft carrier Hornet in the Pacific. We follow the men as they leave loved ones and families to train for something that had never been attempted before: flying a B-25 off the deck of a carrier only five hundred feet long.

While the raid did little damage, it was an incredible morale boost for the United States. As depicted in the film, pilot Ted Lawson (played by Van Johnson), loses a leg in his crash landing, but is able to return home in a wheelchair as a hero. A story told with magnificent integrity. **B.G.**

THREADS (1984), 90 min.

CONTENT: The effect of nuclear war on Sheffield, England.
    This attempt at a realistic portrayal of World War III and
    its effects is not suitable for children. There are some
    obscenities and vulgarities.
INTENDED AUDIENCE: Mature adults
STARRING: Local cast
DIRECTOR: Mick Jackson

Produced by the BBC, this docudrama portrays life before, during, and after a major nuclear strike against Great Britain. The film opens in the countryside surrounding Sheffield, England, and introduces several townspeople. The story follows these citizens as they go about their daily routines, unaware, and ignorant of the gathering holocaust. We follow a host of people, including government officials, who are making preparations for a possible nuclear war. Finally, the crisis becomes full blown when the Soviets, moving to take West Germany, are attacked by B-52 bombers. The Soviets respond with a nuclear missile, destroying the NATO air wing. One hour later, the U.S. responds with one battlefield nuclear weapon on a Soviet base. Protests continue. Intense diplomatic negotiations take place.

The film, like *War Games,* tries to objectively depict a nuclear war, based on what knowledge is available about such a catastrophe. This is a strong film, especially considering it was produced for television. It is recommended for adults only, as there are several scenes of burned bodies and the like. Considerably better than *The Day After,* which was produced for ABC Television in the U.S. in 1984. **B.G.**

THREE AMIGOS (1986)

RATING: PG
CONTENT: Mild off-color language, some crudities,
and some homosexual innuendos
INTENDED AUDIENCE: Adults
STARRING: Steve Martin, Chevy Chase, Martin Short
DIRECTOR: John Landis

Three Amigos is a disappointing movie. It is funny in parts, but the humor is not sustained throughout. This film tells the story of a small Mexican town, Santa Poco, which is being oppressed by a mean bandito, El Guapo. A brave maiden, Carmen, goes searching for help and sees a silent film that features the exploits of the Three Amigos. She mistakes the screen exploits of the Three Amigos for real heroics and sends them a telegram to come to the aid of her town. To save money, the telegram is shortened, and the real-life, Hollywood actors, who have just been fired by the studio, think that they are being invited to Mexico to give a personal appearance.

The three go to Mexico and soon find out that they are expected to be real heroes. After losing the first round against El Guapo, they regroup and destroy him and his gang. As they start to ride off into the sunset, one of them, Lucky Bottoms, says to Carmen that he will come back one day, and Carmen asks, "Why?" This is the best line in the movie. If Steve Martin ever thinks of bringing back these Sad Sacks, the audience should ask, "Why?" A dull, silly, crude movie.

THREE FOR THE ROAD (1987)

CONTENT: Some profanity and obscenity   ★★
INTENDED AUDIENCE: Adults
STARRING: Charlie Sheen, Kerri Green, Alan Ruck, Sally Kellerman
DIRECTOR: Bill Norton, Jr.

Three for the Road stars Charlie Sheen as Paul Tracy, a college student and up-and-coming congressional aide. Senator Kittridge, for whom Paul works, decides to assign Paul to driving his "troubled daughter" to Ashcroft Institute, a maximum security school for girls. The Senator shows Paul bad publicity that his daughter, Robin (Kerri Green), has received, thus putting him in a bad light. He wants her removed from the public eye because he is aiming to be president. The Senator gives Paul enough money for the trip, gives him the keys to a new Mercedes sedan—and handcuffs for his daughter. A number of wild adventures follow showing that a contest of wills exists between the Senator and his ex-wife over how to treat their daughter.

Three for the Road is entertaining. Unfortunately, there is some profanity and one scene where T. S. and Melissa get "acquainted" in the Mercedes. Exercise caution when seeing this film. **P.J.R.**

3 MEN AND A CRADLE (1986)
(Subtitles)

RATING: PG–13   ★★★
CONTENT: Mild bad language (no profanity) and sexual looseness
INTENDED AUDIENCE: Adults
STARRING: Roland Giraud, Michel Boujenah, Andre Dussolier
DIRECTOR: Coline Serreau

This funny French comedy has received rave reviews from critics all over the world. Even though it is flawed and improbable, it is endearing and presents an important message: Hedonism is empty, and the true meaning of life is love and devotion.

It opens on an elegant party in the Paris apartment of three "swinging" bachelors. They learn about a package Jacques is to receive, which turns out to be a baby he fathered. Soon, they are all in love with the baby, and they even give up their friends to care for the child. When the mother returns to claim her child, the men find that their lives are meaningless without the baby. They start to discuss God, love, and devotion. Their former lifestyle of wine, women, and song seems empty to them. They have discovered that love, not selfishness, is the true meaning of life.

Although the film proclaims a positive message to our self-centered age, the problem for Christians is that it starts at the point where the men are moral reprobates, self-centered and foul-mouthed seekers after pleasure. There is no nudity or profanity, but the promiscuity is offensive. Yet it is a positive, uplifting movie with a redemptive plea for the family. It moves toward a moral perspective on life, but never quite gets there. It is interesting viewing, but keep in mind the cautions noted here.

THE THREE WORLDS OF GULLIVER (1960), 100 min.

RATING: G   ★★★
CONTENT: Nothing objectionable
INTENDED AUDIENCE: All ages
STARRING: Kerwin Matthews, Jo Morrow, June Thorburn
DIRECTOR: Jack Sher

Based loosely on the famous Jonathan Swift novel, this imaginative and colorful film rendition is a treat for all ages, especially young children. Matthews, who plays Gulliver, travels to Lilliputian land, where people are no larger than a finger. Here, as a giant, Gulliver meets the emperor of Lilliput, with his doll-like army. Later, Gulliver himself is threatened by giants.

The elaborately scaled, realistic sets add much visual credibility to the story. Most of Swift's social commentary has been excised from the storyline, leaving little for adults other than the visual display. But *The Three Worlds of Gulliver* is a movie your children will enjoy. **B.G.**

THUNDERBALL (1965), 132 min.

RATING: PG ★★★
CONTENT: Sexual innuendo and violence
INTENDED AUDIENCE: Adults
STARRING: Sean Connery, Claudine Arger, Adolfo Celi
DIRECTOR: Terrence Young

Thunderball tells the story of the arch-enemy, terrorist organization Spectre, which has stolen two atomic bombs from NATO forces. Spectre wants 100 million British pounds worth of diamonds or they will nuke a city in America or England. Of course, James Bond is sent in to save the day. Basically, the film is a comic book for adults, and some Bond enthusiasts believe this one is the best of the bunch. The sexual innuendo in the film is mild compared with what goes on today. Any mature Christian viewer should be able to take *Thunderball* lightly, as it was intended to be taken. **L.R.**

TIME BANDITS (1981), 116 min.

RATING: PG ★★★
CONTENT: Minor swearing
INTENDED AUDIENCE: Adults and adolescents
STARRING: John Cleese, Sean Connery, Shelley Duvall, Ian Holm,
    Sir Ralph Richardson, David Warner
DIRECTOR: Terry Gilliam

Time Bandits is a fanciful, light-hearted romp through time with a band of midget rogues and their captive, a young boy named Kevin. This excursion into time takes the viewer on a wild trip to the 1600's, where we meet Robin Hood, a jolly nice fellow played by John Cleese. Then we board the Titanic and enjoy the luxuries of the rich until we hit an iceberg and get thrown into another time and place. The motley crew of midget time bandits and Kevin end up in a showdown between the "Supreme Being" and the "Evil Genius"—good versus evil.

No blasphemy is intended in this final, climactic scene. Rather, it helps illuminate for children the battle between the forces of evil and good. Sir Ralph Richardson portrays the Supreme Being superbly, as if the maxim "God must be an Englishman" were true. Taken for what it is, a pleasant entertainment, the film is light-hearted, whimsical fun. Take it with a grain of salt (on popcorn, of course). **B.G.**

TO KILL A MOCKINGBIRD (1962), 129 min.

CONTENT: The word *nigger* is used in a pejorative manner; ★★★★
    adult situations
INTENDED AUDIENCE: Adults
STARRING: Gregory Peck, Mary Badham, Brock Peters, Robert Duvall
DIRECTOR: Robert Mulligan

Based on Harper Lee's best-selling novel, *To Kill a Mockingbird* takes place in Macon, Georgia, during the depression. A trial attorney, who is also a widower raising his two children, is asked to defend a black man accused of the rape of a white woman. The story is revealed to us through the observations of the children, and they see the ugliness surrounding the case. The attorney admirably defends his client, but he is

200

found guilty by an all-male, all-white jury. Later that night, the black man is killed as he tries to escape the sheriff's deputies who are transferring him to another town.

For a film produced in Hollywood, this is a rare exception in that it addresses the social issues of racism, bigotry, and hatred. The film offers moral lessons throughout; it brims with notions of justice, equality, fairness, and mercy, yet is never heavy-handed or presumptuous. You must see this great movie. **B.G.**

TO LIVE AND DIE IN L.A. (1985), 156 min.

RATING: R
CONTENT: Explicit sex, lesbianism, male nudity, and obscenity
INTENDED AUDIENCE: Adults
STARRING: William Peterson, William Defoe
DIRECTOR: William Friedkin

Great action, good direction, and beautiful craftsmanship cannot overcome the ills of this movie. The violence is horrible—faces are blown off in a number of ways—and explicit sex, lesbianism and male nudity are prevalent. There are no redeeming characters or values in this film. **E.B.**

TOP GUN (1986)

RATING: PG   ★★
CONTENT: Profanity
INTENDED AUDIENCE: Adults and teenagers
STARRING: Tom Cruise, Kelly McGillis
DIRECTOR: Tony Scott

This exciting movie is pure action-adventure entertainment. The personal side of the story is weak, and the dialogue is particularly strained; but the photography is superb, with real aircraft and carriers used instead of models. It's about a navy pilot who is accepted into the elite "top gun" training program for the best-of-the-best pilots and becomes a hero during a mission when two F14's are jumped by five MIG's. Good triumphs over evil.

This film would be recommended if it were not flawed by a sexual affair and extreme profanity. As it is, Christians may want to think twice before seeing it. **E.R.** and **L.R.**

TOUCH OF EVIL (1958) B&W, 93 min.

CONTENT: A vivid, psychological portrait of fallen man   ★★★★
INTENDED AUDIENCE: Adults
STARRING: Charlton Heston, Janet Leigh, Orson Welles, Joseph Calleia,
  Akim Tamiroff, Marlene Dietrich
DIRECTOR: Orson Welles

A Mexican policeman, Vargas, is on his honeymoon when an important American is car-bombed a few feet over the border. The corrupt local sheriff, Hank Quinlan, played magnificently by Welles, fixes evidence to solve the crime easily. Vargas puts his life on the line to bring the sheriff himself to justice.

Touch of Evil is one of the most memorable, best crafted movies ever made. It shows the genius of Orson Welles. In this masterpiece, he paints a vivid, atmospheric, psychological portrait of evil. Recommended.

THE TRANSFORMERS—THE MOVIE (1986)

RATING: PG
CONTENT: Technolatry (worshiping technology) and new-age occultism
INTENDED AUDIENCE: Children
STARRING: (voices) Leonard Nimoy, Orson Welles, Robert Stack
DIRECTOR: Nelson Shin

This animated film is one of those rip-offs from a television program that was the promotional spin-off of a toy. The Transformers are a group of intelligent, superpower robots who can change their shape to perform certain tasks usually associated with war. The Decepticons are forever attacking the Autobots, but even more rotten than the Decepticons is the evil Unicron. The Autobots have the Matrix, which is the energy powerhouse for the universe, and it is used to destroy the leader of the Decepticons and Unicron.

Everyone ends up singing a song that they will all become one in the Matrix—a pretty sad thought that they will all merge and lose their identities—but like Hindus and new-age occultists, they are mesmerized by this vision of the future. This vision is totally opposed to the end God has prepared for us. Avoid this totally anti-Christian movie that combines occultism and the worship of technology.

TRANSYLVANIA 6–5000 (1985)

RATING: PG
CONTENT: Obscenity, profanity, and sexual innuendo
INTENDED AUDIENCE: Teenagers and adults
STARRING: Jeff Goldblum, Joseph Bologna, Ed Begley, Jr.
DIRECTOR: Rudy DeLuca

This is a movie for children that children can't see because of the language and sexual innuendo. This childish story tells about two reporters who search for Dracula and Frankenstein in Transylvania. Glenn Miller would be embarrassed to find that his song "Pennsylvania 6–5000" was mocked for this worthless film. Worse than the language is the fact that evil is not portrayed as evil. Good doesn't triumph; rather, good and evil just continue on into the night. Definitely not recommended. **J.C.J.**

TREASURE ISLAND (1950), 96 min.

RATING: G   ★★★★
CONTENT: Nothing objectionable
INTENDED AUDIENCE: Children and adults
STARRING: Bobby Driscoll, Robert Newton
DIRECTOR: Byron Haskin

Based on the famous tale by Robert Louis Stevenson, this Disney version of the classic story is a colorful rendition. Robert Newton is splendid as Long John Silver. This movie maintains a very glossy look as we follow the characters in search of buried treasure. *Treasure Island* has been made into a film two other times: in 1934 with

Wallace Beery, and in 1972 with Orson Welles portraying Long John Silver as a much more menacing, dangerous, ominous villain, more like the character Stevenson intended. Newton, however, gives an excellent performance in this version with a roguish charm that delights younger viewers. **B.G.**

THE TRIP TO BOUNTIFUL (1985)

RATING: PG ★★★★
CONTENT: Nothing objectionable
INTENDED AUDIENCE: All ages
STARRING: Geraldine Page, John Heard, Carlin Glynn
DIRECTOR: Peter Masterson

The Trip to Bountiful opens with the hymn "Jesus is calling us home" and proceeds to tell the story of an elderly woman who is longing to see her childhood home, a small now-deserted town on the Texas Gulf. Geraldine Page is magnificent as the elderly mother whom Jesus is calling home, and she won an Academy Award for her performance. She seems trapped in her son's house with her daughter-in-law who hates her, hates hymns, and hates children.

The film is a powerful, unique witness to the Christian faith. Because the spiritual, hymn-singing mother is the brunt of the meanness of the selfish, humanist daughter-in-law, the audience is forced to root for and identify with the Christian. It reverses the pattern of most contemporary Hollywood movies, which make the Christian the villain. Go see this great movie.

TROLL (1985)

RATING: R
CONTENT: Foul language, demons, sex, nudity, and witchcraft
INTENDED AUDIENCE: Teenagers
STARRING: Noah Hathaway, Michael Moriarty, Shelley Hack, June Lockhart, Jenny Beck
DIRECTOR: John Buechler

Troll is a second-rate takeoff on the second-rate movie *Gremlins*. Even though it is packed with stars and aimed at the teen market, this portrait of hell, fairies, and demons has nothing to commend it.

Even the plot is weak: A troll is trying to take over an apartment building so that he can take over the earth, but a teenage boy and a hippie witch save the building. Don't let teens see this movie.

TRUE GRIT (1969), 128 min.

RATING: PG ★★★
CONTENT: Minor swearing and some violence
INTENDED AUDIENCE: All ages
STARRING: John Wayne, Glen Campbell, Kim Darby, Robert Duvall, Dennis Hopper, Strother Martin
DIRECTOR: Henry Hathaway

Wayne received the Academy Award for Best Actor (the only Oscar he received in spite of the many films in which he starred), and he is at his best here, still able to shoot straight and go roaring after the outlaws. It is pure Western good versus evil.

John Wayne portrays Rooster Cogburn, a United States marshall who, with the help of fourteen-year-old tomboy Kim Darby, tracks down the killers who murdered her father. This is a good Western made in an age when Westerns had deteriorated to the point of lifting up the villain, not the hero. **B.G.**

TWELVE ANGRY MEN (1957) B&W, 95 min.

CONTENT: Nothing objectionable　　　　　　　　　　★★★★
INTENDED AUDIENCE: Adults
STARRING: Martin Balsam, John Fiebler, Lee J. Cobb, E. G. Marshall,
　　Jack Klugman, Edward Binns, Jack Warden, Henry Fonda,
　　Joseph Sweeney, Ed Begley, George Voskevc, Robert Webber
DIRECTOR: Sidney Lumet

Twelve jurors are deciding the fate of the defendant in a murder trial. At first, the jurors are twelve strangers trapped in the jury room day after day in the heat of the New York summer. As thunderstorms and darkness loom outside, they learn almost too much about each other. In the beginning, only one man stands between the defendant and the death penalty. As the defendant's plight is debated, each one of the jurors changes his vote. In the end, compassion and justice triumph over prejudice and first impressions.

Twelve Angry Men is arguably one of Sidney Lumet's greatest films, an excellent character study. Each performance is a masterpiece. Highly recommended.

---

28 UP (1986)

CONTENT: Nothing objectionable　　　　　　　　　　★★★
INTENDED AUDIENCE: Adults
DIRECTOR: Michael Apted

In 1963, Michael Apted interviewed fourteen English seven-year-olds for a TV documentary. He has returned to interview twelve of them (two dropped out) every seven years so that we can meet them at seven, fourteen, twenty-one, and at the present age of twenty-eight. This is an irresistible, original portrait of people. Some cope well; some are crushed; some succeed; and some stall. It is clear that Apted loves these people.

The film provides an excellent look at the surface of people. The problem is that faith seems to have no part in their lives. This is very disturbing because it means that they have never been touched by the gospel or that religion has been left out of the film on purpose, thereby making it a distorted look at the human condition. It is a movie you will enjoy if you are interested in people. However, beware that God has been left out of this film's universe. **K.K.**

20,000 LEAGUES UNDER THE SEA (1954), 127 min.

CONTENT: Nothing objectionable　　　　　　　　　　★★★
INTENDED AUDIENCE: Families
STARRING: Kirk Douglas, James Mason, Peter Lorre, Paul Lukas
DIRECTOR: Richard Fleischer

This film tells the story of a mad genius, Captain Nemo, who has built the first submarine and is interested in confronting the world that he despises. After destroying their ship, Captain Nemo takes three outsiders on board: Kirk Douglas, who plays Ned Land; Paul Lucas, who plays Professor Arnonax; and Peter Lorre, who plays Conseil. They thwart the Captain's plans and open his eyes to his own evil nature. In the end, they escape and Captain Nemo destroys himself and his island fortress.

20,000 Leagues under the Sea is good entertainment. There's no sex or violence. There is a very obtuse dig at Christianity when Captain Nemo buries a deceased crewman under the sea with a cross and a prayer, which could suggest that the evil Nemo is a Christian. However, good triumphs over evil, and most of the movie is innocuous and acceptable for families. **P.B.** and **J.B.**

TWICE IN A LIFETIME (1986)

RATING: R
CONTENT: Profanity, godlessness, and immorality
INTENDED AUDIENCE: Adults
STARRING: Gene Hackman, Ann-Margaret, Ellen Burstyn
DIRECTOR: Bud Yorkin

This film promotes divorce and provides a sad commentary on the regression of our civilization into immorality. When a middle-aged man dumps his faithful, trusting wife and his loving children for a barmaid, he has no regrets, no sorrow, and no compassion about the pain he has caused his family.

The actors ham it up in this poorly directed film. The script is weak and relies on profanity when short on dialogue. The working-class characters sound like morons, and the scene of the male strip joint is an embarrassment. Protest this antifamily, anti-Christian movie.

2001: A SPACE ODYSSEY (1968), 140 min.

RATING: G   ★★★★
CONTENT: Nothing objectionable
INTENDED AUDIENCE: Families
STARRING: Keir Dullea, Gary Lockwood, William Sylvester, Douglas Rain
DIRECTOR: Stanley Kubrick

A magnificent, grandiose, visionary, spacious, colorful, wide-screen journey into time and space edited with Cinerama in mind, *2001: A Space Odyssey* tells its story from a point of view outside of time and space. The movie opens on man in a prehistoric, mythical past discovering a monolith and moves to the edge of eternity. The major action takes place in the year 2001 where a monolith is found on the moon and astronauts are sent to Jupiter where the scientists detect that there is another one of these strange, ominous objects.

On the way to Jupiter, the computer Hal goes insane and only one of the astronauts survives. However, he is grabbed by an unknown force and ripped through space and time until he reaches the threshold of eternity.

If we take this film as a fantasy, pure and simple, then it is very enjoyable entertainment. If we look at its theology, or history, then we are left with many unanswered questions. Look for the entertainment and leave the theology alone.

UNDER THE CHERRY MOON (1986)

RATING: PG–13
CONTENT: Obscenities and evildoings
INTENDED AUDIENCE: Teenagers
STARRING: Prince, Jerome Benton, Emmanuelle Sallet
DIRECTOR: Prince

This Romeo-and-Juliet fantasy starring that androgynous rock phenomenon, Prince, takes place in Nice, France, in cafés and palaces, pillow-puffed boudoirs, and candle-lit cliff caves. Two young men who are gigolos for wealthy women are the central characters. The action seems to involve scene upon scene contrived for sexual seduction, with each scene trying to prove that Prince is a charming, captivating, experienced lover dressed in gold lamé, silk and satin cutouts, and high heels. All that endless passion appears an exaggerated attempt to prove his manhood.

This film is just short of an actual sex act in the raw. The language *is* raw. Shot in black and white to pretend that it is better than it is, this film should not be viewed by teens—or adults, for that matter. **G.O.**

THE UNSINKABLE MOLLY BROWN (1964), 128 min.

CONTENT: Nothing objectionable   ★★★
INTENDED AUDIENCE: Families
STARRING: Debbie Reynolds, Harve Presnell, Ed Begley
DIRECTOR: Charles Walters

This film tells the somewhat true story of Molly Brown, who by sheer determination, made her way from illiterate waif, growing up in the wilderness, to pillar of Denver society. Early in the story, young Molly heads off to make her way in the world, and meets up with Johnny Brown, a good-looking miner who has staked out a claim in Colorado. He falls in love with her, but she wants to go on to bigger and better things. Brown finally gets his way and marries Molly. Soon thereafter he strikes one of the biggest gold mines in history.

From then on the story focuses on Molly's struggle to be accepted by Denver society. After many adventures, there is a happy ending, as one would expect. This is an excellent film if you like musical comedies; however, beware of some bawdiness. **L.B.**

UPHILL ALL THE WAY (1986)

RATING: PG
CONTENT: Profanity and lewdness
INTENDED AUDIENCE: Adults
STARRING: Roy Clark, Mel Tillis, Burl Ives
DIRECTOR: Frank Q. Dobbs

Uphill All the Way is one of those totally unappealing films that seems to get off on the wrong foot and stays there. This country-and-western comedy is a childish story involving two bums who are trapped in a car theft, are chased around the Wild West, and end up saving a small group of Americans trapped in a Texas border store by Mexican bandits. It is unfunny slapstick at its worst, with profanity and lewdness tossed in to degrade it even more. Don't see it.

UTU (1986)

RATING: R   ★★
CONTENT: Violence and brief native nudity
INTENDED AUDIENCE: Adults
STARRING: Anzac Wallace, Bruno Lawrence, Wi Kuki Kaa, Tim Elliot,
Ilona Rodgers, Tina Bristowe, Kelly Johnson
DIRECTOR: Geoff Murphy

New Zealand filmmakers are emerging as leaders of excellent moviemaking during the last half of the 1980s, and *Utu* is a good example of their art and craft. The photography of the lush countryside is beautiful, the acting is superb, and the story is intriguing and exciting. The problem is that the film canonizes the fierce Maori as noble savages while it criticizes the Christian colonists as pompous dimwits.

The movie opens with an idyllic view of a Maori village in the 1870s. Suddenly, British colonial troops ride through the village and slaughter the natives. Thus, the stage is set for the natives to seek Utu (revenge) and for the soldiers to retaliate. The message is that revenge leads to more revenge, so someone must have the courage to stop fighting. This, of course, is commendable, but it ignores the fact that there is also justice in the world. Revenge is God's, but God has called us to exact justice by punishing wrong and rewarding good. The difference between revenge and justice is clear here, but the filmmaker doesn't seem to comprehend it because he has taken an anti-colonial perspective.

This film is worth seeing if you are aware of its biases and can stomach the realistic violence. There is very brief nudity but no profanity, although there is some sexual laxity. The only real defect in the construction of the movie is the weakness of the actor who plays the main character.

VERTIGO (1958), 128 min.

CONTENT: Nothing objectionable   ★★★★
INTENDED AUDIENCE: All ages
STARRING: James Stewart, Kim Novak, Barbara Bel Geddes
DIRECTOR: Alfred Hitchcock

James Stewart is Scottie Ferguson, a former detective who fears heights. Kim Novak is the woman whom Scottie follows because her husband fears she's suicidal and whom he tries to transform into the man's wife. The story involves acrophobia, murder, and obsession. This is a nearly perfect mystery with each piece of the puzzle coming together at the last moment. A fascinating movie which you will want to see and see again.

VOLUNTEERS (1985)

RATING: R
CONTENT: Gratuitous sex, profanity, and ungodly attitudes
INTENDED AUDIENCE: Teenagers
STARRING: Tom Hanks, John Candy, Rita Wilson
DIRECTOR: Nicholas Meyer

This movie is anti-Christian, anti-American, and antipeople. It is truly a bore full of its own imagined superiority, looking down on everyone and everything else in the universe. The humor stops when the action begins and a playboy joins the Peace Corps. Avoid this film.

THE WANNSEE CONFERENCE (1986)
(Subtitles)

CONTENT: Nothing objectionable ★★★
INTENDED AUDIENCE: Adults
STARRING: Hans Bussinger, Friedrich Beck Haus, Dietrich Mattausch,
  Gerd Boeckmann, Martin Luettge
DIRECTOR: Heinz Schirk

This is a re-creation of a meeting that occurred in a Berlin suburb in January 20, 1942. Nazi leaders, including Adolph Eichmann, head of the Jewish Department of the Gestapo, Reinhard Heydrich, head of the Security Police and Secret Service, and fifteen other state officials met to decide upon and implement the "final solution" of the "Jewish problem."

Beautifully acted and well-directed *The Wannsee Conference* tells how these men came to decide that extermination was the answer. The script is accurately taken from a stenographer's notes that were found after the war. The film is a sad commentary on how evil can control and destroy people. See it. **R.A.**

WARNING SIGN (1985)

RATING: R ★★★
CONTENT: Very little off-color language
INTENDED AUDIENCE: Adults
STARRING: Sam Waterston, Kathleen Quinlan
DIRECTOR: Hal Barwood

This is an exciting, contemporary science-fiction thriller. Pay no attention to the R rating. There is very little obscenity, and even the violence is muted and contained. In fact, there are several references to prayer and to seeking the help of God the Creator.

The acting is good, and the script is tight, making for plausible entertainment. The USA is not the villain that one would expect in this film about germ warfare gene splicing. There are really no villains, only mistakes and circumstances. The happy ending has all the parties reconciled and much wiser. Well worth seeing.

WATER (1986)

RATING: PG–13
CONTENT: Drugs, sex, and profanity
INTENDED AUDIENCE: Young adults
STARRING: Valerie Perrine, Michael Caine, Brenda Vaccaro
DIRECTOR: Dick Clement

This low-life spoof stars Michael Caine as the governor of a Caribbean island that the British want to turn into a waste dump and the Yankees want to exploit for mineral water. The Protestant minister is portrayed as a drunk who has sired fourteen illegitimate children by native women. Nothing good can be said about this infantile, humorless movie.

WEIRD SCIENCE (1985)

RATING: PG–13
CONTENT: Demonic technolatry and profanity
INTENDED AUDIENCE: Teenagers
STARRING: Anthony Michael Hall, Ilan Mitchell-Smith, Kelly LeBrock
DIRECTOR: John Hughes

Weird Science is a teenage, science-fiction, bride-of-Frankenstein sex fantasy with a redeeming premise—"love conquers lust." Aside from the morality of the premise, the movie is a materialist's dream, a portrait of computer-evoked supernaturalism. It is filled with anti-Christian messages and language. Boycott it.

WEST SIDE STORY (1961), 155 min.

CONTENT: Implied promiscuity   ★★★★
INTENDED AUDIENCE: All ages
STARRING: Natalie Wood, Richard Beymer, Rita Moreno, Russ Tamblyn
DIRECTOR: Robert Wise

This film won ten Academy Awards, including Best Picture for 1961. It is the classic Romeo and Juliet story brought into the twentieth century and combined with great music. The acting is excellent, and the choreography is superb, exciting, and lively.

The story tells of two rival New York City street gangs, the Jets and the Sharks, and the love that develops between Tony, who is a Jet, and Maria, who is the sister of the leader of the Sharks, Bernardo. Doomed from the start, the relationship between the couple causes the conflict between the gangs to accelerate. Tony kills Bernardo in a brawl, and Tony is killed by a vengeful Shark. The prayer to Mary may offend some Protestants, but otherwise the film is an entertaining diversion, which implicitly condemns gang warfare. **K.G.**

WHEN FATHER WAS AWAY ON BUSINESS (1985)

RATING: R
CONTENT: Excessive preoccupation with sex
INTENDED AUDIENCE: Adults
STARRING: Moreno D'E Bartolli, Miki Manojlovic, Mirjana Karanovic
DIRECTOR: Emir Kusturica

This is a portrait of postwar Yugoslavia through the eyes of a six-year-old boy who tries to understand why his father is away so long on business. In fact, his father has been sent to the work-concentration camps. The family wants the son and everyone else to think that the father was sent away for political reasons when he really went for philandering.

The characters are not particularly attractive, and there is an excessive preoccupation with sex. God is ignored, and life is reduced to the materialistic minimum. The values are those of a medieval pagan society, where the family stays together while the father gets away with his affairs. **L.B.**

WHERE ARE THE CHILDREN? (1986)

RATING: PG   ★★★

CONTENT: Nothing objectionable
INTENDED AUDIENCE: Adults
STARRING: Jill Clayburgh, Max Gail
DIRECTOR: Bruce Malmuth

Sunbathed Cape Cod is the setting for the Eldridge family home where Ray and Nancy romp through the Autumn leaves with their two small children. During scenes of heightened merriment, an underlying uneasiness surfaces in Nancy. Unknown to her, she and her family are being spied upon. Their paradise playground is focused in a gigantic telescope concealed across the bay.

Later, a boy delivering papers on his bicycle is stopped by a gray bearded stranger offering to pay him for delivering a manila envelop to the local radio station at exactly 10 A.M. This envelope, as it later develops, contains photographs and a nine-year-old California newspaper article exposing Nancy Eldridge as the convicted killer of her two children by a previous marriage—the horror she has tried to bury in her past. The question is: Will she strike again, or is she being framed?

Not for the faint-hearted, this is recommended viewing. **G.O.**

WHERE EAGLES DARE (1969), 158 min.

RATING: PG ★★★
CONTENT: Mild swearing and violence, but not gory
INTENDED AUDIENCE: Adults
STARRING: Richard Burton, Clint Eastwood, Mary Ure, Michael Hordern,
    Patrick Wymark, Anton Diffring, Ingrid Pitt
DIRECTOR: Brian G. Hutton

Smith (Burton) and Schaffer (Eastwood) are dropped behind enemy lines, along with several commandos, to rescue a high-level American officer who knows about the plans for the Allied invasion of Europe. They parachute into the snow-covered German Alps. One of the men dies upon landing with his neck broken, but Schaffer notes that there is no bruise: he was hit by someone. From then on the question preying on Schaffer's mind is: Who is the double-agent traitor in their midst? Based on Alistair MacLean's bestselling novel, this film is as exciting and entertaining as MacLean's *Guns of Navarone*. Action-adventure fans will love it. **B.G.**

WHERE THE LILIES BLOOM (1974), 97 min.

RATING: G ★★★
CONTENT: Nothing objectionable
INTENDED AUDIENCE: All ages
STARRING: Harry Dean Stanton, Julie Gholson, Jan Smithers
DIRECTOR: William Graham

This film centers on Mary Call Luther, a fourteen-year-old girl who keeps a diary to record her thoughts and daily life. Her father, Roy, is very ill and beaten by the vicissitudes of life, so he makes Mary Call promise to hold the family together, not to accept charity, and to keep her older sister from marrying Kiser Pease (Stanton). Pease has bought the farm out from under Roy, and Roy has been a sharecropper ever since, working the two hundred-year-old family farm as a tenant.

When Roy dies the family struggles for survival as Mary Call takes over, preventing the other kids, two younger and her older sister, from being sent to an orphanage. This is an intimate story, which helps children (and adults) better understand death within the family. It talks openly about God, faith, and the Luther's closeness to the land. Highly recommended, especially for children ages eight and up. **B.G.**

WHERE THE RIVER RUNS BLACK (1986)

RATING: PG   ★★★
CONTENT: Some mythic supernaturalism and native nudity
INTENDED AUDIENCE: Adults
STARRING: Charles Durning, Peter Horton, Ajay Naidu
DIRECTOR: Christopher Cain

This is a beautiful motion picture about love and forgiveness. Lazarus, as a young boy, sees his mother killed by the lustful Santos. Later, Santos visits the orphanage where the boy is being taken care of by Father O'Reilly. O'Reilly tries to explain forgiveness to the boy, but Lazarus and a friend run away from the orphanage bent on revenge.

The priest and faith in God are portrayed in a positive light. At one point, Father O'Reilly poses the key question of the movie, "How can someone love God, and yet betray Him." A movie worth seeing in spite of some minor flaws. **T.A.**

WHITE NIGHTS (1985), 216 min.

RATING: PG–13   ★★★★
CONTENT: Very little off-color language
INTENDED AUDIENCE: Adults
STARRING: Mikhail Baryshnikov, Gregory Hines
DIRECTOR: Taylor Hackford

Years after he defects, a Russian dancer finds himself trapped back in the USSR because of a plane crash. He meets up with an American dancer who defected from the USA during the Vietnam war. *White Nights* tells of their escape from the Soviet Union.

The film clearly portrays how totalitarian communism robs everyone of individuality and freedom. Great dance and a great plot make this a winner, in spite of a little off-color language. Highly recommended.

THE WILD BUNCH (1969), 135 min.

RATING: R
CONTENT: Graphic violence, obscenities, and nudity
INTENDED AUDIENCE: Adults
STARRING: William Holden, Ernest Borgnine, Robert Ryan, Edmund O'Brien, Warren Oates, Ben Johnson, Strother Martin
DIRECTOR: Sam Peckinpah

The Wild Bunch marked a pivotal turning point in American cinema with its graphic, gory violence. For the first time on screen, brutal throat slashing and bloodletting, using sophisticated special effects and make-up, were realistically portrayed. Many scenes were overly realistic, with cinematic license allowing bloody mayhem and death to be filmed in slow motion. A trend began that shed the last vestiges of taboos against excessive violence and killed a code of decency, morality, and taste producers had observed since the 1930s.

The story tells of a misfit band of outlaws who join with a Mexican rebel army general and are pursued by the Mexican army in 1913 on the Texas-Mexico border. But the story line is a minor element compared to the violence portrayed. It is not a film to see. **B.G.**

WILDCATS (1986), 146 min.

RATING: R
CONTENT: Foul language (even put into the mouths of children), sexual
    innuendo, immorality, and nudity
INTENDED AUDIENCE: Young adults
STARRING: Goldie Hawn, James Keach
DIRECTOR: Michael Ritchie

At the heart of this movie is a good story of a woman who perseveres to pull a ghetto football team together so they can become champions. However, this film is dragged into the gutter by foul language, sexual innuendo, and nudity. Thievery and other wrongdoings also make it unacceptable for Christians.

THE WIND AND THE LION (1975), 119 min.

RATING: PG   ★ ★ ★
CONTENT: Minor swearing and a very distorted view of history
INTENDED AUDIENCE: Adults
STARRING: Sean Connery, Candice Bergen, Brian Keith, John Huston
DIRECTOR: John Milius

This epic adventure story is loosely based on an event that took place during the presidency of Theodore Roosevelt. A real-life Moroccan bandit named Raisuli kidnapped an elderly, Greek American ex-patriot man named Perdicaris. Theodore Roosevelt's Secretary of State, John Hay, then issued his famous, terse ultimatum to the Moroccan government to have Perdicaris released, "Perdicaris alive or Raisuli dead." Raisuli released Perdicaris. Period.

According to the movie, however, Theodore Roosevelt dispatched the U.S. Marines in 1904, to rescue Perdicaris (who has become a luscious young American woman, played by Candice Bergen) and her two children, who are kidnapped in Morocco and held for ransom by a desert chieftain played by Sean Connery.

The film is full of action, romance, and impressive scenery, even if it has no relation to reality. Enjoyable but nothing like what really happened. **B.G.**

WIRED TO KILL (1986)

RATING: R
CONTENT: Graphic gore and violence; no nudity, but some visual allusions to
    attempted rape, and some profanity
INTENDED AUDIENCE: Adults
STARRING: Devin Hoelscher, Emily Longstreth, Merritt Butternick, Kristina David
DIRECTOR: Franky Schaeffer
212

This is a poorly written, badly directed, bottom of the barrel, futuristic revenge movie, set in a 1998 America that has been decimated by a virus acronymed TAPEX. The mediocre story revolves around a working-class family composed of seventeen-year-old Steve, his widowed mother, and grandmother. They are joined in the film by Becky, a teenage girl seeking refuge from her callous father and his live-in girlfriend.

An early scene shows the four around the meal table, with Steve's mom giving thanks for the food. This is the story's only religious expression, other than Steve's throw away reference to God during a do-or-die situation near the end of the movie. (An example of director Franky Schaeffer's haphazard attention to detail is that, in spite of the barren apocalyptic setting, there is so much food to eat Becky complains of being stuffed.)

After a scene in which Steve shows off his robot-building genius to Becky, we cut to a gang of beefy, moronic, and utterly vile psychopaths who live in a garbage dump and are led by an intellectual demoniac, Reegus, who has a peculiar penchant for Shakespeare. These men spend their days roasting dogs and snorting cocaine by the kilo and their nights performing all types of burglary, robbery, and mayhem to support their drug habit, and as an outlet for their unquenchable sadism. The rest of the film details the conflict between the Reegus gang and Steve and Becky.

Franky Schaeffer, author and son of the late Francis Schaeffer, has gone on the secular and Christian media circuits, hyping his film. To the former, he claims it is "an allegory, a twentieth century version of Homer's 'Odyssey';" to the latter, he speaks as though the film were a poignant portrayal of the apocalypse-to-come.

There is nothing redemptive, or redeemable, about *Wired to Kill*. There is no real hope, only the possibility of revenge. The Christian faith of the family is superficial at best and neither empowers nor motivates their response to events. Indeed, at the beginning and end of the film, one of them says, "If you want history, you gotta make your own." So, in the end, this is a humanistic film about humanistic despair, showing no way out, no alternative.

On an artistic level, the film has an inane script and poor cinematography and sound. The acting is amateurish, but this is probably not the actors' fault, considering the insipid dialogue and actions they've been called to mouth and perform. Stay away from *Wired to Kill* unless you want to weep at how an opportunity for Christian filmmakers was thrown away. **R.C.**

WISE GUYS (1986)

RATING: R
CONTENT: Profanity and obscenity
INTENDED AUDIENCE: Adults
STARRING: Danny DeVito, Joe Piscopo
DIRECTOR: Brian DePalma

Forget this half-baked slapstick comedy about two foul-mouthed Mafia bagmen who can't do anything right. They are sent to the racetrack to make a bet for their boss, but they bet on a different horse. The boss's horse wins, and he is out for revenge. The bums pull a scam on the boss and make off with the loot. The humor doesn't work, and the plot doesn't work. Avoid this lowbrow bomb. **K.K.**

WITNESS (1984), 112 min.
RATING: R

★★★

CONTENT: Brief nudity and violence
INTENDED AUDIENCE: Adults
STARRING: Harrison Ford
DIRECTOR: Peter Weir

Surprisingly sympathetic to the Christian faith, *Witness* tells the story of a little Amish boy who witnesses a murder in the men's room at the Philadelphia train station. The police detective who investigates realizes that the boy's life is in danger and tries to protect him, thus becoming involved in a storm of corruption and cruelty. The detective takes the boy and his mother back to their Amish village to hide out from corrupt police. In the final battle, good triumphs over evil.

The clash of cultures between the faithless police detective and the faithful Amish is truly impressive for its sensitive understanding of the contrast between humanism and Christianity. Furthermore, the respect the Australian director Peter Weir pays to the Amish is beautiful and compelling. Brief nudity and violence may offend some people, but this film is a welcome relief from most Hollywood film fare.

THE WIZ (1978), 133 min.

RATING: G   ★★★
CONTENT: A musical fantasy
INTENDED AUDIENCE: Families
STARRING: Diana Ross, Michael Jackson, Nipsey Russell, Ted Ross, Richard Pryor
DIRECTOR: Sydney Lumet

The Wiz is an extravagant, black musical adapted from the smash Broadway hit play, which was adapted from *The Wizard of Oz*, which was adapted from L. Frank Baum's book! What is interesting about all these adaptations is how powerful the Frank Baum story is. The story ensures that even the movie *The Wiz* is a sure fire hit, although it does not reach the pinnacle of greatness *The Wizard of Oz* attained. Rather, the story has been transformed and placed in a contemporary New York City setting. Dorothy and her cohorts are sure that the sky is blue somewhere over the Brooklyn Bridge, and the Wiz, played by Pryor, is enthroned in the World Trade Center.

Even though this film is not up to the 1939 masterpiece and Diana Ross seems a little old for Dorothy, it is a fun movie your family will enjoy.

THE WIZARD OF OZ (1939), 101 min.

CONTENT: A great musical fantasy   ★★★★
INTENDED AUDIENCE: Everyone who has a heart, courage, and a brain
STARRING: Judy Garland, Frank Morgan, Ray Bolger, Jack Haley, Bert Larr
DIRECTOR: Victor Fleming

The plot of this film is known throughout the world. It is the story of little Dorothy who tries to run away from home because she is hounded by Miss Gulch who hates Dorothy's little dog, Toto. However, Professor Marvel, a flim-flam man sends Dorothy back home where she is caught up in a tornado and carried off to Oz and to adventure.

Volumes have been written about the symbolism in the Oz books. An industry has grown up around the movie that propelled its actors to lasting fame. However, the truth of the matter is that *The Wizard of Oz* is a fun, loving story of good triumphing

214

over evil. There really is no place like home. A monument to love, courage, and wisdom.

WOLF AT THE DOOR (1987), 102 min.

RATING: PG–13
CONTENT: Sexual laxity and some non-erotic nudity
INTENDED AUDIENCE: Adults
STARRING: Donald Sutherland, Gene Jeanyanne, Max Von Sydow
DIRECTOR: Henning Carlsen

Paul Gauguin returns triumphantly from his extended stay in Tahiti with canvas after canvas rich with the soul of the islands. He invests all his money in exhibiting his works, only to be rejected by the artistic community. Gauguin briefly relieves his despair by leaving France and going to England. However, he breaks his leg in a fight; and, returning to Paris, discovers that Anna, a Japanese girl he used as a model, has vandalized several canvases.

Broken and desolate, he finds that the only people who are interested in his paintings are his ex-wife's brother-in-law and his landlord in Britain. Heartbroken, he parts with his treasured Van Gough paintings, which gives him barely enough money to make the trip back to the islands. Because of Gauguin's philandering and the nudity in the film, *Wolf at the Door* is not recommended for Christians.

WUTHERING HEIGHTS (1939) B&W, 104 min.

CONTENT: Nothing objectionable   ★ ★ ★ ★
INTENDED AUDIENCE: Adults
STARRING: Merle Oberon, Laurence Olivier, David Niven,
    Flora Robson, Geraldine Fitzgerald
DIRECTOR: William Wyler

A powerful, haunting film, *Wuthering Heights* retains Emily Bronte's brooding atmosphere and much of her dialogue, but simplifies the complex plot. Thanks to director William Wyler, this movie was a turning point for Laurence Olivier, who played the wild and moody Heathcliff whose love and hate crush all the softness of the Yorkshire countryside. Merle Oberon matched Olivier's performance as Cathy who breaks Heathcliff's heart. A timeless tale with rich romantic sweep.

YEAR OF THE DRAGON (1985), 215 min.

RATING: R
CONTENT: Gratuitous sex, nudity, profanity, and violence
INTENDED AUDIENCE: Adults
STARRING: Mickey Rourke, John Lone, Ariane
DIRECTOR: Michael Cimino

In this tough, old-fashioned, action-adventure movie, the good cop is pitted against evil gangsters condoned by bad politicians. Courage triumphs over evil; however, the hero does not hold a candle to James Cagney, and the good is overshadowed by the excessive, gratuitous sex, nudity, profanity, and violence. This movie is not for Christians.

A YEAR OF THE QUIET SUN (1986)
(Subtitles)

RATING: PG ★★★
CONTENT: Nothing objectionable
INTENDED AUDIENCE: Adults
STARRING: Scott Wilson, Maja Komorowska
DIRECTOR: Krysztof Zanussi

An American soldier and Polish woman, Emily, meet and fall in love in the days that follow World War II. The soldier wants to take his new love to America and marry her, but there are terrific obstacles for people of limited resources to overcome.

The cost of crossing the border is high. Emily's mother, dealing with the guide, can only afford to pay for one person, and she knows Emily will never leave without her. So she purposely exposes herself to the winter cold and dies. But after her mother's death, Emily mistakenly supposes the passage is for two people and offers the other space to her neighbor, a prostitute who is deliriously happy over the prospect of a new beginning. When Emily learns that the passage is for just one person, she tells her neighbor that she has decided not to leave after all, and so another sacrifice is made.

The love of Jesus, though not voiced, is expressed over and over in this touching and tragic film. Compassion, love, and sacrifice are vividly contrasted with man's inhumanity to man. This was Best Film at the Venice International Film Festival. Some film clips of decomposed bodies in mass graves are hard to look at. **D.R.**

YELLOW SUBMARINE (1968), 85 min.
RATING: PG ★★★
CONTENT: Innocuous and ambiguous
INTENDED AUDIENCE: Families
STARRING: The Beatles: John, Paul, George, Ringo
DIRECTOR: George Dunning

It's a sad day in Pepperland when the Blue Meanies move in to take the music away by putting a bubble around Sgt. Pepper's Lonely Heart's Club Band. The Blue Meanies take all of the color out of Pepperland, and the people are frozen in time. In a last ditch attempt to save Pepperland, the Lord Mayor asks the Lord Admiral to go off in the Yellow Submarine to find someone, anyone, to rescue Pepperland. The Lord Admiral goes to Liverpool and talks the Beatles into coming to the rescue. Throughout the movie, John, Paul, George, and Ringo sing memorable songs that are beautifully illustrated.

Yellow Submarine can be seen, as children see it and love it, as a cute movie about bringing music into people's lives. On the other hand, if one is into symbolism, one can read a great deal of sixties hippy culture into this movie. After careful viewing several times, the reviewers concluded that the movie will not insidiously undermine anyone's faith. Recommended for those with discernment. **P.B.** and **J.B.**

THE YOUNG GIRLS OF ROCHEFORT (1968), 126 min.
(Subtitles)

RATING: G ★★★
CONTENT: Nothing objectionable

INTENDED AUDIENCE: Adults
STARRING: George Chakiris, Catherine Deneuve, Francoise Dorleac,
   Gene Kelly, Michael Piccoli
DIRECTOR: Jacques Demy

The Young Girls of Rochefort was the second directorial effort for Jacques Demy and his operetta films. The first was *The Umbrellas of Cherbourg*. Where *Cherbourg* was more moody and low-key, this film is a light mixture of song and dance. No one speaks in these movies; they sing, just as in opera.

The story revolves around two sisters, Deneuve and Dorleac, playing twins, who run a ballet school in Rochefort and dream of meeting with their ideal man. Gene Kelly and his friend dream of meeting their ideal lady. Demy's primary motive seems to be to instill a sense of romantic love in his audiences through a modern day fairy tale. The music, composed by Michel Legrand, is some of his finest work. It is moving and gracious and adds immeasurably to the film.

YOUNG SHERLOCK HOMES (1985)
RATING: PG–13   ★★★
CONTENT: Nothing offensive
INTENDED AUDIENCE: Families
STARRING: Nicholas Rowe, Alan Cox
DIRECTOR: Barry Levinson

There is no offensive language in this entertaining movie, and it is acceptable for children. The problem is that it never captures our imagination, even though there is a neat turn at the end when we discover that the fanatical Egyptian killer is none other than Holmes's archenemy Moriarty. The most serious defect is the unattractive character of young Sherlock.

The story starts out in an interesting direction revealing young Sherlock as a schoolboy, but quickly becomes a retread of a 1930s melodrama telling how he and pudgy Watson stop an Egyptian death cult, which is killing off old school chums. Unfortunately, the script does not have the logic that Holmes's character demands. Instead, the detective work is more of a triumph of coincidence and contrivance rather than mental superiority and impeccable logic. It is encouraging to find this movie pointing out the demonic aspects of esoteric religions that are so in vogue these days, and there is almost a recommendation of the Judeo-Christian heritage. The artistic high point is the computer-generated animation.

YOUNGBLOOD (1986)
RATING: R
CONTENT: Sex, pornography, and violence
INTENDED AUDIENCE: Teenagers
STARRING: Rob Lowe, Cynthia Bigg, Patrick Swayze
DIRECTOR: Peter Marble

Youngblood is *Rocky* on ice without morals. It is about a young hockey player who becomes the star of a small-town professional team. Don't bother with this one, and don't let your children see it. It is laced with sex, pornography, and violence, and it has no emotion or drama.

ZIEGFELD FOLLIES (1946), 110 min.

CONTENT: Nothing objectionable   ★★★
INTENDED AUDIENCE: Families
STARRING: William Powell, Judy Garland, Fred Astaire, Fanny Brice,
  Lena Horne, Gene Kelly, Cyd Charisse
DIRECTOR: Vincente Minnelli

The storyline is practically non-existent, but the segments of music, comedy, and dance "hosted" by Flo Ziegfeld—from heaven!—are superb. The famous showman dreams about a new show and creates a fantasy revue that includes most of the MGM stars: Fred Astaire, Gene Kelly, Esther Williams in an exotic water ballet, Fanny Brice doing vaudeville, Hume Cronyn, Lena Horne singing "Love," Red Skelton, Judy Garland, and many more. A fanciful, fun movie that established Minnelli as the premiere director of movie musicals.

ZULU (1964), 138 min.

CONTENT: Violence and some mild swearing   ★★★
INTENDED AUDIENCE: Adults
STARRING: Michael Caine, Jack Hawkins, Stanley Baker
DIRECTOR: Cy Endfield

A "hold-the-fort-at-all-costs" type of film, *Zulu* awesomely recreates the battle of Rorke's Drift between English soldiers and an overwhelming number of Zulu warriors. Lieutenant John Chard, R.E., takes command of a small outpost when he receives word that British soldiers are being massacred. The encampment prepares for battle, fortifying the outpost with additional walls and barriers. The first attack by the Zulus seems suicidal, as warriors are shot down when they approach the fort but do not try to breach the walls. The battle rages for hours, and then days, as thousands of Zulus attack, probe the walls, and look for weak spots to launch a massive offensive. The Zulus obtain rifles from the dead British soldiers, and use them to harass the troops within the compound.

As the number of British soldiers decreases, last ditch efforts are made to hold the fort on the final assault. The soldiers regroup into an inner walled compound and fight off the attacks until only a few dozen soldiers remain. Seeing that he has only one choice, Chard forms the men into three lines, their backs against a high wall. . . .

This film is recommended with caution because of the violence and minor swearing that is in it.

PART III

IN CONCLUSION

REJOICE!

Scripture says, "Rejoice always, pray without ceasing, in everything give thanks; for this is the will of God in Christ Jesus for you" (1 Thess. 5:16–18). It is our sincere hope and prayer that you have enjoyed *The Movie & Video Guide for Christian Families* and found it helpful for you, your family, and your friends. As you have discovered, there are good movies to see, there are movies to avoid, and there are even certain movies you should see, but you must exercise discretion and discernment that will come through the study of God's Word, prayer, and a sincere desire to walk in His will under the guidance of His Holy Spirit. The key is to be careful, especially where your children are concerned, and remember: "But as He who called you is holy, you also be holy in all your conduct, because it is written, 'Be holy, for I am holy'" (1 Pet. 1:15–16).

It is our plan to expand this guide from time to time by adding both old and new movies so that it will be your most complete reference to movies from a biblical perspective. Please remember that the material here appears as "Movieguide: A Biblical Guide to Movies and Entertainment," a two-minute radio program on many Christian radio stations around the country, and as a column in selected newspapers and magazines. For a complete listing of stations, newspapers, and magazines, please contact us.

If you would like "Movieguide" to air on your local radio station, please send us the name, address, and telephone number of that station, and we will contact them. In addition to writing us, it will help if you call or write your local station and ask them if they want to carry "Movieguide."

Also, "Movieguide" is available for any publications (newspapers or magazines) in which you would like to see it appear. Please write us and send us the name, address, and telephone number of the publication in which you want it to appear, and we will contact them. If you write that publication, it will help them to decide to carry "Movieguide."

Remember, you can make a difference. If Christians would stop supporting immoral, anti-Christian entertainment and programming, producers would quickly change their approach to regain our viewership and our dollars. In the case of movies, our economic support is easy to see—we spend money at the box office for a ticket. In the case of television, the classic saying notes that we pay when we wash, not when we watch. In other words, with TV we support immoral programs when we support advertisers who sponsor immoral programs.

The solution is simple:

- Boycott immoral movies and the advertisers who sponsor immoral programs; let the producer, advertiser, or other key person know of your action and why.
- Witness to those involved in communications whether that person is a videostore owner, a ticket taker, a writer for the local paper, or a big-time producer.
- Support moral programs and movies that are aimed at the mass audience, not just those programs aimed at Christians.
- Encourage Christians who produce programming for Christians to go forth into the marketplace rather than remain in the Christian ghetto.
- Live exemplary, holy lives through the power of His Spirit so that the mass media will be at a loss to find fault with us and will be convicted by the quality of our lives.

Also, join with us in praying that Christians will occupy the mass media for Jesus Christ and that the day will come when you will be able to take your family or friends to a theater and see an uplifting, wholesome movie. Until that day comes we hope that this guide will help you choose the best in motion picture entertainment. "So then, submit yourselves to God. Resist the Devil, and he will run away from you. Come near to God, and he will come near to you. . . . Humble yourselves before the Lord, and he will lift you up" (James 4:7–8, 10 TEV). May God bless you in all that you do.

INDEX BY TITLE

SUBJECT INDEX

ADVENTURE

ANIMATION

BIOGRAPHICAL

CHILDREN

COMEDY

DOCUMENTARY

DRAMA

230

HISTORICAL

HORROR

MUSICAL

NATURE

RELIGIOUS/CHRISTIAN

ROMANCE

SCIENCE FICTION/SCIENCE FANTASY

SWORD & SORCERY

WAR

WESTERN

After using this book, if you would like to subscribe to *Movieguide*, a monthly publication of Good News Communications that keeps you updated on current movies, please write:

Good News Communications
2876 Mabry Road
Atlanta, Ga. 30319